Child Psychology

Published by:
Saurabh Publishing House

Child Psychology

N.M. Tiwari

Saurabh
Publishing House
4735/22, Prakash Deep Building,
Ansari Road, Daryaganj,
New Delhi- 110002

Published by :
SAURABH PUBLISHING HOUSE

Distributed by :
Lotus Press Publishers & Distributors
Unit No. 220, 2nd Floor, 4735/22, Prakash Deep Building,
Ansari Road, Darya Ganj, New Delhi- 110002
Ph.: 23280047, 09811838000
• E-mail : lotuspress1984@gmail.com
www.lotuspress.co.in

Saurabh Publishing House is an imprint of
Lotus Press Publishers & Distributors

Child Psychology

ISBN: 81-89005-08-1

Printed by : **Lotus Press Publishers & Distributors, New Delhi**

PREFACE

Child Psychology deals with mental growth or, what amounts to the same thing, the development of behaviour patterns (including consciousness) up to adolescence, the transitional phase marking the entrance of the individual into adult society. Mental growth is inseparable from physical growth: the maturation of the nervous and endocrine systems, in particular, continues until the age of sixteen. This implies that in order to understand mental growth it is not enough to start with birth; there is an embryology of reflexes) dealing with the movements and responses of the fetus, and the preperceptive behaviour of the fetus, for instance, is relevant to the study of the perception of tactilo-kinesthetic causality. From a theoretical point of view, it also implies that child psychology must be regarded as the study of one aspect of embryogenesis, the embryogenesis of organic as well as mental growth, up to the beginning of the state of relative equilibrium which is the adult level.

Organically as well as mentally, however, environmental influences assume increasing importance after birth. Child psychology, in its search for factors of development, cannot be limited to a study of biological maturation. Other, equally important factors are to be considered exercise or acquired experience as well as social life in general.

Child psychology studies the mental development of the child for its own sake. In this respect it must be distinguished from "genetic psychology," although it constitutes the essential tool of this discipline. To dispel any ambiguity about terminology, let us note first that the word "genetic," as used in the expression "genetic psychology," was introduced by psychologists in the second half of the nineteenth century to refer to the developmental aspects of psychology. Later, biologists began to use the term "genetics" in a more restricted sense. In the current language of biologists, "genetics" refers only to the mechanisms of heredity and does not include the study of embryogenetic or developmental processes. The term "genetic psychology," however, continues to refer to individual development (ontogenesis). One might be tempted to consider the expressions "child psychology" and "genetic psychology" to be synonymous, but there is an important distinction between them: Whereas child psychology deals with the child for his own sake and does not consider his eventual development into an adult, we tend today to use the term "genetic psychology" to refer to the study of the developmental processes that underlie the mental functions studied in general psychology (intelligence, perceptions, etc.). Genetic psychology tries to explain mental functions by their mode of formation; that is, by their development in the child.

The genetic method has become important in all branches of psychology (consider, for example, the major role attributed to childhood by psychoanalysis) and thus gives child psychology a key position in many diverse fields of psychology. In this work, therefore, we will speak primarily from the point of view of genetic psychology. The child is of considerable interest in himself, but interest in psychological investigations of the child is increased when we realize that the child explains the man as well as and often better than the man explains the child. While the adult educates the child by means of multiple social transmissions, every adult, even if he is a creative genius, nevertheless began as a child, in prehistoric times as well as today. This book is a topically organised introduction to child development from conception to adolescence. It examines child psychology from the perspectives of the three principal traditions which characterize the discipline today—the cognitive-developmental, environmental-learning and ethological orientations.

Contents

1. **Child Psychology: Assessing Infants and Young Children**	**11**
Introduction	11
Cultural Definition and Influence	12
Culture Operates Silently and with Voices	14
View of Reality and Experience	16
Culture Influences Expressions of Distress	17
Current Integration of Culture and Clinical Assessment	18
Cultural Formulations with Children	20
Cultural Assessment Framework for Infants and Toddlers	22
Clinical Presentation and Case Description	24
Background	25
Cultural Identity of Child and Caregivers	26
Caregiver Beliefs About Parenting and Child Development	29
Conclusion	31
2. **Prediction and Feeling of Child**	**33**
Introduction	33
Development as a Sequence of Stages	34
New Stages: Gradual or Abrupt?	37
Connections between Stages	30

Arguments for Connectedness 45
Argumets against Connectedness 49
Preservation of Individual Qualities 52
How to Measure Preservation 55
Evidence for Stability of Differences 58
Conclusion 69
3. Guiding Principles in Human Development 71
Introduction 71
Biology and Experience 72
Connectedness and Discontinuity in Development 78
Qualities and Quantities 80
General and Specific Constructs 82
Subjective and Objective Frames 86
4. Experimental Methods in Child Psychology 93
Introduction 93
Some Basic Premises of Experimental Methods 94
Behavioural Research as "Science" 96
Causality 98
Laboratory Experiments 100
Field Experiments 102
Natural Experiments 103
Research Design 104
Internal Validity 104
External Validity 109
Ecological Validity 111
Experimental Approach Evaluated: Advantages and Disadvantages 112
Conclusions 113
5. Language Development in Child 115
Introduction 115
What Makes a Communication System a Language? 116
Features of Language 116
Aspects of Language 117

Different Theoretical Perspectives of Language Development 112
How Children Acquire Language 126
Language in Context 136
Speech Registers 137
Second-language Learning 139
Role of Age in Learning a Second Language 142
Benefits of Bilingualism 143
Critical Period for Learning Language 144
Language and Thought 145
6. Assessment of Parent-Child Relationship **149**
Introduction 149
Conceptual and Theoretical Foundations 151
Reasons for Looking at Relationships 155
Contributions of Parent 156
Contributions of Child 159
Medical Conditions 161
Assessment of the Parent- Child Relationship 162
Interview with Parents 163
Observations of Parent-Child Interactions 164
Parent-child Early Relational Assessment 167
Review of Other Parent- Child Interaction Assessment Methods 172
Diagnosis of Relational Disorders 178
Integrating Culturally Sensitive Approaches 182
Conclusion 182
7. Generation of Thought in Children **184**
Introduction 184
Selection of Terms 193
Cognitive Processes 203
Inference and Categories 208
Memory 220
Evaluation of an Idea 225
The Executive Processes 226

Piaget's Theory and the Executive Processes 230
Conclusion 233
8. Children's Learning, Thinking and Remembering 237
Introduction 237
Learning 237
Learning in Infancy 238
Behaviour Modification 239
Social Cognitive Theory 241
Piaget's Theory 246
Assumptions and Principles of Piaget's Theory 246
Stages of Development 250
Piaget and Individual Differences in Children's Thinking 260
Information-processing Perspectives of Children's Cognition 261
Strategies 265
Memory 267
Children's Theory of Mind 275
Vygotsky's Sociocultural Approach 277
Bibliography 283
Index 287

1

Child Psychology: Assessing Infants and Young Children

Introduction

The inclusion of the Outline for Cultural Formulation in Diagnostic and Statistical Manual of Mental Disorders, a multiaxial classification system has made a significant contribution to the assessment of adult psychological functioning in the context of culture, the field of infant mental health assessment has lagged behind. This is not surprising, considering the newness of the field and the fact that appreciation of cultural factors in development in general has lagged behind other approaches. It is also not surprising that the need to understand culture has come increasingly into our awareness, given the changing demographics of the world population.

Despite current acknowledgment of the importance of culture in our work as psychologists, psychiatrists, and other mental health providers, the concept of culture has remained abstract and therefore difficult to apply in real-world situations. Certain advances are conducive to making culture a more routine element in the assessment, diagnostic, and treatment process. However, as Garcia Coll and Magnuson highlight, academicians and clinicians alike have had what they call and to include in the ass relationship with culture as it influences the lives and well-being of young children. In this chapter, our goal is to discuss the relevance of culture for, and the influence of culture on, infant mental health and, more important, to provide a practical framework to aid in the oftentimes ambiguous task of taking culture into account in the assessment of young children's psychological functioning.

Cultural Definition and Influence

Culture can be defined as meaning that is shared by a group of people. These shared values, assumptions, beliefs, and practices are transmitted across generations and are brought to life through the daily behaviour and interactions of people within a group. Culture supports early development in varied ways, most often operating silently in the background through the mediation of parenting. The supportive aspects of culture are often not appreciated by clinicians, who typically become aware of cultural influences among peoples when they see differences (*e.g.*, in practices, behaviour, etc.) from their own cultural expectations. In addition to reviewing the particulars of cultural difference that contribute to development, we believe it is useful to identify some general features about cultural definition and influence.

Culture as Shared Meaning

First, it is useful to distinguish culture as shared values, beliefs, and practices among members of a group from the terms *ethnicity, race,* and *minority status.* Ethnicity refers to an identity that is assumed, and to some extent chosen, by individuals within a group. Race, although there is controversy over the current usefulness of this term, generally refers to the genetically influenced physical appearance of individuals, while minority status is a descriptive population term often invoked for considerations of social policy. Following others, we advocate that culture is especially important to include in the assessment and treatment process.

Culture Occurs in an Ecology

Second, culture occurs in a setting. As such, it is useful to bear in mind that culture not only occurs in an ecology but also contains adaptations to it. The importance of setting or ecology for culture, and its influence on human development, has been conceptualized in some detail by Bronfenbrenner and by Sameroff and Fiese and given instantiation in the separate studies of rural African caregiving practices by Super and Harkness and by LeVine and colleagues. For example, infants' sleeping and feeding patterns are apt to be shorter but more frequent in a context where mothers engage in culturally supported daily routines that include the continuous carrying of their infants on their backs to soothe and quiet them. Similarly, the environmental demands of work for mothers in rural Africa, along with culturally derived expectations for childbearing and the availability of large family networks, are apt to be associated with routines in which infants and toddlers are cared for by siblings who are not much older. Thus, customs of child care such as how infants are carried and the type and amount of supervision infants receive are governed by assumptions about development espoused by cultures in particular environmental contexts. Furthermore, as Lewis points out, customs of child care influenced by setting also include the ways in which parents respond to infant cues, determinations about the amount and type of stimulation (tactile, verbal, and social) an infant should receive, routines of infant care, and the teaching of skills valued in a particular culture (*e.g.*, smiling, vocalizing, and play).

Culture is Transactional

Third, culture is dynamic and transactional. Evolving history, with its changing norms, roles, and were more available and values, contributes to the dynamic and transactional nature of culture. Moreover, shared meaning changes in the midst of adaptations to technology, influences from other cultural groups, and influences from developing individuals. These factors represent important transactional processes in which culture is both influencing settings and people and is itself being influenced and changed.

Culture is Experienced Subjectively

Fourth, culture is experienced subjectively by individuals. More specifically, culture guides early development by means of subjective experiences that are shared, that is, *intersubjectively* experienced, especially between caregivers and children. Culture not only influences the physical setting and context for parents and young children but also influences attitudes, expectations, and perceptions of safety and appropriate behaviour. Parents share meaning in an intuitive manner with their children as they engage them in everyday learning activities. But parents also share meaning in such activities (*i.e.*, engagement in intersubjectivity) in a special way. Contemporary thinking in the field of child development, following Vygotsky, portrays the parent as providing a psychological scaffolding for the opment through many participatorye child's learning, pulling the child forward in development according to what is sensed as appropriate in a "zone of proximal development. " There is an active process of "guided participation" or "apprenticeship" between adult and child, as Rogoff puts it. That such a process is reflective of cultural support and variation is indicated by the work of Rogoff, Mistry, Goncu, and Mosier, who observed mothers and their toddlers in a rural village of Guatemala and in an urban city of the United States. Guided participation of mothers in rural village occurred in a courtyard setting with a number of mothers watching a number of toddlers as mothers engaged in weaving and other tasks. While mothers in this setting provided fewer vocabulary lessons to their children and engaged in less praise than did mothers in urban city, rural mothers were more available and ready to help any of the children, as opposed to just their own, if there were concerns of safety. Rogoff and Mosier interpreted these differences to be part of a more general cultural respect for autonomy in learning under these particular circumstances in rural village as well as more of an orientation to interdependence among rural mothers.

Culture Operates Silently and with Voices

Fifth, culture operates silently as well as with voices. Rather than being obvious or talked about, much of cultural influence involves procedural knowledge and mental activity. We have come to understand the importance of procedural knowledge as the form of knowledge that refers to information underlying a skill or set of behaviours but that does not need to be represented in conscious awareness in order for the skill or behaviour to be exercised. Knowledge organized procedurally contrasts with knowledge that can be accessed in awareness via processes of recognition or recall (usually referred to as *declarative knowledge*). Most rules that guide behaviour in everyday circumstances have been learned in the course of development through many participatory experiences and are organized procedurally. Common examples include the rules of grammar of a learned first language and the many rules that guide basic moral conduct such as turn taking and reciprocity in social interactions. Thus, while some knowledge about one's culture can be talked about and can be accessed consciously and declaratively, for example in interviews, much culturally guided knowledge exerts its influence through internalized rules that govern routines and social interactions, silently, without reflection and without awareness. Anthropologists have long known that participant observation and immersion in a cul-most cultures support a variety of spiritual expeture often by someone from outside the culture are needed to supplement interviews of key informants in order to access this form of knowledge. In a similar vein, anthropologists have known that cultural models contain rules that regulate behaviour through values, attitudes, and beliefs that are largely assumed by members of a particular group, rather than being explicit or formalized.

The cultural construct *amae,* introduced by Takeo Doi, illustrates the above point. Amae refers to a form of intimacy in Japanese culture that is pervasive and typically oper-toddlers. Similarly, Latin parents who participates outside of conscious awareness. It involves procedures wherein one monitors the feelings and sensitivities of another according to what feels right. While a prototypic form of amae is particularly prominent in the mother-infant relationship, it describes a process of behavioural organization that is motivational throughout life, guiding actions in many social circumstances, most notably when caring is involved. Amae carries with it a sense of dependency, reciprocity, and obligation, and, according to Doi, it operates "sweetly. " Processes of amae guide a good deal of what outsiders see as the routines of courtesy, generosity, and mutuality in Japanese social interactions. Again we are reminded that much of Eastern cultural practice has emphasized mutuality in development and the overlapping connections between the person and the other, whereas much of Western practice and thought, in contrast, has tended to emphasize individuality in development and the separability of the person and the other. Interestingly, recent concepts from infancy research have emphasized the development of mutuality and connectedness as well.

View of Reality and Experience

Sixth, culture provides multiple views of reality and the world. In addition to everyday reality, most cultures support a variety of spiritual experiences that often contain alternative views of reality. These may be important for understanding variations in health behaviours in families with young children (*e.g.*, related to diet, exercise, provisions for safety, and protections from toxins and abusive substances) as well as for understanding variations in opportunities for social connectedness and support. Thus, for example, Native American parents who participate in sweat lodges, ritual dancing, and related spiritual affirmation experiences may be protected from the risk of substance abuse, and hence may be more available for caring activities with their infants and toddlers. Similarly, Latino parents who participate in organized religious activities or other alternate belief systems about protection from evil spirits, curses, or illness may find support and benefit. The forms of play and types of stories that parents tell young children within a given culture also allow for alternative views of reality and, to varying degrees, allow for important "intermediate zones of experience" in which child and parent can try out different cultural views, values, and worlds of belief and "make believe."

Cultural influences on general views of the world may also be important in clinical assessment of the young children. That such influences may change in relation to time and context may make such assessments challenging but no less important. We can illustrate namely the view of individuality versus social connectedness or, in other words, the view of self in relation to others. Although Western views of self have typically been described as "self-contained" and "self-reliant" in contrast to Eastern views of self as more other oriented, there is now substantial appreciation in the West of the self as connected, social, and dialogical.

Moreover, as one might expect, within North America there is now appreciation of significant variations on this cultural dimension. Many Latino families, for example, may feel that maintaining a network of family connections and respect is more important than personal achievement. In a related vein, families also differ on cultural beliefs and practices concerning infant sleeping arrangements. Wolf, Lozoff, Latz, and Paludetto found that cultural differences in cosleeping practices were connected to different values about autonomy, independence, and interrelatedness. Japanese, Italian, Indian and African American families were found to cosleep with their infants more regularly than a U. S. White sample, with the former groups emphasizing the importance of the child learning a sense of interdependence in family and other relationships in contrast to an emphasis on autonomy.

Culture Influences Expressions of Distress

Seventh, culture influences the ways individuals express distress and difficulty. The book *Diagnostic and Statistical Manual of Mental Disorders* takes this aspect of culture into placing a central of account by including a glossary of culture-bound syndromes. Descriptively, many of these syndromes involve the dysregulation of emotions and seem to be supported by cultural forms of belief in the power of strong emotions, such as in the syndrome of *ataques de nervios* in Puerto Rican and related groups. Expressions of grief and depression in some cultures (*e.g.*, Asian) may occur in somatic forms such as gastrointestinal disturbances rather than emotional forms such as crying or mood changes.

Culture is Mediated through the Parenting Relationship

The eighth general feature of cultural influence is at the centre of clinical assessment. This feature acknowledges that in early development, culture is mediated through the parenting relationship. All of the above-mentioned influences occur via parenting. Moreover, the field of infant mental health makes explicit that understanding the caregiving relationship and evaluating its qualities and variations is essential for the prevention and treatment of disorder. How cultural influences result in parent-mediated variations in infant feeding, sleeping, security, and soothing? How cultural influences result in parent-mediated variations in closeness inclinations, caring practices, feeling states, and what is communicated? Next we consider some of these matters in terms of clinical assessment.

Current Integration of Culture and Clinical Assessment

The assessment of infant mental health acknowledges the inextricability of the individual from the context in which he or she functions, placing a central focus on evaluating the parenting relationship. The relationship context as a focus for assessment has dual origins. One origin is clinical experience. It finds itself echoed in the oft-repeated clinical phrase of Winnicott "there is no such thing as a baby" (*i.e.*, there is only baby with mother) and in the equally famous phrases of Fraiberg of "ghosts in the nursery" (characterizing the haunting effects of conflicted internalized relationships across generations) and "it's like having God on your side" (when working in parent-infant psychotherapy while benefiting from seeing the rapid development of the infant). This clinical tradition of infant mental health has led, in a relatively short time, to the creation of parent-infant psychotherapy with both psychodynamic/systems approaches and interaction guidance/educational approaches. Another origin of the focus on early relationships is the developmental sciences and considerations of mental disorder in infancy and early childhood.

A multidisciplinary study group of scientists and clinicians proposed that, based on current knowledge, all mental disorder in the earliest years should be evaluated and treated in the context of evaluating caregiving relationships. They proposed a scheme of relationship disturbances and disorder, which then became influential in the formation of a separately designated axis for this purpose later included in the new diagnostic classification system for ages 0–3.

Cultural variation in the caregiving relationship is therefore a logical topic for us to consider in assessment. Before moving to our suggestions in this area, however, and specifically to our proposed modifications of the cultural formulation as it currently exists in *DSM-IV*, it is important to review our thoughts about diagnosis as a process and the schemes that are available in the current diagnostic classification systems.

Diagnostic Process

It is useful to recognize that the diagnostic process consists of two aspects: (1) assessment of individuals and (2) classification of disorder. The assessment of individuals involves a variety of evaluations of symptoms, suffering, and functioning, and it is considered within the context of family relationships, culture, and stresses that are both biological and environmental. The classification of disorder, on the other hand, involves a way of ordering knowledge about symptom patterns and linking these patterns to what is known in general about etiology, prognosis, and treatment. Disorder classification may also provide a link to services. In other words, such classification allows for communication among professionals about general knowledge, and it is important to remind ourselves that we classify disorders, not individuals.

The *DSM-IV* is used primarily for classification of disorder. It is also, however, a multiaxial system, with the first three axes dealing with disorder and the fourth and fifth axes dealing with individual assessment (psychosocial and environmental problems and global assessment of functioning). The International Classification of Mental and Behavioural Disorders is also multiaxial and similar in many respects to *DSM-IV* Both systems have evolved from initially being concerned with classification only to adding axes dealing with the assessment of individuals. It is therefore noteworthy that both systems, by being multiaxial in this way, have evolved to provide a guideline for clinical formulation. In the applications of *DSM-IV*, Axes IV and V have received little attention although there are indications that in future schemes, increased attention will be paid to the assessment of stressors, adaptive functioning, and the degree of impairment. Along these lines, a substantial innovation of *DSM-IV*, in contrast to earlier *DSM* schemes, is the inclusion of an appendix suggesting a cultural formulation for assessment of disorder within individuals. Although not designed for children (let alone for early childhood), the formulation is appropriate for assessment of parents and is worth reviewing, prior to our suggested modifications.

The *DSM-IV* Approach

The Outline for Cultural Formulation consists of two parts. The first concerns individual assessment and contains a guideline for inquiry that highlights four areas: (1) cultural identity of the individual; (2) cultural explanations of the individual's illness; (3) cultural factors related to the psychosocial environment and levels of functioning; and (4) cultural elements of the relationship between the individual and the clinician. In addition to learning about the individual's cultural reference group and language use, it is important to understand the predominant idioms of distress, explanatory models for illness, and culturally relevant perceptions of social stressors, available supports, sources of care and interpretations of disability. The cultural formulation also acknowledges that differences in culture and social status between clinician and client can introduce challenges for diagnosis and treatment and therefore implicitly recommends that the clinician reflect on this in terms of awareness of his or her own cultural origins and perceptions. In such cases of cultural difference between staff and clients, we recommend the use of cultural sensitivity discussions and workshops to supplement reflective supervision.

The second part of the appendix on cultural formulation makes suggestions for classification, by supplementing the regular *DSM-IV* disorders with a glossary of what are referred to as culturebound syndromes. The term *culture-bound syndrome* is intended to refer to patterns of "locality-specific patterns of aberrant behaviour and troubling experience" that often have local names and connote localized meanings of importance. The appendix points out that some of the syndromes may seem exotic or strange but that there are many subcultures and widely diverse immigrant groups and that the glossary documents syndromes and idioms of distress that may be encountered in clinical practice among these groups.

Cultural Formulations with Children

The *DSM-IV* cultural formulation is clearly aimed at the assessment of adult functioning. As we move to a consideration of children, other schemes are important to review, as they pertain to context and culture. The Diagnostic classification of Mental Health and Developmental Disorders of Infancy and early childhood (DC: 0-3), a multiaxial classification system was developed in response to the need for classification of syndromes experienced in the early years that were not covered in the existing *DSM* system. Similar to the *DSM* scheme, it is multiaxial, with the first three axes dealing with classification of disorder and the fourth and fifth axes dealing with individual assessment (psychosocial stressors and functional emotional and developmental level). Axis I of DC: 0–3 contains an array of regulatory and other disorders that represent particular syndromes for this age period. Axis II is innovative in classification and deals with relationship disorders between caregiver and child. That Axis II in DC: 0–3 is useful is clearly indicated by a number of reports of trials which indicate that a substantial number of referrals are classified within this axis in a way that is meaningful for provision of services. In setting forth a relationship disorder axis, DC: 0–3 targets the evaluation of the child-caregiver relationship as central and goes a step further than *DSM-IV* in assessing context in that sense, but it does not provide a cultural formulation or guide for assessing cultural context.

Two contributions offer suggestions for cultural assessments of children. Novins suggest adaptations to the *DSM-IV* cultural case formulation for use with culturally diverse children and adolescents. Additions to the *DSM-IV* outline are exemplified with four American Indian children (ages 6 years and older). Novins *et al.* suggest accounting for the developmental aspects of cultural identity, the cultural identity of the parents and/or other caregivers, the impact of a biracial heritage, and cultural aspects of the relationship between the parents and/or other caregivers and the therapist. In another effort to promote culturally relevant assessment of children and adolescents, Johnson-Powell proposes a "culturologic interview," and includes the following: country of origin, reason for migration, language use, kinship support, beliefs about causality, child-rearing practices, sex roles, a description of community, life, and home space, reasons for seeking help, description of help-seeking behaviour, educational attainment, occupation, experiences with rejection, degree of acculturation, and degree of cultural conflict.

While Johnson-Powell's culturologic interview and Novins *et al.*'s adaptations to the *DSM-IV* Outline for Cultural Formulation offer useful starting points, both remain limited in their utility for use in clinical practice with infants and toddlers; the former by its lack of detail (as in the *DSM-IV* outline) and the latter because of its lack of attention to issues relevant to infancy and toddlerhood. Considering both the promise and the limitations of existing systems, we propose an outline that represents modifications to the *DSM-IV* outline, which extends features proposed by Novins and

Johnson-Powell. As with the *DSM-IV* outline, its purpose is to provide a framework that will guide both the collection and structuring of culturally relevant information so that an assessment of infant and toddler mental health can be culturally situated, relevant, and useful.

Cultural Assessment Framework for Infants and Toddlers

We have no knowledge about the extent to which the existing *DSM-IV* Outline for Cultural Formulation is routinely implemented by clinicians. However, we regard it as a useful guideline to frame clinicians' thinking about culture and assessment. In this spirit, we present our proposed revision to the *DSM-IV* Outline for Cultural Formulation for use with infants and toddlers.

Proposed Revision to *DSM-IV*

Our revision heavily reflects the eighth general feature of cultural influence discussed previously that culture is mediated through the parenting relationship. In general, we conceive of this revision as both an extension of previous work and also the beginning of an effort to make cultural assessment a formal part of current diagnostic schemes for infancy and early childhood. As is implicit in current multiaxial schemes, we also view this revised formulation as a helpful guideline for clinical inquiry and formulation. Following a discussion of our proposed revisions, we conclude with a case example, utilizing the revised outline.

The *DSM-IV* Outline for Cultural Formulation contains five areas for inquiry, as mentioned previously. The first directs the clinician to describe the individual's cultural identity, noting the individual's ethnic or cultural reference group and the extent to which the individual is involved with both the culture of origin and the dominant culture. The individual's language ability, use, and preference are also noted here. For infants and toddlers, the parents' cultural reference group and degree of involvement with host and dominant culture can be noted. More important, the heavily influenced by our view that culture parents' intentions for raising the child with respect to the culture of origin and the dominant culture are discussed. Following Novins, we suggest including, where relevant, aenvironment, the child'sca discussion of issues of biculturality that may arise for an infant or toddler whose parents come from, and identify with, different cultural backgrounds. Finally, we suggest a discussion of generational issues, such as those that might arise as the infant or toddler grows older and may serve as a cultural mediator or negotiator for the parents (*e.g.*, in terms of language, especially for immigrant groups).

The second area outlined in the *DSM-IV* Cultural Formulation addresses cultural explanations of an individual's illness. The unique ways in which the individual expresses distress are noted here, along with a discussion of how the symptomatic expression compares to normative behaviour in the cultural reference group. Any cultural explanations for the individual's experience of distress are discussed, as well as the individual's past experience with and current preferences for care. For infants and toddlers, we suggest beginning with a discussion of who first noticed the child's symptoms of distress (*e.g.*, the parents or someone outside the family, such as a doctor or day care provider) and the extent to which the parents or caregivers agree that the child's behaviour is indicative of distress. This may be especially important in terms of help-seeking behaviour, because if the parents do not also see a problem, they will be less motivated to seek services for their child. Following this can be a discussion of the parents' perceptions of the child's distress, how the child's behaviour is viewed relative to other children's behaviour in their cultural group, any cultural explanations for the child's distress, and the parents' experiences with and preferences for treatment. The extent to which others are expected to be involved in treatment can also be noted, acknowledging that for certain cultural groups, children are frequently cared for by an extended network of kin.

The third area outlined by the *DSM-IV* Cultural Formulation addresses cultural factors in the psychosocial environment that impact the expression, experience, and treatment of distress and disorder. Our suggested revision for this part of the outline is the most extensive and the most heavily influenced by our view that culture is mediated through the parenting relationship for infants and toddlers. In this section, we suggest addressing three domains: the child's life space and environment, the child's caregiving network, and parental beliefs about parenting and child development. The child's life space and environment refers largely to his or her physical life space in both the home and the larger community. This includes issues such as individuals in the home and their relationship to one another, and community factors such as racial composition and crime. Parental interpretations of social stress and social support within this physical environment are also addressed here. The network is especially critical for placing the child and his or her distress in context. This domain should inventory the significant caregivers in the child's importance of the entire network of both kin and nonkin caregivers involved in raising a child. The child's ers should also be described such as the mobility within the network, noting in particular both continuities and disruptions within this network of care. The final domain addresses parentss'/caregivers' beleifs about parenting and child development not discussed elsewhere—such as any ceremonial practices, beliefs about gender roles, and disciplinary practices. Also noted here are parents' goals and aspirations for their child, which can suggest a positive point for intervention as it provides the clinician with an understanding of potential strengths within the family.

The fourth area outlined by the *DSM-IV* Cultural Formulation address cultural elements of the relationship between the individual and the clinician. Our revision here largely reflects a reframing from the life, acknowledging, as stated earlier, the individual perspective to the parents'/caregivers' perspectiive. In this section the clinician is directed to identify cultural differexperience within this network of caregiv child's ents that may impede the clinical relationship because of difficulties in either communication (*e.g.*, language) or understanding (*e.g.*, different interpretations of the child's distress). In addition, once identified, the clinician must reflect on the significance of these differences for diagnosis and treatment of the child. The fifth and final part of the *DSM-IV* Cultural Formulation calls for an overall cultural assessment for diagnosis and care that is based on the preceding four sections-She considered several options in order to contions. We made no revision to this section, except to frame the overall assessment in terms of diagnosis and care of the child.

Clinical Presentation and Case Description

Here we presented a hypothetical case of an American Indian toddler, intended to demonstrate the utility of the cultural formulation.

Background

Reason for Referral

Thomas was a15 month-old American Indian boy referred for a psychological evaluation by his pediatrician. Thomas was asthmatic and had been seen regularly by the same pediatrician since birth. Thomas's mother brought him in because he was having difficulty in sleeping and was increasingly fussy about what he ate. She thought these difficulties might be due to the new medication prescribed by the pediatrician. During the office visit, the pediatrician noted Thomas's lethargy, relative lack of social engagement, and an apparent language delay. Because the pediatrician could not account for the changes in Thomas's sleeping and eating medically, and because of the additional behavioural concerns noted during the office visit, it was recommended that Thomas's mother seek a psychological evaluation for Thomas.

Developmental History

Thomas's mother described a normal pregnancy and birth, without complications. She described, however, feelings of ambivalence about the pregnancy and about the idea of having a third child after her other children were grown and in school. The ambivalence also arose out of the fact that ceremony. Thomas's father left the family when Thomas's mother became pregnant and that before he left, he had been physically abusive with her. Thomas's mother had just started school and worried that the pregnancy and having an infant to care for would interfere with her progress in school. She considered several options in order to continue school uninterrupted – including having Thomas live with a classmate for a year until she was finished with school, or having Thomas live with relatives on the reservation. She ultimately arranged for subsidized day care through social services.

Since birth, Thomas had spent a great deal of time with his day care provider, who cared for Thomas in her home. Throughout his first year of life, Thomas would spend weeks at a time with his day care provider, without seeing his mother. At most, Thomas would spend weekends with his mother, having spent the entire week, including nights, with the day care provider. Several months prior to the evaluation, Thomas's mother finished school and decided to sharply curtail his time with the day care provider because she not only had more time to spend with him, but because she was also concerned that he was becoming "too attached" to the day care provider and needed to spend more time with his family. The clinician was impressed with the likelihood of attachment problems between Thomas and his mother, and was concerned about the consequences of a disrupted attachment relationship for symptoms of regulation and affect.

Cultural Identity of Child and Caregivers

Thomas's mother was American Indian and had grown up on a Northern Plains reservation. She maintained strong ties with her tribal community. Even though she had moved away ten years previously, she returned to the reservation frequently to visit family and to attend powwows and other community gatherings, such as ceremonies. She enrolled Thomas as a member of her tribe when he was born. She intended to introduce Thomas to his American Indian culture by having him dance at powwows when he was old enough, by having him spend time with extended family on the reservation, and by having a naming ceremony. Thomas's father was Mexican American. Thomas's mother acknowledged his Mexican American heritage by giving Thomas his father's last name, and hoped that one day he would know his father's side of the family and learn about his Mexican heritage. Thomas's mother spoke English as her first language but knew some of her tribal language and would occasionally speak to Thomas in their native language. She hoped that Thomas would learn more of the tribal language than she had, by spending time with family elders on the reservation.

Cultural Explanations of the Child's Presenting Problems

Thomas was referred for a psychological evaluation by his pediatrician subsequent to the pediatrician noticing Thomas's lethargy, relative lack of engagement with his physical and social world, and apparent delays in language acquisition. At home, Thomas's mother noticed a change in his behaviour, observing in particular that he was sleeping more and was more "fussy" about eating. Though Thomas's mother was the first to notice the changes in his sleeping and eating, she noticed little of the lethargy, lack of engagement, and language delay noted by the pediatrician. She believed that what the pediatrician observed was, in actuality, evidence of Thomas's easy and nondemanding nature. In her family and home community, she said that children were taught to learn through quiet observation of their surroundings and by listening to adults and elders. Thomas's quiet nature, she believed, was evidence that he was a "respectful" child a quality highly valued in her reservation community. When asked what she thought the effect of Thomas's separation from his day care provider might be, Thomas's mother stated that she had been around many different adults as a child, and that whatever reaction Thomas might have would pass because he was "strong, and would grow out of it." She believed in general that facing some challenges was good for a child's character. Furthermore, she respected Thomas's ability to "be on his own," to respond as needed to what he faced in life.

Cultural Factors Related to the Child's Psychosocial and Caregiving Environment

Thomas was living in a three-bedroom apartment with his mother and two older half siblings, in a low-income urban housing complex designed specifically for families with parents who were either working or in school full-time. Parents were also required to volunteer for one of the complex's programmes, such as evening child care or tutoring other children. The complex was situated in a racially diverse community; however, there were few other American Indian families nearby. Thomas's older siblings had their own bedrooms, while Thomas shared a room and a bed with his mother. Thomas's mother valued this sleeping time with Thomas, and said that it made her feel closer to him. During times of hardship, her relatives would stay with the family. Most recently, Thomas's maternal uncle came from the reservation to escape legal trouble. However, he was causing problems for Thomas's family because of his disruptive behaviour and because his residence there was in violation of the complex rules, jeopardizing the entire family's ability to remain in the apartment. Thomas's mother struggled with her sense of duty to her extended family versus her duty to her own family, because these duties often pulled her in opposite directions. Growing up on the reservation, and as the oldest daughter in her family, Thomas's mother was raised with a sense of obligation to help family members in their times of need. This was a heavily ingrained value, and when she considered asking her brother to leave, she felt conflicted and feared being judged negatively by other family members, especially her mother. She worried that the stress she felt about this situation made her more impatient and irritable with her own children.

Infant's Caregiving Network

Thomas's day care provider had cared for him most of the time since he was born. This woman took care of Thomas in her home, and would keep him for weeks at a time, during which he did not see his mother. Thomas's mother trusted this woman and readily agreed to let Thomas stay for extended periods of time because she felt her time was already consumed with work, school, and her other two children. As mentioned, she was so busy when Thomas was born that she considered letting a classmate take Thomas to live with her until she was finished with school. She decided against this, however, when subsidized day care became available. Thomas was also cared for by a maternal aunt who lived nearby, who would occasionally keep him over weekends. Thomas's older siblings provided some care for Thomas; however, the pediatrician expressed concern about their ability to care for him, having observed them handling him roughly several times during office visits. Just prior to being referred for an evaluation, Thomas's mother said her cided to put him in the child care facility located in the complex where they lived. She did this because her child care subsidy had been eliminated, the location was more convenient, and also because she wanted to have Thomas with her on a regular basis. At the time of referral, Thomas's mother had made no arrangements for him to see his previous day care provider. Thomas's mother stated that during her childhood she was often cared for by people other than her biological mother, staying variously with her grandparents, her aunt, and a family friend. She also stated that when she was growing up, little distinction was made between cousins and siblings, or between aunts and uncles and parents. Additionally, close family friends were often considered family and at times were ceremonially adopted into the family rendering their relationship the same as if they were biologically related. Thus, the fact that Thomas was variously cared for by herself, the day care provider, and her sister was not unlike her own experience growing up. In fact, she saw it as a positive experience that Thomas had a close relationship with three "mothers."

Caregiver Beliefs About Parenting and Child Development

When observed with Thomas, Thomas's mother seemed to engage in a hands-off style of parenting. She stated that this reflected a general respect for the fact that her children were autonomous and separate individuals, free to learn about the world through exploration and direct experience. She believed it was her duty to tell her children something once, but that it was up to them to follow that guidance after that—learning "the hard way" if they chose not to heed her advice. Her greatest aspiration for Thomas was that he would one day go to college, have his own family, and lead a drug- and alcohol-free life. She also hoped that he would be respectful and strong. Her belief that children were largely autonomous and separate individuals who needed to find their own way in life stemmed in part from what she said was a tribal belief that children, before birth, had been taught many things about life by the spirits, and also chose their families based on what they needed to accomplish on their path here on earth. Thomas's mother said her family elders had taught her these things about children, and that when she needed advice about parenting she turned to these elders as well as to other elders in her home community.

Relationship between the Parents or Caregivers and the Clinician

In Thomas's mother's tribe, discussing problems from the past is believed to give them new energy in one's present life. Thus, there are prohibitions against speaking of past problems lest they be brought to life again. In collecting a family history, which involved the discussion of some past trauma that Thomas's mother experienced (*e.g.*, domestic violence), additional care was taken to gather only the most pertinent information in this regard. When asked about previous experiences with therapy, Thomas's mother said that she had some mistrust of psychologists because she had heard stories that if they did not agree with how a mother was raising her children, they would take her children away. She also remembered how, in her reservation community, word would get out if one was seeing a mental health specialist. She was thus concerned about confidentiality. She and the clinician espoused different views of attachment relationships and Thomas's strength to endure the challenges he faced on his own. This was an area in which the clinician needed to bring her understanding and expertise about child development to bear in a way that respected the mother's cultural beliefs but also served the needs of the child, who seemed clearly to be reacting to a disruption in his network of attachment relationships.

Cultural Assessment for the Child's Diagnosis and Care

The foremost issue in Thomas's case was to support his mother in her culturally derived belief that an extended network of kin (whether biological or "fictive") would benefit both her and her child. The challenge, however, was to help her understand the importance of continuity in this network of care and the relevance of Thomas's attachment to individuals in this caregiving network. The other challenge was to help Thomas's mother find ways that she could maintain her respect for his "being on his own" but also intervene and provide stimulating engagement for Thomas.

Cultural Case Formulation: Overview

The case presented above is intended to highlight several issues in conducting a mental health assessment of an infant or a toddler that is not only culturally sensitive but, more important, is culturally relevant and meaningful to the point that it enhances the care that is delivered. First and foremost, cultural assessment places the presenting concern within the larger cultural context that provides for greater understanding of the disorder and also suggests points for interventions. The case formulation presented above also points out that for clinicians, there are several important issues to consider in conducting a cultural case formulation, often involving the balancing of two apparently opposite poles. First, clinicians must balance cultural sensitivity on the one hand with useful concepts from Western psychological practice on the other. In Thomas's case, the clinician needed to be sensitive to the fact that Thomas's mother believed that her son's mobility within his network of caregivers not only made him "stronger" but provided him with the advantage of having several "mothers." To the clinician, however, it seemed clear that Thomas was having an emotional reaction to his curtailed involvement with one of the attachment figures within this network of care, which made sense from the perspective of attachment theory. The challenge, as stated in the overall assessment; was to help Thomas's mother understand the importance of continuity in this network of care and the relevance of his attachment to individuals in this caregiving network, while still respecting the fact that she saw this as an experience that would strengthen his character.

The case also highlights that, on the one hand, cultural assessment requires a general working knowledge about the process of assessment, while on the other, it requires specific knowledge about a given culture. General knowledge about process involves the "how" of assessment that is, how one approaches a situation of cultural differences in a way that transcends the particulars of any one cultural group. General knowledge about process involves not only a basic acknowledgment and respect for the relevance of culture but also the utilization of such tools as the *DSM-IV* Outline for Cultural Formulation, which can be applied to the spectrum of cultural groups that one might encounter in practice. In order to address the relevance of culture to a particular case, however, one must also possess specific knowledge about the cultural group from which the child and his or her family comes. However, this specific cultural knowledge must be held loosely, as parents may or may not espouse those particular beliefs, which also points to the fact that not all parental beliefs are culturally supported and that there will always be individual differences in the understanding of broader cultural constructs.

Conclusion

The undertaking of cultural sensitivity is not an insignificant exercise in the field of mental health. As Good warns, the danger of crosscultural misunderstanding in the psychiatric process means that "at stake is not only the integrity of psychiatry's claims to knowledge as a science of the human mind but also, more importantly, the care of many of the most disadvantaged members of American society psychiatric patients who are recent immigrants, members of minority populations, or persons who are poor and living on the margins of our society". Good further points out that such misunderstandings can have deleterious consequences for those who are misunderstood such as inappropriate intervention, the withholding of effective interventions, or even greater social injustices.

We presented an outline of eight general features of culture that provide a background for understanding the role of culture in the assessment of infants and toddlers. Those eight features define culture as shared meaning, distinct from ethnicity, race, and minority status, as occurring in a setting or ecology, as dynamic and transactional, as experienced subjectively, as operating silently as well as with voices, as providing multiple views of reality and the world, as influencing the ways in which individuals express distress, and, for infants and toddlers in particular, as mediated through the parenting relationship.

We distinguished the classification of disorder from the assessment of the individual, and the role of current systems such as *DSM-IV* and DC: 0–3 in these pursuits. Both *DSM-IV* and DC: 0–3 are multiaxial systems, which allow for the classification of disorder and the assessment of the individual. By including a specific relationship axis, DC: 0–3 acknowledges that to understand the infant, one must understand the context of his or her development and experience. In this chapter, we argue that to understand the infant, it is also necessary to understand the larger cultural context in which the infant's development, and development in relationship, takes place. As a cultural tool, *DSM-IV* has made a significant contribution to the assessment of the individual with the inclusion of the Outline for Cultural Formulation; the thrust of this chapter is to adapt this outline for use with infants and toddlers. By presenting a cultural case formulation based on these revisions, we hope to demonstrate the relevance of culture for infant mental health assessment as well as to highlight the challenge for clinicians to apply general knowledge about the classification of disorder in the process of assessing a particular individual who is situated in a particular sociocultural context.

2

Prediction and Feeling of Child

Introduction

Human beings have longed to know something of the future and have searched for signs of it in nature. They have looked to the colour of the rising and setting sun to predict the weather, to the thickness of a squirrel's fur to guess the harshness of the coming winter, to the presence of a thin membrane on the face of a newborn girl to know whether she is destined to be a midwife. Although most societies believe in some special sign that foretells a child's future, contemporary American parents are unusual in the depth of their commitment to the view that the psychological qualities of the infant, inborn temperamental characteristics as well as those shaped by experience, might be preserved for an indefinite time. A lusty cry, low tolerance for frustration, and hyperactivity at twelve months are possible signs of athlete or criminal, while gentleness and timidity might mark the beginnings of artist or anxious adolescent. Exposing the infant to many caregivers is assumed to create permanent emotional insecurity; physical affection and reliable care by a single caregiver, especially the biological mother, are supposed to inoculate the young child against an easy vulnerability to later threats.

Faith in a connection between early childhood and the succeeding years also permeates our views of the growth of those qualities that are characteristic of all children, for most theorists believe that each of the universal milestones grows out of earlier competences. But there is another way to view the changes that characterize psychological development. One can maintain that, even though all children pass through the same sequence of milestones for example, babbling, speaking single words, and then complex conversation there is no dependent relation between successive abilities: that is, the capacity that underlies the speaking of sentences might not require a prior capacity to speak single words. This view is not as preposterous as it sounds. All children crawl before they stand, but a child would stand at about one year of age, even though he was prevented from crawling. In a classic experiment, salamander larvae were anesthetized and prevented from practicing any swimming movements. When the anesthetic was removed and the larvae were transferred to fresh water, they swam as well as those that had never been anesthetized. The swimming movements require only maturation of the central nervous system; they are not dependent upon the opportunity to practice the immature swimming movements that occur in normally growing larvae. Thus, the fact that one behaviour always occurs before another does not mean that the earlier behaviour is necessary for the later one.

This more loosely connected conception of growth has never been as popular as its complement, which assumes a fixed series of increasingly complex competences, occurring at similar ages, that are sequentially related to each other so that a later capacity cannot occur without an earlier one. The quieter intervals between the appearance of new competences are called *stages*, and the transition from one stage to the next is supposed to be provoked by a combination of maturing functions and information that is extracted from conditioning experiences, discrepant events, reflective thought, and active interaction with people and objects.

Development as a Sequence of Stages

The course of a life, like the cycle of the seasons, consists of a set of inevitable, genetically determined phenomena which, depending on time and place, are exhibited in a local script whose surface details can take on remarkable variety. The Eskimo infant living near Hudson Bay remains physically close to its mother for most of the first year; the infant born on an Israeli kibbutz is cared for by a hired caregiver; the Mayan infant of northwest Guatemala, wrapped in tattered pieces of woven cloth, spends much of the first year sleeping in a hammock hung from the roof of the house. But despite the differences in affectivity, alertness, and maturity of motor coordination produced by these varied rearing conditions by three years of age, children from these three cultures share the capacity to recognize the past, to become frightened by the unusual, and to understand the significance of an adult prohibition a trio of talents that emerge in that order.

The hypothesis that the transformation of a babbling, poorly coordinated newborn into a loquacious ballerina involves a set of hidden stages unites three separate assumptions a special organization, slow growth, and connectedness. The quintessential criterion of a stage is that it consists of a special constellation of necessarily related qualities. Biology supplies many exquisite examples. When the original fertilized egg becomes two cell layers thick, a stage in which half the cells are outside and half inside, subsequent growth of the cells is determined by the spatial relation between the two layers. The cells on the outside grow to become skin and brain; the cells on the inside become stomach and lungs. Thus, all the neurons of the newborn's brain are derived from the outer layer of cells that emerged at a stage of development nine months earlier.

There are good reasons for positing stages in psychological growth, in addition to the rationales put forward by Freud and Piaget. The infant becomes capable of retrieving the past and relating past and present and, as a result, shows obvious signs of fear in response to the same events that were innocuous a few weeks earlier. One way to interpret the changed reaction is to assume that the maturation of a new competence permits the infant to retrieve the past and to work at understanding unfamiliar or unexpected experience (the stranger and the unexpected maternal departure). Failure to understand provokes a special emotional state.

During the era Piaget calls the concrete operational stage of intelligence, which emerges in a majority of European and American youngsters by seven years of age, children appreciate that the quantity of clay in a ball does not change despite a major alteration in its shape. The child knows that she can pound the same ball of clay into a broad, flat pancake and put it back into its original shape. Additionally, the child knows that names for objects can be nested into categories that have a logical relation to each other. Dogs are members of the category pets, pets are animals, and animals are living things. Piaget claimed that these new talents are due to the emergence of the ability to manipulate the relation between an event and its category, and the relation between categories.

A new psychological organization need not require the maturation of new functions. The loss of loved one, a drug experience, or repeated school failure can produce deep insights and changed moods that permanently reorganize beliefs. The popular idea of "stages of adulthood" rests on this phenomenon. Historians and sociologists use the idea of stage in a similar way. A new idea, invention, or law changes the relations among people, groups, or institutions. The introduction of factories and machine labor led many men and women to leave their rural agricultural settings in order to live in the cities. In time, this practice led to new social structures, including a large group of middle-class, nonworking mothers committed almost entirely to raising their children, and-in the contemporary West of fathers who were away from their families for many hours every day.

I shall use a restricted definition of stage: namely, a changed set of relations among psychological dispositions resulting from the maturation of a new competence. But even this definition implies the possibility of many more stages than Freud or Piaget imagined. Why, then, did these two theorists single out the second year, the sixth year, and puberty as being transitional to new stages and ignore equally significant changes that occur at other times?

The consensus that the second year marks a special transition is not surprising, for language, pretend play, self-awareness, and the appreciation of right and wrong all appear at this time. Even cultures without formal knowledge of human behaviour regard the two-year-old as qualitatively different from the infant. The transition at six years is more subtle. Piaget used changes in reasoning to mark this era; while Freud generated the idea of the oedipal stage from the fact of sex-role identification and from the appearance of guilt over violation of standards, which begins to rival fear of parental punishment as a basis for socialization.

There is a possible relation between the cognitive competences of Piaget's concrete operational stage and the emergence of guilt and identification with the same-sex parent. The emotion of guilt requires a conscious appreciation that one could have acted other than the way one has acted. In order to recognize this possibility, the child must be able to reverse in thought an act issued in the past and to consider an alternative script. This is precisely the ability Piaget posits as being central to the concrete operational stage. Identification with other members of one's biological sex requires the ability to appreciate that one is a member of a set of categories boy or girl, male or female that nest into each other. According to Piagetian theory, the appreciation that categories are related to each other in a hierarchical way emerges in most children between five and seven years of age.

A boy's fear that the father might retaliate in response to the child's hostility toward the parent, which is the heart of the oedipal conflict, requires that the child put himself in the mind of another and imagine how the father might feel if he knew the boy's thoughts. Although two-year-olds are able to appreciate some of the psychological states of others, these states are typically feelings produced by external events and not motivational ideas conditional upon the child's behaviour. According to Freud, the sixyear-old is in conflict because he believes the father knows his motives. But equally important, the child believes he can mute the father's hostility and reverse the course of the parent's resentment by becoming similar to him. In each of these examples, cognitive advances are the bases for new emotional phenomena, not the other way around. The universal fears of infancy are due, in part, to enhanced retrieval memory. Hence, new emotional and motivational states, especially those that mark a stage, often follow the emergence of new cognitive abilities.

But the idea of stage in Western writing on development usually contains two additional assumptions that are not necessary to a change in organization: the first is that the movement into a new stage is always gradual; the second posits a material connection among the elements that compose successive stages.

New Stages: Gradual or Abrupt?

Most theorists assume a slow, continuous growth of the structures that define a stage, with gradual transitions between successive stages. Although the infant's spontaneous smile to a human face appears rather suddenly at about three months of age, psychologists believe that the structures and processes that make this smile possible have been changing in tiny steps since birth. The velocity of growth of the qualities that characterize a new stage is a matter of perspective: the suddenness of an event is always relative, be it the first snow or a dogwood's first blossoms. Although no one denies that some events intrude abruptly into conscious experience, controversy centres not on the subjectively perceived event but on the suddenness of the inferred, underlying processes hidden from unaided perception that are described in the objective frame. Although a wave breaking on the beach is relatively discrete and short-lived, an engineer measuring the changes in hydrostatic pressure a hundred yards out from the beach would note a gradual, continuous phenomenon. Analogously, although the one-yearold's first word "Bye-bye" seems to appear without much prior warning, its display is assumed to depend on an association between the word and the gesture established slowly and imperceptibly from the first days of life.

The degree of gradualness in the growth of structures represents a specific instance of the general, and historically ancient the wisdom of reducing all qualities to quantities. Although a fair proportion of qualities that appear with suddenness must have taken a long time to grow, it is as reasonable to suppose that many equally abrupt characteristics have a shorter history. Reproductive fertility, for example, emerges between twelve and fourteen years of age in most well-fed girls when the brain's sensitivity to blood-circulating estrogen is changed, and the normal inhibition of pituitary secretion of gonadotrophins by the hypothalamus fails. As a result of these relatively abrupt events, sex hormones are released and the visible signs of puberty appear.

Modern historians have become friendly to the idea of sudden societal change. War, natural catastrophe, or a technical innovation may have only a brief preceding aura that is not always traceable to the deep past. For example, some historians claim that the disillusion among European intellectuals over the failure of political and economic reforms after the First World War made it easy for fascist ideas to take root quickly in the decade after Versailles.

Even evolutionary biologists, who traditionally have claimed that changes in the morphological characteristics that define species are slow and gradual, now entertain the possibility that, on occasion, a major alteration in the environment can lead to relatively rapid changes in a species. For example, as a result of a major drought on one of the islands in the Galapagos in 1977, a species of finch that did not breed that year suffered an 85-per cent decline in population, presumably due to a serious reduction in the availability of seeds. One year later, the ratio of males to females had changed from parity to six males for every female. Further, the birds that survived were considerably larger than those that had disappeared. In only one year, an infinitesimal interval of time on the scale of evolution, a dramatic change had occurred in the character of the finch population on this island.

In August 1980, a Caribbean hurricane severely damaged the shore and coral reefs on the northern coast of Jamaica. Biologists were surprised by the amount of change in plant and animal species:

> the effects of Hurricane Allen on the reef populations were impressive for their magnitude, speed, and patchiness. Organisms were unevenly affected, and the reefs are now a mosaic of areas that differ in the amount of open space and in the relative abundance of surviving species. Overnight, Hurricane Allen created patterns of distribution and abundance of organisms that are strikingly different from pre-existing states.

It has been argued that the mass protests against the Vietnam War in the 1960s had a serious, long-lasting influence on high school youths' attitudes toward authority and, by extension, toward the purposes of educational institutions. Those cynical attitudes were established over just a few years, not even a decade.

But despite these examples of serious change with a fast onset, the majority of psychologists have preferred gradual, continuous transitions. Consider some popular concepts that assume slow growth to lie behind psychological novelties. The famous nineteenth-century "law of practice" was invented to extend the time it took for will and self-consciousness to emerge; the gradual relocation of libido, through the mechanisms of fixation and regression, smoothed the sudden appearance of an adult phobia; the "law of effect" removed the surprise from the child's first words;

and Piaget's stages of intelligence transformed the abrupt display of conservation of mass into an extended, seamless, achievement that originated in the play of the infant. The distinguished biologist C. H. Waddington has written:

> The orderly minded orthodox biological world closed its ranks against [the] suggestion that revolutionary processes may happen. It became accepted that the only respectable doctrine is that evolution never involves any thing but step-by-step Fabian gradualism, plodding along a weary way similar to that by which the annual milk yield of dairy cows or egg yield of hens has slowly improved.

Connections between Stages

The preservation of a structure across stages is perhaps the most controversial property of a stagelike conception of human development. This Aristotelian idea, amplified by medieval scholars and present in modern essays, declares that each natural state contains within it the seeds of the next higher state. One obvious advantage of assuming such a material connection is that one can preview what is to come by examining only what is.

The possibility of a connection between early and later developmental phases takes two related forms. One involves only a dependence of one structure or process upon an earlier one, as fingernails require the prior existence of fingers. Does the appearance of language by two years of age, for example, depend upon the prior capacities for symbolism and enhanced memory that are present by one year? Piaget, together with many contemporary psychologists, believed the competences of one phase to be closely interdependent with those of preceding and succeeding ones. Although this form of connectedness between stages occurs, one should remain open to the possibility that some competences may be relatively independent of earlier functions.

A second stronger meaning of connectedness assumes not only interdependence but, in addition, the belief that a particular structure is preserved through succeeding stages, as the same forty-six chromosomes are preserved from the original fertilized egg to the end of life. Are the schemata that a three-year-old has created of the mother's face preserved in any form, or are they replaced completely by the many different exposures to the mother between three years and adolescence? Because the profile of manifest characteristics changes dramatically over the first dozen years, all psychologists agree on the impossibility of finding preservation at the level of the phenotype. If it is present, it must be found in hidden essences that undergo transformation at the surface. Thus, it is assumed that the insecurely attached infant who becomes a delinquent twelve-year-old has done so because fear and hostility to parents have remained as deep qualities from infancy to adolescence.

William Stern, a nineteenth-century observer of children, believed in a connection between the babbling of the five-month-old and the speech of the two-year-old. Other scholars suggested that a person's aesthetic sense is dependent on early exposure to attractive toys. Modern authors have argued for a connection between the harshness of toilet training during the second year and conformity during adulthood, or between multiple caregivers during infancy and a fragile emotional security in adolescence. Some observers even believe that the five-month-old's ability to detect the difference between two and three black dots is the first sign of a future appreciation of the concept of number.

The assumption of connectedness imposes a significant bias on what is observed and described. An observer who believes that a hidden structure is preserved between two points in time is likely to look for actions that can be classified (usually on the basis of physical resemblance) with ones manifested earlier. Piaget, for example, grouped the newborn's grasping of a finger placed in her palm with the eighteen-month-old's imitative opening and closing of the hand: that is, some residue of the act displayed on the first day is participating in the later response. Piaget's insistence on the preservation of remnants of old structures can be traced to his first scientific papers on the classification of snails written before he was twenty years old. The young Piaget defended the hypothesis that morphological changes can be induced slowly by the organism's continued commerce with the environment, and disagreed sharply with those naturalists who defended sudden mutation as the primary basis for evolutionary change (the genus in question was *Limnaea*). These morphological changes, according to Piaget, occur gradually over time and eventually become hereditary and preserved.

These views of snails, remained key premises in his writings on the origins of intelligence in children:

> Thus, when we studied the beginnings of intelligence we were forced to go as far back as the reflex in order to trace the cause of the assimilating activity which finally leads to the construction of adaptive schemas, for it is only by a principle of functional continuity that the indefinite variety of structures can be explained.

Following the spirit of Piagetian theory, Jonas Langer suggests that the origins of adult logic can be detected in the object manipulations of infants six to twelve months old. When a six-month-old raises an object to her face with the left hand while her right hand slides a second object to the right, Langer writes, "The most advanced binary mappings produced at this stage consist of two-step sequences of simultaneous but different transformations". A child who bangs a block three times on a table is displaying a "three unit equivalence which is an instance of two distinct pmto-responding reproductions".

These strong claims for preservation of structure are reasonable only if one already believes in connectedness. When Freud's writings were more popular, many scholars accepted as probable the suggestion that the verbal aggression of a twenty-two-year-old woman toward her professor rests on structures whose establishment began with premature weaning from the breast at nine months of age. Faith in a connectedness between the distant past and the present remains an essential premise in theories of development, as it has been since the beginning of formal study of the child in the decades following Darwin's great work. All theorists assumed a structural link between all phases of development and wrote in affirmation of Bertrand Russell's bold assertion, "The chain of causation can be traced by the inquiring mind from any given point backward to the creation of the world". Many theorists implied that no part of the child's past can ever be lost; that every psychological property in the adult can, in theory, be traced to a distant origin.

But there seems to be no manner of doubt, among those whose studies have best qualified them to speak with authority, that the mind of any person, child or adult, is made up of the sum total of all of the experiences through which he has passed since birth, plus every impression that has ever touched him in passing, no matter how fleeting and transitory some of these may have seemed. That is to say, that every thought, feeling, experience, or image that has ever impinged upon one's consciousness becomes, once and for all, a component part of a great, constantly growing, indestructible body, his mind, which is to say, his real self.

P. H. Mussen, J. J. Conger, and I suggested, that there is a connection between harsh toilet training in the second year and later conformity: "Excessive timidity and over-conformity may also stem from unduly severe toilet training"; and, "Toilet training is a learned situation in which the mother-child relationship may deteriorate, handicapping subsequent, healthy emotional and social adjustment".

All of the preceding statements contain the same premise evident in John Locke's writing several centuries ago:

> The little, or almost insensible, impressions on our tender infancies, have very important and lasting consequences: and there it is, as in the fountains of some rivers, where a gentle application of the hand turns the flexible waters into channels, that make them take quite contrary courses; and by this little direction, given them at first, in the source, they receive different tendencies, and arrive at last at very remote and distant places. I imagine the minds of children as easily turned, this or that way, as water itself.

Most of the declarations of a connected relation between a quality of early childhood and one seen later in development have been based on a single element of possible similarity between the behaviour of infants and actions seen in older children or adults. Humans are remarkably adept at inventing a theoretical reason for a relation between fundamentally different phenomena simply by detecting one feature that is shared, or seems to be shared, by two events. Such inventions are so easy that they cannot be sufficient to prove or even to imply a true relation. The pseudopod of amoeba is as similar to the newborn's penile erection as the infant's grasp reflex is to Silas Marner's grasping of coins. It is only the culture's assumptions that make the former assertion far less credible than the latter. A century ago, the protesting cry of the one-year-old following maternal departure was classified as similar to the willful disobedience of the adult. Today the same act is linked with the anxiety and sadness that follow loss of sweetheart, spouse, or parent. As this century began, Havelock Ellis postulated a similarity between a nursing infant and adult sexual intercourse – to which Freud later referred in *"The Three Essays on Sexuality"*:

The erectile nipple corresponds to the erectile penis: the eager watery mouth of the infant to the moist and throbbing vagina, the vitally albuminous milk to the vitally albuminous semen. The complete mutual satisfaction, physical and psychic, of mother and child in the transfer from one to the other of a precious organized fluid, is the one true physiological analogy to the relationship of a man and woman at the climax of the sexual act.

Why is this analogy, which seemed reasonable in 1900, much less compelling today? Why has the event of nursing become, in this generation, analogous to adult trust rather than to sexual passion? The reasonableness of an analogy between two disparate domains requires, first, a heightened mood of uncertainty over the larger category of experience to which the analogy points; and, second, an *a priori* belief in the root basis of the similarity between the two phenomena. To many scholars at the turn of the century, sex and hunger were closely related by virtue of being the two major human drives around which all of society was supposedly organized. Hence, the mind of the community was prepared to regard an infant nursing as a partially sexual act.

Contemporary theorists award sex and hunger less importance and regard the individual's needs for a trusting, loving relationship and for control of anxiety as more potent forces in human behaviour. Lack of trust between adults has become, in this century, a major source of uncertainty. Hence, to contemporary minds, Erik Erikson's suggestion that the act of nursing contains elements resembling the bond of trust between adults is more attractive than is Ellis's equally poetic idea. All current theories that posit a structural connection between early childhood and adult life are essentially hypotheses about possible histories. They are sentences that attempt to make a coherent story out of a multitude of events and, therefore, resemble both *On the Origin of Species and The Decline and Fall of the Roman Empire*.

But in developmental psychology, as in history and biology, the biases of the observer determine the details selected for the story that is told. Between any two points in time lie many more events than can be seen or recorded; of these the scholar selects a few and ignores many others. In the nineteenth century, the automobile, the television, the nuclear warhead, the laser, and the contraceptive pill were invented; the Germans lost the First World War; there was an economic depression; Germany was divided following the end of the Second World War; the Peoples' Republic of China was created; there was a long, bitter struggle in Vietnam; an American president resigned; the prices of oil and postage increased dramatically. Which of these events are part of a coherent sequence, and which are not? Only theory can produce an answer to that question. The same problem confronts psychologists. Between one and fifteen months of age, most infants will smile at a face, show anxiety toward a stranger, sit, stand, walk, run, reach for a toy they have seen hidden under a pillow, engage in symbolic play, and begin to speak single words. Which of these phenomena are connected, and which are not? The theorist determines which phenomena are structurally related by the plausibility of the reasons given for the relations noted. But these reasons, as well as the initial selection of phenomena, are guided by assumptions that are not always made explicit.

Arguments for Connectedness

There are good reasons, sentimental as well as rational, for assuming connectedness in development. First, this doctrine renders original forms useful and rationalizes the maxim that one must prepare for the future. Ministers and statesmen urged mothers to care for their young children, and implied that a conscientious attitude toward the infant was not unlike gathering wood in August to prepare for December's frigid winds. If the origins of adult properties occur during later childhood or adolescence, then the first years of life would appear to have no special purpose. However, if a person's future is determined by early experience, then the future is, to some degree, knowable through careful attention to each day in the infant's life. It is a parent's responsibility to provide the proper environment for the young child, and the earlier the better.

Second, arguments for connectedness have the illusion of being mechanistic. When each new function is preceded by another that makes a substantial contribution to it, one is better able to state the cause-effect sequence than if a function emerges relatively rapidly as a result of a new endogenous change. In the latter instance, the mind is left with an explanatory gap, as it was for early nineteenthcentury biologists who had to deal with the suggestion that there was spontaneous generation of new life forms an assumption that was troubling to minds who insisted on knowing the mechanisms that generate new forms. Similarly, the hypothesis of the egg as the origin of the fetus created theoretical problems, for no one could see the bodily organs in this tiny cell, and the organ, not the cell, was the primary theoretical entity. It was not until the cell as a unit and mitosis as a process were accepted that the continuous view became ascendant once more, and the nineteenth-century microbiologist and minister William Dallinger could write that there is a "continuity an unbroken chain of unity running from the base to the apex of the entire organic series".

Many scientists believe that a mechanistic account of development is easier if one assumes that all psychological experience involves changes in neurons and synapses. The facts that experience can affect the weight of the brain, and that early stimulation can add tiny spines to brain cells or alter the sensitivity of the visual cortex to vertical lines, have led many scientists to regard the central nervous system as a malleable surface which accepts material marks that are difficult to erase. The belief that experience produces a permanent change in the brain, wedded to the premise that the brain directs thought and behaviour, implies that since the structures first established are likely to direct the later ones, early experience must be important, even though most modern research on the brain also indicates inconstancy. Many synapses vanish; some are replaced; and new ones are being established throughout the life span. Indeed, the waxing and waning of synapses in the canary's brain, which accompanies the annual song cycle, has been likened to the growth and shedding of leaves in May and October.

A third source of the persuasiveness of connectedness is more speculative. During each historical period, there is a dominant philosophical view that most scholars try to avoid confronting an intellectual electric fence. From the Renaissance to the nineteenth century, philosophers and scientists were reluctant to deduce or infer propositions that would refute or contradict biblical statements on man and nature. Although few contemporary scientists worry about the implications of their results for Christian teaching, many social scientists are concerned, often unconsciously, with the implications of their data and ideas for the doctrine of egalitarianism. The criticisms of Arthur Jensen, Richard Herrnstein, and E. O. Wilson have less to do with the data they discuss than with their implications for the idea of equality.

The assumption of connectedness in the growth of human characteristics is in greater accord with egalitarian principles than is the possibility of discontinuous growth, for the latter is likely to be due to maturational changes in the central nervous system. Emphasis on the role of biological changes in the brain implies that an individual's biology has formative force. Since each person is biologically unique (except for one-egg twins), scholars are forced to assume different rates of psychological growth which have their roots in biological processes. This conclusion is regarded by some theorists as inconsistent with egalitarian premises, although it need not be. By contrast, the assumption of continuous development is taken to imply the formative action of experiences that gradually establish new properties. Because most psychologists believe that the life experiences of children are potentially controllable, the connected view implies, but does not prove, that one can arrange similar experiences for all infants. Legitimizing discontinuity in development due to biological maturation, genetic variation, or revolutionary social arrangements implies that the benevolent products of early experience might be abrogated by peer groups, quality of schooling, social unrest, or changes in physiology. Awarding power to the latter forces is regarded by some theorists (incorrectly, I might add) as inconsistent with egalitarian suppositions, for it seems to make it more difficult to arrange similar benevolent experiences for all young children.

Fourth, the belief in the permanence of characteristics is sustained by our language habits, for English contains a bias favoring continuity in an individual's qualities. The adjectives used to describe young children rarely refer to the age of the actor or to the context of action. Like the names of colours, they imply a permanence over time and place. Adjectives like *passive, irritable, intelligent*, or *labile* are applied to infants, children, and adults as if the meanings of these terms were not altered by growth. This is not the case in all languages. In Japanese, for example, a different word is used to describe the quality of intelligence in a child from that in an adult.

There is always a strong temptation to assume that entities with the same name are of the same essence: hence, sixteenth-century herbalists classified wheat (a grass) with buckwheat (which is not a grass), because both had *wheat* in their names. Thus, use of the same word to describe a characteristic in children and adults makes each of us receptive to believing in a hidden disposition which survives, unchanged, over the years.

Fifth, the appeal of connectedness to Western minds may be due, in part, to the significance of formal, written knowledge in our lives, as compared with the daily experiences of most humans for whom many significant events are transient or cyclical. Hunger and satiation, pain and pleasure, rain and drought, illness and health, anger and grief are salient in the consciousness of those who live under conditions where survival is the immediate and primary requirement. In technological societies, reasoning and written knowledge assume a greater importance in daily life. Knowledge printed in books generates a feeling of permanence, unlike the continually changing flux of human moods and desires. The knowledge that influenza is caused by a virus that will run its course imposes some stabilizing certainty on what is an unpredictable sequence of changes in feeling tone. To put it more plainly than is proper, living in a world of scientific explanations composed of abstract ideas that are printed on paper imposes on experience a sense of stability that may be less compelling for those who live closer to events.

A sixth argument for the belief in the connectedness of earlier experience is based on our ranking of children on valued traits both in and out of school. This practice sensitizes every parent of a pre-school child to the fact that the child will be ranked at the end of the first grade, and that that evaluation will influence the quality of education the child will receive from that time forward. Few societies practice such a severe grading of children with such zeal.

American commitment to a meritocratic system forces us to select candidates from the best trained a decision that is made early, perhaps by age ten or eleven. Most parents know this sequence, or sense it; hence their goal is to guarantee that their child is ahead early in the race. Most people believe that a seven-year-old who is more talented in reading, art, or mathematics than other children of the same age is more likely to remain more skilled, rather than to plummet. This belief is true to some extent; the school-age child who gets off to a good start is likely, other things being equal, to remain ahead. Parents assume that the half-dozen years prior to school determine that initial evaluation, and interpret the child's characteristics at age seven as a complex derivative of all that has gone before.

Arguments against Connectedness

Despite the appeal of connectedness, modern biology supplies substantial counter examples. The development of the embryo contains frequent discontinuities in which some structures disappear after their mission has been accomplished, leaving no structural residue. In the metamorphosis of the tadpole, for example, a particular class of sensory cells in the dorsal spinal cord vanishes, to be replaced by the more typical dorsal root ganglion cells. Similar examples have led some biologists to suggest that each life stage requires special temporary structures and functions that facilitate maximal adaptation for that specific developmental period. When the next stage is reached, and these adaptive functions are no longer needed, they are inhibited, replaced, or lost. In most modern psychological writing, for example, the crying of the one-year-old at separation from the caregiver is treated as an index of the infant's attachment to that adult, a state that is assumed to persist indefinitely. The infant's attachment is regarded neither as a temporary process that serves to keep the mother close during the helplessness of the first year, nor as an accompaniment to the maturation of new cognitive talents that have produced separation anxiety as a consequence. In neither of these latter scripts does the phenomenon called separation distress have an important future role. It is similar to the reflex actions of birds that are about to hatch. The special behaviour accompanying hatching is used once, and once only, and has no future function. The hatching behaviour is like the stepping reflex of the fetus whose presumed function is to ensure normal positioning of the head for delivery (an improperly positioned fetus "walks itself" around the uterus until its head is against the cervix). During the first year of life, the helpless infant needs to have the caregiver near. Absence of the caregiver is dangerous, at least until the second and third years. Thus, separation distress may occur toward the end of the first year because children are crawling or beginning to walk and may need a way to recall a caregiver when they move away and confront a dangerous situation. But by age three, when children are more self-reliant, there is no need to cry if a caregiver is not present. In this script, the separation anxiety of the one-year-old is adaptive for that period of development and has no future function. It might even be omitted from the experiences of the first year with no untoward consequences. The normal suckling of young rat pups appears to be of no consequence for the efficiency or the quality of the adult rats' feeding habits. Infant rats prevented from suckling (by being fed artificially) do not differ from normally reared rats in eating or in appetitive learning for foods. Similarly, even though the initiation of play behaviour in juvenile squirrel monkeys is believed to facilitate later social behaviour, the absence of play in some troops of juvenile squirrel monkeys does not prevent the appearance of normal social behaviour.

Each life phase makes special demands, and so each phase is accompanied by a special set of qualities. Succeeding phases have a different set of demands; hence, some of the past is inhibited or discarded. The new pattern may contain none of the elements of the earlier, but often functionally similar, competence.

Faith in the material preservation of human qualities across the life span resembles the pre-Darwinian belief in the fixity of species. Darwin's great insight was to see the history of animals as dynamic, with some species vanishing and new ones emerging. If the analogy between evolution and ontogeny is fruitful, a structure or a process is likely to be preserved if it is adaptive. The demands of the first two years are so different from those of later childhood and adolescence that one might expect many of the qualities of the early period to disappear and leave no trace of their temporary ascendency.

All aspects of growth are not analogous to a relay race where batons are handed in sequence from one runner to another. Rather, some developmental sequences are more like the creation of a painting in which an artist decides when and where a new figure will be added to the canvas. The presence of a row of trees on a canvas does not give rise to the later insertion of a figure reclining by one of the trees, even though the latter follows the former. Despite the attractiveness and seeming utility of regarding development as being composed of slowly growing, connected stages, we should remain open to the velocity of the transitions and the degree of connectedness among them.

I do not claim that there are no structurally preserved elements in development there must be some; I suggest only that it is unlikely that every actor in the first scene of the play has a role in the second act.

Paul Baltes of the Max Planck Institute in West Berlin has invented a useful heuristic conception of the balance of both early and late forces that monitor the development of a life. He suggests that if one were to study the behaviour of a single person every day for fifty years cognitive talents, social behaviour, emotional reactions one would discover times of transition when the person's behaviour changed in a major way. Each of the four major conditions for change assumes differential potency during successive periods of development.

The effect of maturation slows during later childhood, changes in behaviour will be more obviously correlated with environmental demands. Hence, a second set of conditions resides in the normative regimens of a particular culture. Maximum children go to school between four and six years of age; that normative event produces a major change in the child's behaviour. Most youths learn to drive a car, and about half go on to college at seventeen to eighteen years of age. And each of these socially normative events leads to significant changes in a person's behaviour. Although such norms persist through early adulthood, by the third decade they have become weaker. For new normative constraints are imposed on the behaviour of a thirty-year-old.

A third set consists of historical events that affect the entire society but are most influential on adolescents and young adults. These historical events include economic depression, war, revolution, natural catastrophe, or inventions, like the automobile, radio, or television. It is argued that the children who were five to fifteen years of age when television was introduced were more influenced by that medium than were younger children or adults. Similarly, it is believed that Americans who were between fifteen and twentyfive years of age during the Vietnam war were more seriously influenced by the anti-war demonstrations than Americans who were younger or older in the 1960s. The children who are now between seven and seventeen years of age will be influenced more profoundly by the widespread use of computers than their parents will be.

A fourth set of forces are unexpected or unpredictable events, like a divorce, illness, accident, or the meeting of a certain person. Although these rare events are always potent, they become increasingly significant in controlling change in a particular person's behaviour after age thirty, when the other three factors wane in significance, and behaviour, beliefs, and moods have become relatively fixed.

Preservation of Individual Qualities

The theme of connectedness assumes a much different meaning when we consider the preservation of those special psychological qualities that distinguish one child from another. This meaning of connectedness is of great interest to parents who wish to know whether their child's personality provides a preview of his or her adult character. Before we can answer this question, there first must be some agreement on the individual qualities that might enjoy the privilege of preservation.

Unfortunately psychologists do not have the benefit of consensus on primary theoretical entities. Biologists begin each day's work with that advantage: at the core of the three major theoretical ideas in biology inheritance, growth, and evolution is a different hypothetical entity or unit. The gene is the major unit in inheritance; the cell, in growth; and the individual organism, in evolution. Each of these three entities has different qualities and functions.

The major theoretical entities in psychology are not things, like genes or cells, but processes. Hence psychologists must make nouns out of predicates, as do physiologists who write, "Respiration aerates the blood." Although psychologists have not yet discovered any theoretical entities comparable in significance to the gene or the cell, it may be helpful to suggest some candidates. As in biology, the primacy of a theoretical entity is a function of the use to which it is put; and the candidates I shall nominate are most useful for descriptions of the preservation of psychological qualities. These entities may be less helpful in theoretical discussions of language or reasoning, for example.

I also recognize that the primacy of an entity is a function of the discipline's level of progress; and, therefore, its status is impermanent. In the eighteenth century, the organ, not the cell, was a primary entity in biology; and earlier in this century, the nucleus of the atom, not the quark, was a primary entity in physics. Perhaps a century from now, neither the cell nor the quark will be as fundamental as each is today. Considering the current immaturity of psychology, there is little risk in predicting that none of the five units I suggest will be fundamental a century from now.

The units invented to explain preservation have to accomplish five important psychological functions. First, we need a unit that stores an experience in a form sufficiently faithful that a person can recognize most events encountered in the past. The *schema* fills that function. A schema is the infant's way to represent an event, whether it be the father's face, an internal feeling, or the anticipation of the mother. Schemata allow older children and adults to recognize that a voice, a room, a melody, or a fragrance that is now in the perceptual field has been encountered previously.

But schemata do not lend themselves well either to linguistic description or to logical reasoning; hence, we need a more discrete unit that can be communicated easily and is amenable to manipulation in thought. A *category*, defined as the symbolic representation of the qualities shared by a set of events, fills that function. Each person has a large number of schemata for the distinctive qualities of separate adult females, but the category *woman* is a stabilizing force permitting the person to talk about the whole class of previously encountered women. When schemata are sorted into the symbolic categorical bins of food, justice, and joy, the concrete differences among the originally varied experiences are muted. Some schemata become equivalent, while others become part of something larger. When I place my schema for my ten-year-old green Volvo into its appropriate category *car*, it loses its colour, dents, and squeak from the rear wheels; when placed in the category *vehicle*, it even loses its shape and size.

Categories are the essential components of beliefs, for a belief is a relation between categories. The belief, "Boys are tough," for example, represents the relation between the categories *boy* and *tough*. Linguistic philosophers and psychologists treat beliefs as part of a larger class of units called *propositions*. Because many beliefs are preserved, some for long periods of time, it would seem wise to make propositions basic units. Such a decision would not be an error. However, I can avoid positing this extra unit by suggesting that a belief like, "Boys are tough" can also be regarded as meaning that the category *boy* has toughness as one of its salient qualities. And most propositions can be treated as statements about one or more salient attributes of a concept. When a person's belief changes, the salient attributes of the underlying categories change too. A girl whose attitude of hostility toward her mother is transformed to one of respect alters a salient attribute of the category *mother*. There are few propositions that cannot be transformed this way. For this reason, I treat category as the basic entity and *proposition* as derivative.

Schemata, categories, and propositions are mental units, and we need to provide the person with entities that will allow him or her to stay alive and out of danger. Thus, a third primary unit is an *action* which produces some change in the environment. Smiling, talking, hammering, and conforming to a command are potential examples, but dreaming is not. I do not wish to minimize the psychological significance of processes like dreaming, but I suspect that these acts are less significant because a behaviour that produces a change in the environment provides the person with information that can be used to perfect the action so that the behavioural surface can move toward adaptation. I suspect that the *operant*, defined by behaviourists as an action that produces a change, has been behaviourism's most important idea.

Each person, however, possesses many actions, schemata, and categories, and we need to invent a unit that selects the relevant few from the larger array. The nineteenth-century scholar nominated *will* to serve this function. But will is purely cognitive in its connotation; and chronic emotional states, or moods, which control the selection of behaviour, can be preserved for a long time. Thus, a *state of consciousness*, which includes perceived feeling tone and the intentions that dominate awareness at a particular moment, is a fourth unit. Although specific states of consciousness are more transient than schemata, categories, or actions, a state of consciousness is the executor, or executrix, of a large but limited proportion of an individual's behaviours, desires, and emotions.

Finally, psychologists find it useful to invent categories for coherences of schemata, categories, acts, and states of consciousness. These four elementary units form clusters that are regarded as *classes of persons*, our fifth entity. An adolescent who feels anxious in test situations, and avoids situations that contain intellectual challenge, is classified by the scientist as "one who is afraid of failure." One who generates schemata in which one is in a higher status than another, who categorizes most interaction as either facilitating or blocking one's access to status, and who experiences pleasure from dominating another, is classified as a "person with a motive for power." Because investigators who study preservation of human qualities theorize about such coherences, we need to posit a class of person as a fundamental unit.

Almost all the available studies concerned with the preservation of human qualities from childhood forward have concentrated on actions and classes of persons because psychologists do not yet have sensitive ways to measure schemata, categories, or states of consciousness. As we shall see shortly, when actions and classes of persons are the primary units, long-term preservation is minimal until late childhood. But it remains a possibility that when scientists are able to evaluate with greater sensitivity the other three units schemata, categories, and states of consciousness they may find evidence for the folk belief that some early memories and intense emotional states are preserved from infancy to adolescence and adulthood. We will have to wait and see.

How to Measure Preservation

Evaluating whether a psychological quality is preserved over time is much more difficult than it may seem on the surface. One reason for the difficulty is that no living creature remains exactly the same; hence, all statements about degree of preservation must be relative. But relative to what or to whom? An example will clarify the problem. Imagine that, for one hundred successive mornings, we have filmed a woman's behaviour in her home for the first hour after she awakens, and wish to know if her actions during this hour are preserved across the one hundred days. That is, does the woman perform the same acts in the same order on a majority of mornings? But we cannot know whether the woman's behaviour is preserved to a significant degree unless we have some point of comparison; that comparison might be her behaviour during another part of the day, her behaviour in another place, or the early-morning behaviour of another person. If we study only her behaviour during the first hour, it is likely that we might find that, on one morning, she makes her bed, bathes, dresses, and then eats breakfast. But, on a second morning, she dresses and eats breakfast but neither makes her bed nor bathes; and, on a third morning, she does not eat breakfast at all. If we demand a repetition of the same acts or the same acts in the same order, on every morning, we might come to the counterintuitive conclusion that the woman's behaviour is not stable from day to day. But her morning behaviour will seem stable if we compare her actions during the first hour with her actions at another time of the day, or her behaviour at another place, like a hotel resort in the middle of summer. Now we find that bathing, dressing, and eating breakfast are much more likely to occur in that order during the first hour at home than at any other time of day, and that these three acts are more likely to occur at home than at a holiday hotel. Thus, once we supply a comparison time or place, we see that there is considerable preservation of her behaviour during the first morning hour. But in actuality our conclusions refer to the preservation of *differences in behaviour* between times and places.

A third point of comparison might be a less frequent action that occurs during the first hour let us say, listening to the radio. If the woman was always more likely to bathe than to listen to the radio, we would conclude that the former act was better preserved than the latter. This way of assessing stability that is, comparing the relative frequency of one behaviour with another is often used by parents when they reflect on the consistency of their child's personality. For example, children either obey or disobey maternal commands. One might reasonably ask whether a particular child's tendency to obey rather than to disobey is preserved over time. If, for each set of one hundred maternal requests, a child obeys 75 per cent of the time and disobeys 25 per cent of the time, we could conclude that the child's preference to obey, rather than to disobey, is preserved. But note that the frequency or form of the obedience or disobedience might be very different over time and situation. The child might protest on one occasion, ignore the mother on another, or delay acquiescence on a third. Parents who say that their ten-year-old has always been obedient do not mean that their child has consistently conformed to their requests or is more conforming than other children. I suspect they mean that their child's tendency to obey is usually stronger than the counter tendency to disobey.

The most frequently used comparison is the behaviour of another person or persons in the same context. When other persons are the referent, the psychologist draws conclusions about the preservation of differences in behaviour among a particular group of persons. But the selection of the "other person" is extremely important. A comparison of the morning routine of our woman with a neighbour's routine will reveal small differences in behaviour, while comparing her with an Eskimo wife living at Hudson Bay will reveal dramatic differences. Once again, depending upon the comparison chosen, the conclusion drawn about the degree of preservation will vary.

The vast majority of scientific investigations of preservation of human qualities over time rely on differences among persons in some attribute or set of related attributes. For example, if the statures of one hundred children are assessed every six months from one to five years of age, the correlation between height at age one and height at age five is likely to be 0.5, and the scientist concludes that relative height is a stable attribute of children. However, this statement does not mean that a child's height does not change, or that height is better preserved than another attribute, like weight. Rather, it means that the differences in the heights of the one hundred children have remained somewhat constant. When textbooks state that children's intelligence is stable from five to ten years of age, they do not mean that a child's basic intellectual abilities are stable they are not but that the differences in I.Q. test scores among a group of children are preserved, despite dramatic changes in the intellectual talents that accompany growth. A serious problem with drawing conclusions about the stability of an abstract quality from the results of such a strategy is that it is easy to invent a hypothetical quality that might account for the differences among individuals in two markedly different behaviours observed at two different times, especially when many years intervene. Alan Sroufe believes that the positive relation between behaviour in Ainsworth's Strange Situation at one year (some children cry at maternal departure but greet the mother upon her return) and a three-year-old's tendency to explore new toys in a novel environment reflects preservation of the quality that Sroufe calls a "secure attachment."

Although this hypothesis about what disposition is preserved might be correct, it is neither intuitively obvious nor empirically certain. Indeed, the positive relation between two classes of behaviour at two points in time is likely to be the result of many intermediate changes that occur between the two measurements. A middleclass three-year-old with an unusually large vocabulary is more likely to become a successful lawyer than is a working-class threeyear-old who has just begun to speak. But it is as reasonable to suggest that these different outcomes in adulthood are due to the maintenance of their respective environments for three decades, as it is to suggest that the differences in each child's original cognitive abilities were preserved from the third year to adulthood.

Evidence for Stability of Differences

Scientific study of the preservation of psychological qualities has a short history, fragile facts, and is typically based on comparisons among children. Hence, conclusions must be viewed with great caution. Additionally, the primary psychological entities typically studied have been actions and classes of persons, not schemata, categories, or states of consciousness.

In general, the differences among children in specific action profiles – like aggression toward or dominance with peers, dependency upon parents, sociability or shyness with unfamiliar people, and intellectual accomplishments – are preserved from age five or six through adolescence. The very shy, timid six-year-old is likely to become an adolescent who is tense and quiet with strangers, and an adult who prefers a secure job to one that entails risk. When a group of extremely shy, withdrawn three- to eight-year-olds boys were interviewed as adults twenty years later, the vast majority were working for large institutions, and few had chosen an entrepreneurial vocation with its attendant risk. These men stressed the importance of job security, and many more had married outgoing women who complemented their personality than women who were shy and retiring like themselves.

The aggressive seven-year-old is likely to be an adolescent bully. Over fourteen different longitudinal studies, from both American and European laboratories, reveal stability of aggressive behaviour over periods of two to three years, especially among boys. Although there is a gradual drop in the degree of preservation of aggression as the age interval increases, even for intervals as long as twenty years, the differences in aggressive behaviour are preserved. There is, therefore, preservation of some acts and classes of persons from childhood to adulthood.

However, the existing data, albeit vulnerable to criticism, are far less supportive of the belief that the characteristics displayed during the first two to three years of life, with the exception of the temperamental qualities of inhibition and lack of inhibition, provide a sensitive preview of the future. Although the results of each investigation are too weak to bear the burden of proof alone, the findings of many related studies can be woven into a more persuasive fabric.

An international social service agency arranged for middle-class American families to adopt homeless children who had led uncertain lives in Europe during the World war. When the children arrived in the United States, they ranged in age from about five months to ten years. A group of thirty-eight of these children were followed in their new homes. About 20 per cent of the children initially displayed severe signs of anxiety, like overeating, sleep disturbance, and nightmares. But, over the years, all of these symptoms vanished; the vast majority of the children made good school progress; and there was no case of academic difficulty among them. The authors of this study wrote:

The thing that is most impressive is that with only a few exceptions they do not seem to be suffering either from frozen affect or the indiscriminate friendliness that Bowlby describes. As far as can be determined their relationships to their adopted families are genuinely affectionate. The present results indicate that for the child suffering extreme loss the chances for recovery are far better than had previously been expected.

In a later but similar study, 229 Korean girls who when they were between two and three years of age had been adopted by middle-class American families were followed for at least six years. At the time of admission the children were divided into three groups based on their degree of malnutrition and were studied again about six years after admission to their foster homes, when all were in elementary school. The average I.Q. of the severely malnourished group was forty points higher than the scores reported for similar Korean samples who were returned to their original home environments. This degree of recovery of intellectual skills, as well as of physical health, does not occur among malnourished children who are returned to their originally poor environments after a period of rehabilitation.

Even children with symptoms serious enough to lead to their referral to a child guidance clinic at nine years of age can become adequately adjusted young adults. The authors of a relevant study wrote:

> Except for extreme personality deviations, that is, psychoses and extreme anti-social behaviour, there seems to be little continuity between child and adult disturbances. Most children can be expected to improve in adjustment into adulthood with or without therapy.

It may be that the difficulty in predicting from childhood characteristics to adult adjustment is due at least in part to the influence of certain life experiences intervening between the two points in time. As research evidence accumulates, however, to cast doubt on previously favoured theories of the continuity of personality development and of the great importance to be attached to the experience of the first three years of life, the issue of the effects of intervening events, particularly of trauma and stress, has also been open to debate. It now seems probable that life experiences intervening between early childhood and adulthood may counteract or reinforce earlier positive and negative experience and thereby influence adjustment in complex ways.

Psychologists have been following the development of a girl named Genie who at thirteen and one-half years of age was removed from a home where she had been immobilized, isolated from contact with others, and physically beaten for most of the first thirteen years of her life. When discovered, she was malnourished, unable to stand erect, and without language, an unsocialized victim of extreme deprivation. After only four years in a normal environment, she developed some language, learned some social skills, was able to take a bus to school, and began to express some of the basic human emotions. On some of the scales of a standardized intelligence test, she obtained scores close to those of the average child. Although she is still markedly different from an average California eighteen-year-old, Genie has grown remarkably in a short time.

Studies of normal children reveal that most behaviour normally undergoes alteration with development. The results of several longitudinal investigations of working-and middle-class American children, most of whom were growing up in relatively stable and supportive homes, indicated that variation in psychological qualities during the first three years of life was not substantially predictive of variation in culturally significant and age-appropriate characteristics five, ten, or twenty years later; while variation during the early school years, especially five to ten years of age, was predictive of adolescent and adult profiles. For example, children from working- and middle-class parents living in the Boston area had been evaluated extensively four times during the first three years of life. In the first part of the study, the infants' attentiveness, vocal excitability, activity level, tempo of play, irritability, and disposition to smile were evaluated at four, eight, thirteen, and twentyseven months of age. With only one exception, variation in these classes of behaviour prior to one year was not highly predictive of a small set of theoretically related qualities at twenty-seven months of age. These children were evaluated again when they were ten years old, in order to determine if variation in the infant qualities would predict intelligence test scores, reading ability, or a tendency toward reflection-impulsivity at that age. The educational level of the family and therefore the family's social class was the only robust predictor of a child's I.Q. and reading skill. When children from the same social class who were markedly different on both reading ability and I.Q. were compared, there were no major differences between them during the period of infancy.

A major long-term study of seventy-one children who had grown up in southwestern Ohio revealed little relation between variation in activity, dependency, tantrums, or aggression during the first three years of life and variation in a variety of culturally related and relevant qualities during adolescence and early adulthood. Infants who were extremely irritable did not differ in a major way from those who were less irritable when they were of school age; active infants did not turn out differently from less active ones. The only hint of preservation held for the quality I call "inhibition to the unfamiliar": some infants initially withdraw from the unfamiliar, from threat, and from obstacles, while others are more disposed to approach, attack, or retaliate to threat. When the inhibited infants were of school age, they displayed behaviour that seemed to reflect the same quality. They avoided dangerous activities, were less aggressive with peers, and were more withdrawn and less spontaneous with other people. The adult males who had been the most inhibited infants chose vocations that minimized competitiveness and were less traditionally masculine. By contrast, those men who had been the least inhibited infants chose more competitive and traditionally masculine occupations (athletic coach, salesman, and engineer).

But even if there is a biological contribution to this behaviour, these qualities will not persist if they are totally maladaptive. This statement finds support in the fact that about one third of a group of extremely inhibited twenty-one-month-old children were less inhibited when they were four years old, while no uninhibited twenty-one-month-old was markedly inhibited at the older age. As most American parents do not like timid, fearful children, they promote courage and boldness and consistently discourage timidity. A child can change from being inhibited to uninhibited, even though such a change might be more difficult for a child whose behavioural inhibition rested, in part, on biological constitution.

Similarly, most school-age children who are extremely aggressive or withdrawn, and who are therefore subject to both anxiety and social rejection, are likely to grow toward less extreme behaviour. Fewer than one third of three thousand children, six to thirteen years of age, who were nominated by their classmates as being unusually aggressive or withdrawn, remained as extreme three years later. That fact does not mean that the extremely aggressive children were no longer aggressive, but it does imply that the majority were less aggressive than they had been three years earlier.

A similar investigation studied thirty-year-old adults who had been nominated by their peers when they were eight years old as either minimally or maximally aggressive. Although the extremely aggressive children, compared with the less aggressive ones, became adults who described themselves as aggressive and had more criminal offenses, the correlation between the degree of childhood aggression and these two indexes of aggressive behaviour at age thirty were low: only about 0.3 for men and 0.2 for the women. Apparently, most aggressive children became less aggressive, and many minimally aggressive children became more aggressive, over the intervening twenty-two years.

Each child's tendency to acquire the qualities the social environment demands, in spite of an earlier history that might be inconsistent with adaptative abilities, has a nice analogue in evolution. Biologists suggest that those morphological features that are involved in the animal's adaptation are poorer guides to its phylogenetic history than are those qualities that are minimally or only indirectly, related to its adaptation. Thus, the shape of a bird's beak, which is important for the acquisition of food, is a less useful sign of its closeness of relation to other avian species than are its internal organs or biochemistry. A sociable and easy manner with strangers is a desirable human characteristic in modern society; hence, similarity among adults in this quality may not be a sensitive index of similarities in earlier histories. But school failure and extreme timidity, which are not adaptive, are likely to be more revealing signs of a person's past.

Even among laboratory-reared animals, there seems to be minimal stability from infancy to adulthood of individual differences in qualities like aggressiveness, activity, or excitability. For example, the differences among young monkeys in excitability or social interaction were not stable over periods as short as eighteen months; and differences in dominance behaviour among a group of laboratory rats were not preserved over twenty months of observation.

After an extensive review of the evidence on preservation of behavioural differences in animals, R. B. Cairns and K. E. Hood concluded that the preservation of differences in behaviour only became obvious as the animal neared reproductive maturity:

> The findings offer meagre support for the idea that significant features of social interactions at maturity are fixed by experiences in early development. The qualities that are predictable are not in the organism but in the developmental context; its relationships and its likely course of subsequent development.

The young organism is remarkably plastic, and much of what is acquired "from the social environment is transient and is relevant primarily for the organism's immediate adaptation".

Preservation of a quality over a shorter period one to two years occurs often. For example, some infants who were extremely irritable and hard to quiet during the first month of life remained harder to placate at three months. But it is likely, from all the evidence reviewed, that if these children were seen again at five years of age, they might not differ in irritability or in related behaviour.

Some psychologists and psychiatrists resist this conclusion, arguing that infants who are extremely irritable at six months should remain different in some way from those who are less irritable, because the basis for the initial behaviour cannot vanish. These theorists suspect that certain schemata or vulnerabilities to anxiety units that are difficult to measure are preserved, even if the surface actions have changed. This belief is at the heart of the controversy on connectedness. One can always claim that if scientists measured these subtle properties, they would find theoretically appropriate differences between irritable and non-irritable infants ten years later. This is a possibility, but I am suggesting it is also reasonable that no such difference would occur because the bases for the infant irritability may have vanished. Some babies are irritable because of transient conditions, like colic or a temporary allergy to milk. As each of these conditions disappears with growth, so, too, does the tendency to be irritable. There is no more reason to assume that irritability during the first six months will leave persistent structural residues than that a child who has perspired a lot during her first three months, because she was born in the middle of July, will take with her into late childhood psychological remnants of the bouts of excessive perspiration. Every quality need not leave structural heirs.

A second reason that we might not see derivatives of early irritability is that parents do not react in the same way to highly irritable or to minimally irritable babies. Some mothers ignore irritable infants. Other mothers become overprotective, thus creating different dispositions in these children. Similarly, some parents react to non-irritable infants by letting them play alone for long periods; others interact with them a great deal.

The behavioural profile created in children by differential treatment invites special reactions from other people. By the time the child is ten years old, it is unlikely that there will be any common outcome of the simple fact of extreme irritability at three months, even though it is possible, if the entire child's history were known, to create a story that seems to explain why a particular quality of a ten-year-old say, shyness with peers has been influenced by excessive irritability during the opening year of life.

In contrast to the difficulty of using an infant's qualities to predict his or her future, a family's education, vocation, and income are excellent predictors of many aspects of a child's behaviour at age ten. Thus, discovery of a relation between variation in a quality during infancy and one seen in a five- or a ten-year-old need not mean that some aspect of the original quality has been preserved; rather, it could indicate that the same forces that produced the behaviour in the first year continued to operate for the next decade. For example, infants who are very attentive to discrepant stimuli have higher I.Q. scores five to ten years later than do less attentive babies. This finding appears to imply that a quality related to intelligence has been preserved; it is assumed that the "intellectual ability" of some children led them to detect the discrepant events and to look longer in order to understand them. However, both prolonged attention during infancy and a higher I.Q. are more often characteristic of infants from better-educated families. Many inattentive infants born to middleclass families will have a high I.Q. when they are ten years old.

Consider an analogy. Well-nourished, physically healthy infants play with more vitality than malnourished or sickly infants, and healthy adults are likely to engage in more athletic tasks than ill adults. Yet no one would suggest that there is a quality called playfulness that is stable from the first year through adulthood.

Rather, if a sickly child stays in an environment that does not support health, he or she will be ill and weak as an infant and unlikely to engage in athletic activity later in life. The relation between the two qualities is due to the continued operation of a specific external influence, not to the uninterrupted possession of the property of playfulness. If a marble placed in a narrow trough rolls in a straight line, one does not attribute a sense of direction to the marble but appropriately concludes that its linear roll is fixed by the environmental constraint of the trough. In most areas of the world, children born to parents in poverty grow up to be povertystricken adults, not because they possess an inherent incapacity to acquire property, but because they cannot escape their villages.

In general, about 10 per cent to 20 per cent of adolescents in a typical modern community fail to adjust to the demands of the school or to other local norms for socialized behaviour. The best predictor of these apparent failures in adaptation is continued rearing in a family that is under economic stress and believes itself powerless to change its status. Children who grow up in such settings are less well prepared for school mastery and, as a result of identification with their social class, grow to doubt their potency. Hence, they lower their expectations and create defenses against middle-class standards. A child's social class constitutes a continuing set of influences on development. It is this constancy in the envelope of daily events that determines the degree of stability of a psychological quality. The more stable the environment, the more likely the preservation of those properties that are adaptive in that context. It is claimed that, over the last one hundred thousand years, clams have changed far less than terrestrial animals because there have been fewer serious changes in the ecology of the clam compared with that of the horse. Thus, one should not view the infant as possessing a set of prerecorded tapes embedded deep within the brain labeled "intelligent," "irritable," "dependent," "labile, or "passive." Although children present different behavioural surfaces to their environment during the opening years of life, each accommodates to the pressures imposed from without and is altered in accord with those forces.

When a behaviour persists it is often a silent attempt to communicate a wish, a resentment, or a request, either because words are inadequate or because the person is unaware of the message he feels pressed to declare. Many of the adolescents who vandalize stores, smear paint on statues, or steal purses are trying to tell the community they are angry. The scribbled note that warns of a suicide is a request for help; the twelve-year-old girl who refuses to eat is trying to say she does not want to grow up. Of course, each culture imposes special meanings on an action. Among a group in New Guinea, a sudden display of unprovoked aggression by a twentyyear-old man is not a sign of anger, but an announcement that the new burdens of adulthood are too heavy.

Thus, a behaviour is preserved if the underlying message remains urgent. With growth, many messages lose their urgency. Although some stubborn habits resist replacement, many more are symbolic greetings, which, we know, are altered when conditions change.

The existing corpus of data is not firm enough to permit the conclusion that the early experiences or the qualities of infants are of no consequence for later childhood. But the evidence does imply that if the profiles created by early encounters are not supported by future and current environments, change is likely. Some parents resist this conclusion because they want to believe that a particular recipe of experiences in the home is an elixir young children need in order to grow up healthy and happy. Many citizens fear that if the experiences of infancy do not contribute substantially to the future, parents may become indifferent to the needs of their young children. Because the way infants are treated does affect their mood and behaviour, some clarification is needed.

There is probably a broad range of early environments that have similar effects on infants. As long as caregivers provide food, protection from pain, and playful interaction with children on a regular schedule, it is likely that the small differences among twoyear-olds raised on such regimens will have little predictive consequences for differences among them five or ten years hence. But there is no question that infants who frequently experience prolonged periods of distress, and do not enjoy playful interaction with adults, will be more fearful, irritable, and perhaps more aggressive and less cognitively proficient at age three than children treated in more benevolent fashion.

Consider an analogy to colds. It is reasonable to suppose that infants who contract only two colds during the first year will not, other things being equal, be healthier at age six than infants who contract six colds. But children who have had chronic respiratory infection throughout the first year will probably be less healthy at age six. And, indeed, the evidence indicates that the number of acute bouts of self-limiting illnesses in early childhood is not very predictive of the future health of middle-class children. There seems to be a threshold function: up to a point, quality of experience is of minimal importance for the future. But once that threshold is crossed, the consequences are more serious. Because most American parents provide adequate care for their infants, they may not need to worry excessively about the potential impact of every missed hug or impulsively administered punishment. But that suggestion does not condone indifference, aloofness, or lack of love.

Infants whose experiences have created pathology are likely to continue to grow anomalously only if they remain in the same environment. However, two-year-olds are receptive to change if their neglecting environments become benevolent and facilitate more desirable development. Nature has supplied a nice example of this hypothesis. If a pregnant mother is tense or ill for most of the pregnancy, the probability of a premature birth is increased. And infants born prematurely are different psychologically during the first year or two of life. But if the environment is supportive of growth, psychologists are unable to find any differences between six-year-old children born prematurely and those born at term. The experiences of the intervening six years are able to repair or change the psychological profile of the premature infant.

Another example of this principle is seen in a long-term study of over six hundred children growing up in the Hawaiian group who were followed from birth to eighteen years of age to see whether infants born with perinatal complications were at risk for later academic problems or psychiatric disorders. Only a small group of fourteen infants were born with serious perinatal stress. Of this group, four were mentally retarded at age ten, two had mental health problems, and three were delinquent. Thus, serious perinatal stress does place an infant at risk. But, of the sixty-nine infants born with mild perinatal stress, the occurrence of mental retardation, schizophrenia, neurotic symptoms, or delinquency was not greater than it was for infants born without risk, because a supportive home environment can ameliorate the vulnerabilities imposed by perinatal stress. More important, the stressful nature of the home environment was more predictive of later psychological problems than was risk status at birth. Children growing up in homes that had minimal psychological stability or economic disadvantage were more likely to have problems during adolescence than were those born with some form of biological risk.

When these children were ten years old, about sixty10 per cent of the original group were anxious, had neurotic symptoms, or were in need of psychiatric treatment. But these problems proved temporary, especially for the adolescents who came form economically secure families. The combination of biological stress at birth and an economically stressed family environment was the best predictor of later psychological problems; either condition alone was far less potent. The authors wrote: "As we watched these children grow from babyhood to adulthood we could not help but respect the self-righting tendencies within them that produced normal development under all but the most persistently adverse circumstances".

Conclusion

This discussion of the two forms of connectedness challenges two favourite assumptions in Western views on human development. Many observers want the past to seriously constrain the present through material links that join the universal milestones of growth into a forged chain. Each child must step on every link no skipping permitted as he or she journeys into maturity. It is odd that, in a society that celebrates originality, many social scientists prefer psychological novelties that are so dependent upon the past they seem almost determined.

The second popular assumption, captured by the motto "Well begun is half done, holds that the qualities acquired first will be the last to go. Hence, by looking at an infant, we not only obtain a preview of what is to come, but we are also justified in explaining a particular adult's personality as a necessary product of the distant past. These two suppositions ignore the power of the many social forces and maturing abilities that appear later in life.

The evolutionary tree may be a good metaphor for psychological development. Biologists do not explain the appearance of man by pointing to protozoa, even though in the remote past the existence of protozoa made humans a little more likely. Rather, scientists point to the entire evolutionary sequence. Similarly, one cannot explain a ten-year-old's phobia of horses or Proust's aestheticism by listing their respective experiences as infants. Each person can be understood only as a coherence of many, many past events.

The satisfying quality of an explanation that relates two psychological qualities separated by a long period of time depends on the degree to which the theorist can fill the temporal space with possible mechanisms. The older the child, the less satisfying are explanatory propositions that rely too heavily on early experience.

Each developmental journey contains many points where one can move in any one of several directions. Each choice modifies, in however small a way, the probability of a particular outcome. A perinatal trauma alters the probability of future academic failure by some very small amount. The affection of the mother, the arrival of a sibling, the authoritarian quality of the father, and the degree of success in first grade comprise successive events that move a child toward certain choices and away from others. Once a choice is made, the child will resist being detracted from that path.

The embryological development of the neural crest cells provides the most informative analogy. Early in the growth of the nervous system, the cells surrounding the future spinal cord begin to migrate to various locations in the tiny embryo. Some of these cells will end up serving the eye; some, the gut; some, the heart. Their final fate is determined by the cells they will encounter in their journey; it is not inherent in their intrinsic structure before their migration begins. But once the cell reaches its destination whether eye, gut, or heart it assumes a form that eventually becomes impossible to change. This principle seems to apply to psychological development. I suspect that it is only when the child interprets experiences as having implications for his talent, gender, virtue, and acceptability that his dispositions become more resistant to change. As we shall see in the next chapter, the first components of a sense of self do not emerge until late in the second year.

3

Guiding Principles in Human Development

Introduction

It is so natural to suppose that there is a special purpose hidden in the facts of growth that most scholars who posit a universal scenario add, as a statement of faith, that children are moving toward a higher plane where they will be more free, more logical, more loving, more moral, or more detached, depending upon the favoured metaphysical theme.

All sciences first select phenomena to study and then gather evidence in order to explain why certain events occur together-whether the joined events be the presence of bacteria and a high fever, or the association between an extra chromosome and mental retardation. But the scientists who study human nature, especially psychologists and sociologists, often add an additional question.

They ask, To what end, or, For what purpose, are the events related? and usually have a favoured purpose in mind before they begin their work. A great many child psychologists, for example, believe that maternal love toward a child should produce a less anxious and more self-confident adolescent. They expend a great deal of energy trying to prove that this idea is correct, and far less effort in trying to determine *how* maternal love might create any set of consequences. I shall try to keep these two questions separate and will stress the *how* of development over the *why*. Thus, a second pair of questions seeks the reasons for the phenomena of development. Why do the abilities and moods of children exhibit similar changes, and why are children of the same age so different? It is understood that we will need different explanations for these two kinds of variation.

The final pair of questions springs naturally from a desire to predict the future. Which of the many qualities observed in infants and children are preserved for years, and what conditions maximize the stability of a belief, a talent, a desire, or style of behaviour?

The attempts to solve this trio of conundrums are guided, as is all scholarship, by deep premises that the physicist Gerald Holton calls *themata*. Each theme is defined by a pair of complementary assumptions that can be neither proven nor refuted. Each scientist is loyal to one or the other of the assumptions, and his or her research gains coherence through that point of view. Five themata currently guide developmental inquiry.

Biology and Experience

The first theme involves the balance between biology and experience. There have been two contrasting views of the child. One emphasizes the strong hand of maturation, which releases new talents as it gradually relaxes its hold over the first dozen years. The complementary view places the formative power in the richness of encounters and comes very close to claiming that almost anything is possible if adults are clever enough in the way they handle children. Theorists who side with Aristotle and modern behavioural geneticists award considerable potency to the qualities that are inherent in the biological nature of the child. These potentials guarantee the appearance of speech and reason in all youngsters and vulnerability to fear or psychosis in some. The most important biological influences on psychological development are contained in the maturation of central nervous system structures that permit motor and cognitive abilities such as walking, speech, symbolism, and self-awareness to appear at regular times. The brain is still completing its growth during the early years, and the cortex of the young infant resembles that of the adult rat. Nerve fibres must still finish their growth, important connections must be made, and all of the neurotransmitters that are essential to adult functioning may not be operative in the infant.

Contrary to popular intuition, brain growth during childhood is characterized by the elimination of synapses that were laid down during the months before and immediately after birth. This pruning of connections permits the surviving cells to expand their contacts with neighbours, much as an animal species comes to dominate an ecological niche as its competitors are eliminated. The victor in the neuronal competition is determined, in part, by asymmetry of stimulation and use. If the right hand is used more than the left, the neural connections that serve the right hand expand their sphere of dominance; those serving the left lose some power. There may be a material basis for the folk belief that those who are unusually skilled at languages are a little less proficient with their hands. Although loss, as well as gain, is inherent in the growth of the brain, the loss of synapses is accompanied by greater specificity of response, decreased malleability, and a capacity to inhibit an automatic reaction. The qualities that are direct consequences of maturation are inevitable, as long as children are growing in any reasonably varied environment where minimal nutritional needs are met and children can exercise emerging abilities.

These two caveats are necessary, for the competences that are dependent upon growth of the nervous system can be affected, often seriously, if animals or children are deprived of stimulation or an opportunity to act. Although rhesus monkeys raised in isolation, with no visual access to humans or monkeys, eventually display to a human face the same signs of fear that are shown by normal monkeys, the fear occurs about a month later than it does in animals who are exposed to other monkeys and humans. But almost all children, save for an unfortunate few who are locked in empty rooms or housed in barren institutions, experience sufficient variety to permit the biological changes natural to our species to occur. As brain structures reach certain levels of organization, new cognitive abilities emerge which make new motives possible. For example, it is not until after the second birthday that the child appreciates that her behaviour is evaluated by others with respect to standards of excellence. When the child becomes aware of these evaluations, a motive for task mastery emerges. By age seven, when the child can compare some properties of self with those of others, he generates either a motive of hostility toward, or a motive for acceptance by, those peers who possess desired characteristics he does not have. Finally, cognitive abilities that appear at puberty generate a motive for logical consistency between beliefs and between beliefs and behaviour. Thus, the emergence of cognitive talents during the first dozen years is accompanied by motives that, although they may appear to be the same as, or derivative of, earlier ones, are often novel desires.

Scholars who regard the environment as more formative treat evolution through natural selection as a generative model for growth, because that perspective emphasizes the child's malleability in response to challenge and the potential for change that follows an individual's attempt to cope with real or imagined threat. But the environmentalists also see history as limiting change. Each person lives simultaneously in nested social spheres extending from the home to the neighbourhood to the fuzzy boundaried culture that constrain what the child values, believes, and dreams. Karl Marx saw this principle operating on the large stage of class membership. B. F. Skinner's script is written for a pair of players in a smaller theater. But both theorists have insisted that because each person is partly imprisoned by his or her past, the potential for change is not limitless.

The main catalyst for environmentally mediated change is information. One source of information is contained in those events that have become associated with strong feelings. A child looking outside a window at a large red bus is startled by an unexpected clap of thunder, feels frightened, and cries. The next time she sees a large red bus, or perhaps any bus, she may re-experience the feeling of fright. Sometimes the child's own behaviour becomes predictive of a desired goal. A one-year-old cries when his mother tucks him into bed, turns out the light, and leaves the room. The cry provokes the mother to return, turn on the light, and go to the infant's side. The return of the mother, regarded as a rewarding event, increases the likelihood that in the future the child will cry when the mother puts him to bed.

However, it is not possible to specify the characteristics of the rewarding events most likely to change the probability of actions that precede them. In the past, most scholars stated, without argument, that the important component of the rewarding event was its ability to provide pleasure to an actor. But because one does not feel pleasure every time one performs an action that attains a goal, many psychologists argue that if a response is simply followed by any change in experience especially one that is alerting the probability that the behaviour will occur again is enhanced. But that conclusion is not quite accurate either, for new actions always produce changes. I move my pencil to produce a change in experience, but that sequence of events does not necessarily increase the probability of my repeating that action. The depth of the enigma is apparent when we watch a baby who has just acted in a way that seems to provide pleasure. The baby strikes a balloon full of beads, causing it to move and make a noise. The baby laughs and repeats the action. The movement and noise occur again and again, and the baby smiles. If this sequence were an example of the principle of instrumental conditioning, the baby should repeat the act until exhausted. But after only a few minutes, the baby stops smiling, as if she were bored. The common phenomenon of boredom following attainment of a goal suggests that we must know something about the motivational state and knowledge of the child. If the child does not desire the goal, the response that ordinarily gains it will not occur.

A third source of information is contained in the unfamiliar and the unexpected, for such events provoke the child to attempt to relate them to his knowledge in a process that changes what he originally knew. Consider a five-month-old whose only representation of a human is the mother's form and face a structure we call a *schema.* The infant scans the face and form of the first unfamiliar adult he has seen, detects a relation between the stranger and the schema of the mother's face, and, in relating the former to the latter, becomes sensitized to the possibility of unfamiliar faces. This single experience with the novel face probably alters the child's ability to assimilate the next stranger more rapidly.

A two-year-old notes her first animal with horns and tries, at first unsuccessfully, to relate it to a schema of the dogs and cats she has often encountered in the past. As a result, she changes her schema for animals to include the possibility of one with horns. Encounters with new information change beliefs, too; an eightyear-old who learns that her friend's father locked her in a room may brood for the first time on the possibility of cruel fathers and deeply angry children.

New ideas are also created through reflective thought. The child is continually making inferences from information that is not immediately comprehensible. An incompletely understood event provokes a child to generate hypotheses that facilitate understanding. If one of the guesses is followed by a sense of resolution, whether or not it is valid, the child treats it as correct, until it is disconfirmed by experience. A twenty-month-old child is shown a toy cup, a car, and a cat and correctly gives the examiner the toy requested on three successive occasions. The examiner then replaces these three toys with two new, but equally familiar, objects and one odd-shaped piece of wood that is totally unfamiliar. The examiner waits a few seconds to permit the child to scan the toys and then, in a matter-of-fact tone, asks, "Give me the zoob." The child pauses for a moment and then gives the odd-shaped piece of wood to the adult. The confidence of the child's reply implies that she regards the question as reasonable and assumes that the unfamiliar object must be the correct referent for the unfamiliar word.

Reflective thought is often provoked by communications from others. The child tries to maintain consistency among his beliefs and actions. Discovery of an inconsistency leads the child to change one or the other. The child who believes reading is an important skill but fails reading tests for three years in a row is troubled by the implication that he might be incompetent at a task he values. Since this conclusion is inconsistent with his view of self as capable, he may reclassify the task as unimportant. Failure does not generate disparagement of reading skill in all children; some continue to treat it as sacred and live with the anxiety that comes from acknowledging their incompetence.

The structure of beliefs about self and world that are most resistant to change is called a *frame*. The frame determines the events that will be selected for accommodation and imposes biases on the conclusions drawn from experience. Most children hold a frame that assumes their parents are wise, competent, just, and affectionate. For a much smaller group, the premises of the frame are reversed. Hence, a particular event will not be interpreted similarly by these two classes of children. A chastisement, for example, is viewed by a majority as motivated by the parent's desire to raise a socialized child, and is treated as serving the child's welfare. A smaller group of children interpret the punishment as a sign of parental hostility.

Although the maturation of cognitive functions can initiate a change in frame for example, adolescents examine their beliefs on a topic as a related set and, when they detect inconsistencies, change some of these beliefs most of the time, new experiences produce a change in frame. One of the most significant experiences for an only child is the arrival of a new baby, especially if the older child is between two and five years of age. Many mothers report changes in the behaviour of their three-year-old that do not occur as often in three-year-olds who remain only children. The former child first shows a brief period of anxiety; he may lose bowel and bladder control and want to be with the mother continually. But soon a spurt of more mature behaviour appears, characterized by more initiative and a loss of fearfulness. One basis for the new boldness is the realization that, for the first time, there is a person less potent than the child, not unlike the lightening of mood that follows discovery of someone who carries a more serious burden. The basis for change is not based primarily on special interactions with the sibling or on new patterns of behaviour with the parents. The new qualities are a product of the mental comparison of self with sibling and a realization of the differences in size, strength, and competence. Thus, it is necessary to assume, with John Locke and Leon Festinger, that the mind is prepared to be altered simply by detecting novelty in the world or inconsistency among one's ideas. It is reassuring to note that recent essays on conditioning also acknowledge that a discrepancy between what the animal wants and what happens is fundamental for a conditional association.

But we must never treat the biological and the experiential as separate, independent forces. The complementarity of the two is best illustrated by the early growth of the brain. Although the number of neurons a particular species will possess seems to be determined strictly by its genetic constitution, the locations of those nerve cells and the pattern of final synaptic connections in the central nervous system are influenced by both local physical and chemical conditions and experience and, therefore, are much more variable. Indeed, whether a particular cell appearing in the earliest phases of neural development becomes part of the spinal column or part of the eye depends in large measure on the cells it meets as it travels from the neural crest to its final destination.

Some social scientists have accepted the unprofitable and misleading dichotomy between biology and experience, in part, because they inherited statistical models that assume that influences due to endogenous forces can be separated from those due to exogenous ones. Biologists and physicists have more successfully avoided the fallacy of treating complementary forces as having independent causal status. An embryo capable of cell division is formed when the sperm and egg unite; neither is the more important cause of the first division of the fertilized egg. Or, consider a pond in the process of freezing. Water has one set of inherent properties over 32 degrees Fahrenheit and another set when the outside temperature falls below that point. Physicists do not explain the pond's freezing by assuming that the formation of ice can be apportioned into one set of factors attributable to the inherent properties of water and into another ascribable to external change in temperature. Freezing is a unitary event resulting from a particular quality of the outside air acting upon a closed body of water. In a similar vein, the cognitive development of a premature infant who grows up in an economically disadvantaged home will follow a different developmental course than will that of a premature infant who grows up in a middle-class home. It is not possible to determine the differential importance of being born premature and subsequent family experience on a child's profile of intellectual abilities.

Connectedness and Discontinuity in Development

A second theme contrasts the belief in continuous, connected growth from infancy to adulthood with the possibility of serious discontinuity, where some earlier characteristics vanish completely and new ones emerge with relatively short histories. Put plainly, what qualities of infants and children are preserved, and for how long?

No era in the history of Western society is without its share of scholars, ministers and statesmen who declare that part of the adult character is formed during the opening years of life. Plato believed that the baby who is rocked frequently becomes a better athlete; German Reformation leaders declared that the hand that rocks the cradle shapes the destiny of a society; nineteenth-century New England ministers in Sunday sermons told parents that the way they handled their infants would determine the child's future character. Rousseau's diagnosis of society's problems is modern in tone:

> When mothers deign to nurse their own children then will be a reform in morals; natural feeling will revive in every heart; there will be no lack of citizens for the state; this first step by itself will restore mutual affection. As women become good mothers men will be good husbands and fathers.

Concern with the initial period of development, which is part of a general curiosity about the origins of natural phenomena, rests on the premise that each life is an unbroken trail on which one can trace a psychological quality from any point back to its beginning. Each child provides the discerning mind with clues that are subtle previews of adolescence and adulthood. Hence, parents fear that their quiet, timid three-year-old will become an adolescent loner, or anticipate that their effusive energetic six-year-old will be elected president of her high school class.

The possibility of serious change in psychological profile complements the theme of stability. Classic Chinese premises form a compelling contrast to those of the West, for an emphasis on change, rather than on permanence, has dominated philosophical writings during most of Chinese history. An important third century essay the "Chuang-tzû Commentary" captures this theme: "Of the forces which are imperceptible forces, none is greater than that of change. All things are ever in a state of change therefore the I of the past is no longer the I of today".

Despite the Western preference for stability, Americans invest so much of public and private resources in purchasing the services of psychologists, psychiatrists, and counselors, and in supporting government intervention programmes, they must believe that a child's behaviour can be changed through benevolent intervention.

Americans, from colonial times, have trusted the power of education to remove incompetence and to civilize the vagrant and the criminal. A threatening consequence of the scientific evaluations of benevolent efforts like Head Start and increased expenditures for schools is the general pessimism regarding their permanent benefit to the child. On the other hand, some delinquents do stop stealing and apply to college, and some successful executives leave their jobs and families to write poetry in isolated mountain cabins. Even though these cases are not the rule, their existence forces us to acknowledge the possibility of some change at any point in the life span.

Qualities and Quantities

A third theme deals with our descriptions of human characteristics. There are two ways to think about natural events. A tree, the taste of salt, the sound of a crashing wave, and a suicide seem to be qualitatively distinctive events, not parts of a graded series. By contrast, the depth of blue in a morning sky, the temperature of a cup of tea, the perceived speed of our heartbeat, and the feeling of fatigue in a particular moment seem to be points on a continuum of similar events that differ from each other only in degree.

Most of the properties of matter that are of concern to physicists are continuous, like weight, length, temperature, and, for an object in motion, velocity. But the biological qualities of living creatures irritability, reproduction, disease are generally not continuous. A nerve cell is or is not in an irritable state; a female is or is not reproducing an offspring. There is no state of "partial pregnancy."

This dichotomy between qualitatively discrete properties and continuous quantities has been a persistent source of debate in essays on the essence of natural phenomena. On the one hand, there was Aristotle's insistence on qualitative differences among events; and, on the other, Plato's view that the unique qualities that seem to compose phenomenal experience are derived from invisible continuities in their basic elements. The status and intellectual power of mathematics, which were enhanced in the subsequent two millenniums, persuaded most Enlightenment scholars to side with Plato and to declare, with Galileo, that God used mathematics as the language of nature, even though the power of mathematics in the natural sciences remains mysterious and defies rational explanation. Therefore, the best scientific explanation should eventually rest on continuous mathematical functions. Explanations that rely on qualities are preliminary, less powerful, and always less pleasing.

Despite the fact that many psychological phenomena seem to be best described as discrete qualities, psychologists prefer, whenever possible, to flatten the bumpy qualities into tiny points on a graded series. Consider the perception of colour. Qualitatively different cells in the retina and the thalamus respond selectively to light of different wavelengths, even though the physicist describes the light in a continuous metric of nanometers. And infants, like adults, treat the differences between the hues as discrete categories rather than as visual experiences on a continuum. After becoming bored with a circle that is crimson in colour, infants show far less excitement when a pink circle replaces the crimson one than when the change is from pink to green, even though the physical changes are of equivalent wavelengths, as measured in nanometers.

Similarly, psychological phenomena like schizophrenia and Down's syndrome are not instances on a continuum of psychic disturbance or intelligence, but coherent sets of distinctive qualities. A biologist who correlated the speed of completing a mating episode with the size of reproductive organs in a variety of species of animals, and invented the continuous concept of "mating efficiency," would probably invite a sarcastic critique from colleagues. Yet most social scientists do not deride a scientist who computes ratios of brain to body weight in different species in order to infer a continuum of intelligence, because psychologists are attracted to characteristics like intelligence that fall on a continuum, and are less friendly than biologists or linguists to the idea of distinctive classes. One of the sharpest controversies in modern linguistics concerns whether human language is a distinctive characteristic of our species, or a talent that lies on a continuum with the communicative competence of apes.

One of the unfortunate consequences of regarding discrete qualities as points on a continuum is the practice of comparing children of vastly different ages on the same characteristic (for example, the number of ideas that can be recalled or the magnitude of increase in heart rate to a threat), with the assumption that the conditions that produced the behaviour are identical for all age groups and differ only in intensity. But infants are qualitatively different from older children and should not be conceptualized as having less of some quality than ten-year-olds possess.

One reason psychologists prefer continua is that the statistical techniques available to them correlations, analysis of variance, and path analysis assume an underlying continuum of causation, with both extreme and less extreme values produced by the same forces.

General and Specific Constructs

The selection of the most appropriate level of analysis, which lies at the heart of the fourth theme, contrasts broad with narrow concepts. Until recently, psychologists have preferred very broad ideas. Freud, for example, felt he needed only three basic forces – id, ego, and superego to explain most behaviour. Both Piagetians and behaviourists also base their explanations of behaviour on a very small number of concepts. Their strategy is to use a limited empirical fact to invent a broad explanatory idea – a leap away from specificity. I suspect that one reason for this ambition is traceable to the sociology of science. Disciplines, like individuals, imitate those with higher status. Mathematics, acknowledged to be the queen of sciences, enjoys the greatest respect in the academy, and most mathematicians, especially those who call themselves formalists, regard complex deductive arguments from a small set of axioms as the ideal of scholarship. But biology provides a productive counterexample. There are only a few broad ideas in biology, but many powerful specific ones. The concepts of cell, nucleus, and DNA were all inductively derived, and each has a specific set of functions that cannot be deduced from a small set of assumptions. I believe psychology should follow biology, not mathematics, at this point in its short history.

There is, therefore, a tension in psychology over how general or specific psychological concepts should be. Most contemporary psychologists prefer constructs that are minimally constrained by local conditions like setting, incentive, and target. Descriptive terms such as "need for achievement," "anxiety," "hostility," "working memory," and "intelligence" are popular examples. But people do not possess these abstract qualities in all situations. No one desires to achieve in all settings or is hostile to all people. A psychologist friendly to the view that names for human competences or dispositions should be constrained by context, would use constructs that include a clear reference to the locus of action, and replace "need for achievement" and "hostility" with "need for intellectual achievement" and "hostility toward male authority."

Every psychological procedure is a specific context in which a person reacts. Therefore, the meaning of a quality inferred from a person's reactions often must be limited to that scientific procedure, as we shall see in chapter 6. But psychologists habitually use seriously different procedures to measure what they think is the same quality. One scientist asks the child if she is afraid of her father; another watches the child's behaviour with the parent at home; a third puts electrodes on the child to see if her heart rate changes when she sees a picture of man punishing a small child. It is not surprising that each procedure yields a different answer. But rather than conclude that there is no single meaning to "a child's fear of the father," investigators throw stones at the procedures they distrust.

The relation of procedure to conclusion is nicely illustrated in the work of particle physicists who wish to determine the elementary constituents of the atom. When scientists build a more powerful accelerator that increases the velocity of the stream of protons striking a target, they typically discover new particles that were not present when they used the less powerful machine. The new particles are to be viewed as the joint product of the structure of the atom and the energy of the bombarding protons, and not as parts of the atomic target that had always been there just waiting to be released.

Each method elicits from its target of study a special profile of characteristics. Many of these characteristics are not stable components of the target as wetness is a continuous characteristic of the ocean but rather potential qualities that are actualized under very specific experimental conditions. An adult who is told by a white-coated experimenter to administer shock to a stranger in an adjoining laboratory room will do so, even though the stranger protests vigorously. The compliance does not mean that most American adults have a stable disposition to conform to the inhumane requests of authority; rather, it means that the combination of this special procedure and the person's characteristics create the conformity and apparent indifference to the distress of another human being. A different procedure would not have produced the conformity. Hence, the unquestioning obedience is not a continuous property of the adult, but a characteristic that is provoked only under specific conditions. That is why the physicist Freeman Dyson has written, "It is hopeless to look for a description independent of the mode of observation".

When a nineteenth-century observer made a statement about a child's lability or fear, his colleagues knew that the source of the statement was the child's overt behaviour, for this was the method of choice. Today psychologists use questionnaries, interviews, projective tests, memory problems, and polygraphic display of neural discharge. Even if we ignore the fact that these methods may not be accurate evaluations of either lability or fear, scientists who use any of them make statements about the degree to which a child possesses these properties, and are often indifferent to the real possibility that the measurement methods are not equivalent. The proposition "the newborn is labile" has one meaning if it is based on watching the baby in a crib for two hours, quite another if one is looking at the infant's heart rate, and still another if the evidence comes from the amplitude of the baby's brain waves in response to one hundred brief flashes of light.

The intimate relation between a procedure and a description of a child's qualities becomes increasingly relevant as social scientists begin to study physiological correlates of psychological states. The construct that best fits the biological data often has no obvious synonym in terms used to describe what seem to be related psychological characteristics.

I recently studied a large group of three-year-old children and their mothers. One of the most striking differences between the children was based on their heart-rate profiles when they were being administered a series of tests. One group had high and stable heart rates across all the test procedures. The contrasting group had low and variable heart rates. Experimental work with older children and adults has shown that, when a person is doing mental work (for example, listening carefully to a list of numbers in order to remember them), heart rate rises and stabilizes; but this pattern does not occur when the person is simply listening to words or looking at pictures. It is believed that the profile of an increasing and more stable heart rate is due to an increase in physiological arousal.

How shall we describe the children who show these two different patterns? Terms like "motivated," "anxious," and "hopeful of success" which historically have been used to summarize similar data do not seem to be appropriate for the states associated with the heart-rate profiles. The facial expressions or bodily movements of the children with the higher and more stable heart rates, for example, do not reflect more intense motivation or greater anxiety. Because the mothers of the children with the higher and more stable heart rates told an interviewer that they held high standards for their children's intellectual competence, we might suggest terms like "amused," "uncertain about quality of performance," or "involved in the tasks." But no aspect of a child's behaviour warranted those labels; hence, these descriptions originate in and take their meaning from the heart-rate evidence. This situation is not unlike that of the electroencephalographer who says of a subject with closed eyes that his brain-wave pattern indicates a state of alertness. Indeed, the phrase "paradoxical sleep" was invented to account for the odd phenomenon of a sleeping subject whose brain waves resemble those of an alert person at high noon.

Consider the following hypothetical situation. One person is allowed only to see an apple at a distance; two others are blindfolded, and one is permitted to taste the apple but not feel it, while the other can only feel it. After all process their source of information, each declares, "This object is an apple." These statements do not have the same meaning because the sources of the experience are different. If this example does not seem persuasive, change the apple to a gold harp to which three persons have access through only one sensory modality: sight, sound, or touch. Should all three declare, "This object is beautiful," it should be more obvious that the three statements have different meanings.

The psychologist more often uses terms to name hypothetical qualities like beauty than to label concrete objects like apples. The idealist who believes there is a unitary essence of "apple" or "beauty" behind the different sensory experiences should be reminded that phlogiston and witches do not exist, despite initial signs that were persuasive of their reality.

The scientist's task is to detect the relations among events and, subsequently, to apply names to the events and the newly discovered relations. But the best scientific procedures reveal only a portion of the total phenomena to be understood; and the names, therefore, denote what has been revealed by the procedures and not the events as they occur in nature. The position of empiricists is much like that of two blind persons, one with scissors and the other with a jackknife, who, after being told the characteristics of a rose petal, are instructed to find one and to separate it from its surroundings so that the product is perfectly faithful to the original petal. Even if our blind adventurers should be fortunate enough to find a rose bush, it is unlikely that they would cut away one complete petal and nothing more. Each would probably detach part of a petal, part of a stem, and perhaps a bit of the bush and return with these non-identical products, convinced that each of them had found the perfect rose petal.

This argument may appear to be a restatement of Percy Bridgman's philosophy of operationalism, which had a brief period of high popularity after the First World War and is now in disrepute. Bridgman and some other philosophers urged that the meaning of all theoretical terms, including the qualities of organisms, rested only on their measurement operations. Application of that view to modern psychology would mean, for example, that intelligence is only a particular set of answers on the Wechsler Intelligence Scale. There are good reasons to reject this conclusion as too restrictive and obstructive of theoretical progress. I favor a more permissive mood. The investigator has license to ascribe qualities to organisms for settings that were not observed, but he or she is obligated to specify the nature of those unrealized settings.

Subjective and Objective Frames

Description and explanation of psychological phenomena can be constructed from the frame of the subject or the frame of another who is trying to understand the subject. Although there can be as many "other" frames as there are observers, the special perspective of the scholar who is trying to improve theoretical understanding by using evidence to eliminate incorrect hypotheses is usually called the *objective frame*. The objective frame is not always more correct, but it does try to be more consistent in its application of rules of inference. The subjective and the objective frames have different functions and different criteria for validity, and the two need not be consonant.

Although statements cast in an objective frame, usually based on empirical data gathered by an observer or a machine, are only one source of understanding (intuition is an equally valuable source), such statements need not have a relation to the subjective experience or explanation of the agent being described. The truth of this statement is obvious when animals are the targets of description. Karl Von Frisch's elegant reports on the dance of returning honey bees describe a lawful relation between the distance of the pollen source from the hive and the movement patterns of the returning bees. Von Frisch need not tell us what the bees' experience might be. From the perspective of the person what Wendell Garner calls the primary epistemology of the subject perception is holistic, immediate, and unanalyzed. But the psychologist, loyal to an objective epistemology, self-consciously analyzes into separate mechanisms what was unanalyzed by the subject.

Students of perception regard the distinction between the two frames as a contrast between appearance and reality. When a bullseye of alternating black and white segments is rotated rapidly, people have the subjective impression that the thin segment of black bordering the white is darker than the rest of the black segment. However, objective measurements reveal that the entire black segment is at the same level of brightness. In this case, the two frames are irreconcilable.

The philosophical distinction between a person's belief and knowledge also acknowledges the two frames, but philosophers would like to see more consonance between the two perspectives in order to avoid legitimizing individual beliefs that are not shared by the community. After infancy, each person has a subjective awareness and interpretation of his or her behaviour, wishes, and feelings. From the perspective of an objective description, this private interpretation is to be regarded as an event to be understood, and not as a competing account or one to which the statement in the objective frame must accommodate. If not, there would be no need for the diagnostic categories of the psychiatrist, which, most of the time, bear little relation either to the patient's description or explanation of his symptoms.

The problem is not only that a person's private experience does not contain events unavailable to conscious awareness; but, more important, the person's description of his private experience to another has a unique structure (objects followed by predicates, rules of sentence construction which respect temporal order and causality, and no terms that refer to fragments of experience) that is unlikely to be faithful to the structure of the processes being summarized. Sentences are not finely tooled to the events they are supposed to describe. When a person exploring the interior of a deep hole with a stick is asked to describe what she is experiencing, she will talk about the shape of the hole. But the original perceptual information on which the description is based, which is not in awareness, is composed of a mosaic of pressures between the stick and the hand. Each linguistic description of one's conscious experience can be likened to a pair of mechanical hands attempting to retrieve a set of small fragile forms of clumped sand whose shapes are so imperfectly matched to the mechanical hands that they cannot be grasped easily. Hence, what is retrieved represents an odd fragment of what is present. Although one's report of one's experiences or thoughts has validity in the subjective frame, it may not have much validity in the objective frame. Some contemporary concepts "a feeling of anonymity," for example have their clearest meaning in the subjective frame; while others like "relative dominance of left over right hemisphere " only have meaning in the objective frame. One form of resolution of the conflict between the determinism of natural science and the humanistic belief in an individual's free will is to view the former premise as belonging to the objective and the latter to the subjective frame. Because the two frames need not be consistent, there is no conflict between the two views.

The complementary relation between the two frames is illustrated in the area of human motivation. Most persons do not think about their motives in the terms chosen by the psychologist. An adolescent girl, for example, wants to become the friend of a specific person; the psychologist says she has an affiliative motive. Another adolescent wants an A in English or an athletic letter in tennis; the scientist says he has an achievement motive. Whereas the individual's motive is typically for a specific event, the scientist's term embraces a broad class of events, because the investigator assumes that the motive to spend an hour drinking with a specific person is only one instance of a more inclusive desire that includes the potential to seek a different person and a different activity if the first is not available. But the more abstract category is in the objective frame of the investigator, not the subjective frame of the individual.

Consider the robust phenomenon called *interference* in human memory. When you ask a subject why he cannot remember a set of animal words after he has listened to, and successfully recalled, two prior sets, he simply says, "I can't remember." He does not feel as though anything is interfering with his ability to remember the words. A psychologist might say of the same phenomenon, that there was elimination, replacement, dampening, or simply forgetting. The point is that use of interference in the objective description is not regarded by the subject as the reason for his forgetting the words.

Objectively framed explanations of the relation between social class and early school achievement in children rely on heritability of intelligence, lack of preparation for school tasks, motivation, and expectancy of success. But a ten-year-old boy who is asked why he is failing is likely to reply that the work is too hard or that the teacher is unfair or incompetent. The boy is not likely to say that he has inherited inferior intelligence, or did not learn the alphabet at home, or does not want to succeed. Although psychologists may regard the child's interpretation as a defence a way of externalizing the failure many ten-year-olds do believe that an unjust teacher is the reason for their poor achievement. The child's subjective report that the teacher is unjust is a fact that might be used in an objective explanation of the relation between social class and past experience; but it is not necessarily inconsistent with the objective interpretation, or less true.

The difference between the two frames is revealed in a comparison of the stability of personality traits based on objective observations of adolescents, on the one hand, and on self-reports, on the other. Most longitudinal research in an objective frame, using observations and tests, finds that qualities like intellectual achievement, sociability, and dominance are moderately stable over the period of ten to fourteen years of age. But when adolescents were asked on three occasions (grades nine, ten, and eleven) to rate themselves, in a subjective frame, on twenty-one adjectives dealing with such qualities as degree of anxiety, feelings of intellectual ability, kindness, sociability, and dominance over others, there was no relation between the self-reports given in grade nine and those given in grade eleven. The youngsters felt subjectively that they had undergone a great deal of change in these qualities. However, empirical data on similar groups of adolescents, summarized in an objective frame, suggest far less change in these qualities.

Another illustration of the two frames is revealed in a comparison of office workers' subjective reports of how often they talked with fellow workers during a particular week, and the objective accounts of observers who walked through the office area every thirty minutes of the working day. There was a serious discrepancy between each person's impression of how often he or she communicated with others and the objective information.

The different meanings of descriptions that emanate from the two frames are clearly illustrated in studies that ask children or adults to talk about their personal characteristics. Of a large group of nine-year-old boys who were regarded uniformly by their classmates and teachers as extremely unpopular, over one third insisted that they were well liked and popular with all of their classmates at school. This discrepancy between the opinions of others and that of the self is not troubling, for it is always possible for a person to hold a positive, subjective opinion of self despite less flattering perceptions by friends. The special quality of the subjective evaluation, however, was revealed when the psychologist attempted to evaluate the child's conception of self in the objective frame. Each child was given the names of three children in his classroom and asked to select the two that were most similar in personality. In some of these trios, the child under study was a member of the trio being evaluated. Because many of the children who said they were popular placed themselves consistently with the less, rather than with the more, popular children, it is reasonable to infer that they did not regard themselves as popular. But that conclusion is in the objective frame. It is not necessary to determine whether the subjective or the objective conclusion is more correct, for the two conclusions are not logically inconsistent. The meaning of the statement "John believes he is popular" depends on the frame adopted a special case of the earlier conclusion that the meaning of a conclusion always depends upon the method used.

Thus, psychologists must be careful about attributing special significance to verbal replies to their questions. A person's verbal report of private feelings is one datum in a puzzle, and few scientists would wish to make judgements on a single fact. A zoologist who wanted to assign a newly discovered animal to its proper species would never rely on only one characteristic, be it the shape of the beak, the length of the forelimb, or reproductive behaviour, but would use a combination of characteristics. So, too, with the classification of a child's beliefs, hopes, or feeling states. No single piece of evidence is likely to be sufficient.

Subjective reports have a special quality, for they pass through consciousness and are transformed in that passage. Psychologists use varied probes to detect the presence of beliefs, intentions, feelings, and competences; each imposes a unique distortion on the information desired. A drawing of the self is not an accurate representation of what the person believes he or she looks like, because the child may have poor artistic skills. A story told to a picture is influenced by the objects in the picture. But because a verbal reply travels through consciousness, it is subject to two serious influences: it must be rational and logical and should not reveal too much that is undesirable about the self. The original information used to construct the answer is altered to fit these requirements. Because so much information is viewed by the person as evaluative of self, a verbal report is often an extremely distorted sign of the essential quality the scientist wishes to know in its less disguised form.

The hard-nosed natural scientist usually wants to dismiss subjective evidence as being unreliable, while some social scientists wish to make it the central explanation. But the latter ignore the fact that each person's frame is unique and limited in scope and illuminates only a small part of the event to be understood in the objective frame three criticisms that were also levelled eighty years ago at those who believed that the primary problem in psychology was the contents of consciousness, and that introspection was the method of choice.

The reader is not to interpret this discussion as an attack on the utility of the subjective frame. Quite the contrary. Most of each day's decisions flow from that frame, and the coherence that each of us feels compelled to impose on a day, a week, or a life originates in the subjective frame. But the goal of science is to generate statements in the objective frame; hence, subjective information is to be regarded as having the same degree of disguise as rapid eye movements during sleep or a rise in heart rate to an insult. However, treating a person's subjective report of her mood or explanation of her behaviour as a datum whose significance is to be discovered is different from regarding it on the same level as the explanation in the objective frame. Thus, I shall try to be careful in my discussion to distinguish these two sources of information and the complementary explanations they generate.

4

Experimental Methods in Child Psychology

Introduction

The researchers try to elicit information from children by putting them in a contrived, or analogue, situation. Typically the conditions under which these methods are used are controlled. These methods are easily contrasted with the more naturalistic approaches. In naturalistic approaches to child study, children are observed in their natural habits, not controlled situations. Although each set of methods has positive and negative dimensions, the ultimate choice for a method of child study should be guided by one's question and the most effective method to answer that question should dictate choice. Ultimately, however, we think that the complexity of children's lives cannot be understood with only one method. Consequently, a multiple method approach to the study of children is probably most fruitful and the experimental method should represent one of many strategies used.

Despite this commonsense approach, there seems to be a "paradigm war" raging between experimentalists and interpretive, naturalistic researchers, especially in the area of educational research. Although polemics are helpful at the beginning of major disagreements between groups so that they can each define themselves clearly, at this point we should recognize that there is no one "silver bullet" or crystal ball that will provide all the answers. We should draw what we can from each approach to help us better understand the complexities of childhood.

Some Basic Premises of Experimental Methods

Whereas naturalistic approaches attempt to study children in the everyday environment, the experimental approach attempts to create an experimental, often contrived, environment in which to examine children. Aspects of the environment thought to affect children's behaviour are manipulated and controlled. Through manipulation and control researchers can make causal inferences about these manipulations.

Experimental environments can be real classrooms, as in the cases of field experiments of curriculum and design, laboratories, where children are taken from their natural habitats and studied, or hybrid designs where parts of classrooms are experimentally controlled and manipulated. These terms *manipulate* and *control* are crucial to the experimental method, because they help us make causal inferences about sets of variables.

Generally, experiments are conducted in order to isolate specific cause-effect relationships. That is, experimenters attempt to identify the effects of certain independent variables (*e.g.*, crowding) on behaviour, or dependent variables (*e.g.*, children's aggression). The independent variables are manipulated to examine their effect on the dependent measure. Other, extraneous, variables are controlled so that they do not influence the relation between independent and dependent variables, and thus cloud the causal picture. Experiments that give us insight into the effects of an independent variable on a dependent variable, without confounding effects of extraneous variables, are said to be *internally valid*.

Experiments are thus most beneficial where the investigator is interested in identifying such cause-effect relationships. Further, experiments can be conducted only in situations where investigators are free to manipulate and control aspects of the children's environment. For example, to investigate the cause-effect relationhip between certain styles of teachers' reading books to children and children's literacy, the investigator must be free to vary, or manipulate, different reading environments.

Two types of experiments are relevant. True experiments are defined as those in which participants and conditions are randomly assigned to groups and data collection schedules are standardized, whereas quasi-experiments do not have the benefit of randomization or standardized data collection schedules. True experiments are difficult to conduct in most applied settings because one cannot usually randomly assign children and manipulate environments at will; quasi-experiments, however, can be implemented in many applied settings.

This chapter is intended to familiarize the reader with the process of conducting experiments. In this way, the reader can intelligibly consume the experimental literature that addresses issues in child study. In addition, the chapter serves as a general guide to conducting an experiment and outlines some basic assumptions about the experimental approach. First we discuss the experimental approach as an extension of the scientific method. In the next two sections, we discuss laboratory and field experiments. Then we discuss research design, outlining the basic premises involved in designing experiments, and examine important concepts related to research design: internal, external, and ecological validity. Generally these concepts refer to the truthfulness of the results obtained (internal validity), the extent to which these experimental results are interpretable in the world outside of the laboratory (external validity), and the extent to which demands of the experimental laboratory match the demands of the situation to which results will be generalized. We also discuss ecological validity of experiments, or judging experiments in terms of their approximations of the actual worlds that children inhabit.

Most experimenters examine their results through a variety of statistical techniques. Although we do not outline specific statistical procedures here, the reader is referred to a number of excellent introductory books that discuss experiments and appropriate statistical analyses of experimental results. We discuss some of the underlying principles, however, that should be applied to experiments in order to apply certain statistical analyses. In the final section we discuss the advantages and disadvantages of the experimental approach in comparison with the naturalistic approach.

Behavioural Research as "Science"

A common aim of scientific inquiry is to know about a phenomenon, and an assumption behind many different forms of enquiry is that truth can be uncovered, or is knowable. A general rule of thumb for using scientific enquiry to know involves the elimination of false ideas. First, however, the idea must be put in terms that allow it to be tested for "falsifiability." A common example involves discussions over the origins of man. The creationist view that man was created by God in the Garden of Eden, for example, cannot be subjected to test of falsifiability. An alternative idea, natural selection, can be tested, and evaluated in terms of the consistency of the evidence with the theory. The methods used to expose falsehood are indeed varied. Different modes of inquiry typically include observing naturally occurring behaviour, asking others questions, or both. We then make inferences about the meaning of those behaviours as part of our quest to know.

Another approach to knowing is the experiment. Experimental methods originated in the physical sciences and were adapted by the behavioural sciences. A basic assumption behind the experimental approach is that we have a theory, or explanation, for the way in which something works. For example, following massed versus distributed practice theory, we might posit that providing children with a recess break after prolonged periods of classroom works to improve their performance on those tasks. We could design an experiment where children's attention to classroom tasks is measured before and after recess. We then manipulate the duration of time before recesses are provided. It may be that on certain days recess is every 2 hours and on other days it is every 3.5 hours. Our idea, or hypothesis, would be supported if children in the 2-hour group were more attentive than the other group. This procedure, however, also affords the possibility of not having our hypothesis supported (falsified). Consequently, the extent to which theories and their data are capable of tests that deem them true or false is, *the* hallmark of science.

Experimenters manipulate aspects of situations in order to produce their predicted effects. Extraneous variables, or those not of interest, must be controlled, or made to not influence the results. An example of manipulation and control may help clarify the point. Researchers have a theory that recess, and other types of breaks, maximizes children's attention to tasks and possibly learning. The prediction is that the frequent, compared to infrequent, breaks should result in increased attention. In order to test this experimentally we would have to manipulate, or systematically vary, subjects' exposure to the independent variable different recess timing regimens or the dependent variable attention to classroom tasks. Different groups, or the same groups at different times, would experience different recess regimens. Extraneous variables, which could effect results, should be controlled. For example, different teachers or different types of tasks may influence children's attention; thus teachers and tasks musts be controlled. Extraneous variables are not directly relevant to our theory but could influence results. For example, one can easily imagine cases that teachers who allow more frequent recesses might have other attributes that relate to children's attention. Similarly, there are clearly some tasks that are more interesting to children than others. Thus we should control tasks and teachers so that their effects do not "confound" or contaminate the effects of recess timing on attention.

Aside from manipulation, another feature of experimental inquiry is objectivity. Indeed, naturalistic, psychometric, and experimental approaches all aspire to obtain objective data. By objective we mean two things: First, an observation or datum is objective if it can be observed by more than one observer; second, results are objective if they can be replicated by other researchers. The importance of replication is the reason for the elaborately described Methods sections of most experimental reports. For example, descriptions of the exact age of the children involved in a study, as well as the number and types of toys that children play with in an experimental setting, are necessary for replication attempts.

Replication is also important in making policies that affect children. We as researchers should be clear that our programmes can be replicated before the lives of children, parents, and teachers are affected. Relatedly, programmes that are implemented before they have been replicated have a negative effect on the likelihood that other innovative programmes might be adopted. Why should policy makers and taxpayers, the reasonable person might ask, support adoption of a programme that has uncertain effects?

The third hallmark of behavioural science is the reliance on evidence or data. Again, reliance on data is not only advocated by experimentalists, but by all empirical researchers. Reliance on data simply means that interpretations and conclusions should be based on the data obtained from objective observations, experiments, or both. Again, the data should guide policy and implementation of programmes.

Causality

Most researchers would agree that the hallmark of experimental research is the ability to infer cause-effect relationships. Causal inferences can be made when our experimental manipulations result in predicted outcomes. Of course, they must be embedded in a theory to the extent that experiments are designed to test theories. In short, causal inferences are only as good as our theories. Experimental manipulations and predicted results are not, however, unequivocal. Although we may conduct an experiment and the results might support or hypotheses, there may be room for discussion about the meaning of the results. First and foremost, we should recognize the fact that just because kids do something in an experiment, or in any other situation where we choose to study them, does not mean that they will also do it in other situations. It may be, as Robert McCall, noted 20 years ago, that experiments tell us what children can do; they may not tell us what they actually do in their lives. Relatedly, it may be that the observed experimental effects only explain a portion, albeit it a statistically significant portion, of our results. There is the real possibility that other children in other situation reach those same outcomes through very different means. Thus, an experimental treatment may result in a child learning a certain strategy; this result does not preclude the possibility that other treatments may have similar results.

We offer these qualifiers as a prologue to our discussion on causality. Human being are very complex beings and defy simple explanation. We should remain equivocal in our examination of evidence. This stance should not, however, result in nihilistic responses that there is no meaning anywhere. We should continue to try and find out what works for certain children in certain situations, recognizing that we always have more to learn, remaining open to alternative explanation, and testing those explanations.

Of course, poorly designed experiments tell us little if anything about the veracity of ideas. For example, suppose we found in an experiment that children exposed to sugar were more hyperactive than the children in a sugar-free group. Our causal inference regarding the effects of sugar may be inaccurate. The differences in children's behaviours may have been due to the food that the sugar was put on, not to the sugar itself; thus the food confounded the effects of the sugar.

Correlations between variables are often confused with causal relations. Rather, they show the extent to which they are interrelated (in a linear way) with each other. Thus there is usually a positive correlation between the amount of time children spend studying and their achievement scores; the more one studies, the higher the score. A common negative correlation involves the relation between aggression and popularity: The more aggressive a child is, the less popular he or she is (usually). Correlations, however, do not show causality. It may be, for example, that children are aggressive because they are disliked, not vice versa. Only through experimentation do we know that aggression does cause children to be disliked.

A necessary, but not sufficient, condition for causality is the existence of an antecedent-consequence relationship. That is, one variable, the antecedent, must precede the outcome, or consequence, in time. Thus aggression must precede rejection within a specific peer group. Obviously, these antecedent-consequence relations can be observed outside of the laboratory, and longitudinal research design, or studying children across a time span, is one excellent way to accomplish this.

Causality involves more than antecedent-consequence relations, however. Causality can be established only when extraneous variables are controlled and theoretically relevant variables are manipulated. Although these conditions can be met with naturalistic studies utilizing a form of statistical testing, or *structural models*, they are usually accomplished through laboratory or field experimentation.

Laboratory Experiments

An experiment attempts to construct a controlled, analogue model of the world inside of the laboratory. The environment is constructed such that the researcher is manipulating aspects of the environment relevant to the hypothesis being tested. For example, a researcher may be interested in the effects of specific museum exhibits on children's social behaviour; an experiment would thus be designed to approximate a museum. The specific exhibits (or independent variable) are experimentally manipulated to determine their causal effects on certain social behaviours (the dependent variable). The children may be exposed to dinosaurs and then to prisms. Inferences regarding the effect of these exhibits on behaviour are based on the observations of children interacting with each exhibit. As such, the first purpose of laboratory experiments is to discover relations between variables under "uncontaminated" conditions. In the experimental museum exhibit example, children's free choice of exhibits is controlled, and thus it does not contaminate the effect of the exhibit. Exposure to specific exhibits is manipulated and we can judge their effects on behaviour, without the contaminating effects of children's self-selection into exhibits. Self-selection must be controlled because it would probably affect behaviour. That is, there probably are real differences in children who choose to go to museum and those who choose not to go; similarly there are probably differences between children who choose to interact with different exhibits within a museum, and these differences probably affect behaviour.

By controlling extraneous variables and manipulating relevant variables we can make reasonable, although cautious, inferences about the effects of the independent variables on the dependent variables.

Laboratory Experiments: Strengths and Weaknesses

A real strength of experiments is the ability to make causal inferences. We can manipulate and assign in many different ways; quasi-experiments exist when we cannot randomly choose and assign subjects. As such, they are probably a more realistic choice for most applied settings, and we can thus make precise tests of theories. We can be more sure that our results are due to our manipulations than we could if we utilized other research approaches.

The main weakness of the experimental approach is equally as obvious as its strengths. The artificiality of the experimental situation may mean that the subjects behave differently in the laboratory than they do in "real world" situations. Indeed, we might argue that the more controlled the experiment, the further it is from an approximation of a real world situation. Children may act one way in a laboratory playroom but very differently in their classroom. Recall McCall's warning: Laboratory experiments tell us what children can do, not what they actually do.

Taking a point repeatedly made in cross-cultural psychology theorizing, the specific context in which children development affects their development. By examining children in different contexts we become aware of possible causal mechanisms in development. In order to design such different experimental contexts, however, we must be aware that such differences exist and design experiments that are appropriate for the question under consideration. An example will clarify. We are interested in what causes some infants to walk earlier than others. In order to study this, we be aware of the different ways in which infants' sensorimotor development is treated in cultures that have different walking onset periods. Differences are typically due to specific context differences; in cultures with early onset, infants' sitting and walking are encouraged, crawling is not. In short, the choice of the context that we think will elicit behaviour is all important.

Probably more relevant to studying children in laboratory experiments is the fact that young children are extremely vulnerable to the effects of strange situations. As we noted in our discussion of testing, when children are put into a strange situation, they become anxious. Anxiety, in turn, relates to children exhibiting low, rather than high, levels of competence.

So what to do? Simply, make the experimental environment as familiar as possible. The discussion on ecological validity to follow will be most helpful here. Children should be observed in experimental settings on numerous occasions or, if that is not a possibility, observe them for a prolonged period. For example, if we are interested in the differential effects of toys on children's play behaviours, we should observe a child repeatedly in each of the toy settings. A useful rule of thumb has been presented by Wachs. He suggested that if we observe one occasion it should be for 90 minutes; two occasions should be 45 minutes each. Repeated or prolonged exposure to the experimental setting will make it less strange and anxiety-producing to the child. Of course, experimentally manipulating dimensions of those contexts that children usually inhabit, such as schools or clubs field experiments is a preferred option.

Field Experiments

We noted that all aspects of the environment had to be randomized and controlled in order to make causal inferences about our treatments. To say the least, randomization and control are very difficult to achieve in applied settings. We offer field experiments as a compromise in that they are more realistically achieved in applied settings.

Field experiments are experiments that take place in real situations. The researcher, however, manipulates these environments. Some of the best examples of field experiments involve research in preschool settings. The work of Johnson and his colleagues, Lawton and P. K. Smith and Connolly with preschoolers is illustrative of excellent field experiments where the differential effects of curriculum was studied. In other cases with primary schools, researchers have manipulated children's exposure to different recess timing regimens to determine their effect on children's attention to seat work. In one Johnson study, for example, preschool curriculum (traditional-didactic vs. open-exploratory) was systematically manipulated in each classroom to determine the effect of each on children's play behaviours. Lawton and Fowler compared Piagetian and Ausubelian programmes on teachers' and children's language. In the P. K. Smith and Connolly study, classrooms that differed on aspects of social and spatial density as well as types of toys were designed. Pellegrini and colleagues compared the effects of long versus short periods during which children were deprived of recess.

A major advantage of field experiments over those in a laboratory is that the children are being observed in a realistic and familiar setting. As a result, the conclusions made about children's observed behaviour also are likely to be supported by observations in similar, nonmanipulated settings.

The field experiment also has its disadvantages. Experimenters typically exercise control on an external institution, like the classroom, as they can in an experimental situation. For example, teachers in a field experiment, because they were often hired for reasons other than their ability to act as experimenters, may not be consistent in their use of a particular experimental technique. As a result, the actual experimental treatment may not be consistent with the ideal treatment. Experimenters who are trained and retrained to implement a specific procedure may be more reliable.

Natural Experiments

Moving down the ladder of control from true laboratory experiments we come to the interesting case of "natural" experiments. Natural experiments exist when important natural events occur which may have an effect on children's behaviour. Examples of such events include: a family moving from one neighbourhood to another, a fetus' in utero experience, or a group witnessing a traumatic event. We then gauge the effect of these events (considered independent, or predictor, variables) on theoretically relevant behaviour. Take the case of a child who is having behaviour problems in one school. His parents move house and he attends another school, one with fewer boys having behaviour problems. The boy's problems then decline. We conclude that if we statistically control the effect of extraneous variables, such as income, the move and school change contributed to the decline.

Another case: A mother is having pregnancy difficulties and her physician prescribes hormones (androgens). These male hormones represent a "treatment" on the fetus' development and they typically result in girls exhibiting more male-typical behaviours than comparisons. These cases are interesting because they involve manipulation that researchers either could not or would not execute. Given the "natural" occurrence of the interventions, however, they becoming interesting cases. Of course a number of other variables, other than those listed as "treatments," may also be influencing the dependent variable. In the boy moving example, it might be the case that more affluent, compared to less affluent, parents tend to move out of areas where there are "problems" in schools. Parents' SES and their desire to "move up" probably have added effects on children's problem behaviours. In the hormones cases, mother may be aware of the relation between male hormones and children's behaviour and thus treat their daughters differently.

Practioners and researchers alike should take advantage of natural experiments as a way of studying something that otherwise would be impossible to study. However, because of the probable influence of numerous other variables, various explanations should be systematically explored and rejected where appropriate.

Research Design

Research design is the procedure by which experiments are designed and actually implemented. They are most relevant to both laboratory and field experiments, and less relevant to natural experiments, as we do not design them. Issues of design are relevant here, however, to the extent that they inform us as to the multitude of forces that affect the dependent measure.

Experimental designs are blueprint-like plans describing the plan of the research. The concepts of internal and external validity determine different types of research designs. Experiments should be designed such that they are internally, externally, and ecologically valid.

Internal Validity

Experiments should be designed such that threats to the internal validity of the experiment are minimized. Internally valid experiments are those in which the stated experimental manipulations (or independent variables) are the main factors causing variation on that which is being measured (dependent variable). In other words, internally valid experiments control the effects of extraneous (of nonmanipulated) variables on the dependent measures. In the example previously outlined about the effects of sugar on hyperactivity, we noted a scenario wherein the causes of hyperactivity may have been due to the food on which the sugar was applied. The food, therefore, was not controlled and, as a result, confounded the effect of the sugar. In this case the food was an extraneous variable. In order to control this extraneous variable we should have used exactly the same food for both groups, adding sugar to food of one group.

Campbell and Stanley, in their classic monograph on experimental design, outlined eight extraneous factors that could affect the internal validity of experiments.

History, or specific events occurring between two measurement points, can have an extraneous effect. For example, in the case where students are given an experimental science curriculum to improve their achievement, inclusion of their regular science curriculum may be an extraneous variable affecting achievement. In order to prevent history from affecting results, or controlling history, we should have members of all experimental groups be exposed to virtually the same experiences over time. Following the sugar example previously given, children in both groups should be exposed to the same curriculum so that they have equal experiences that might elicit hyperactivity. The groups should differ only in the experimental treatments they receive.

Table 4.1. Threats to the Internal Validity of Experiments

1. History	5. Instrumentation
2. Maturation	6. Differential selection
3. Testing	7. Experimental mortality
4. Statistical regression	8. Selection-maturation interaction

Maturation is the effects of passing time on subjects. For example, children may be more tired at the end of an experiment than at the beginning. As a result, fatigue has an extraneous effect. Maturation can be controlled in a way similar to history. Have all students in all conditions experienced the same time span and events between the data collection points?

Testing is where students' exposure to a pretest affects their performance on a post-test. For example, students may show improvement from one test to the other simply because they remember test questions. This knowledge of the test has an extraneous effect on their measured growth. Testing can be controlled by extending the time span between the pre- and post-test.

Statistical regression occurs when students score very low or very high on the pretest. They tend to "regress toward the mean" (or score more near the average) on the post-test. As a result, differences between pre- and post-test scores may be due to regression, not the treatment. Regression to the mean can be controlled by administering pre- and post-tests to all groups in the experiment.

Instrumentation is when changes occur between pre- and post-test due to a change in measurement instruments. For example, for the pretest a student may have been given a test using machine-scorable answer sheets; the post-test may have used interviews. Differences between these scores are probably due to the different procedures used. Instrumentation can be controlled by administering the same, or parallel, form of a test for pre- and post-testing purposes.

Differential selection means that between-group differences may be due to the procedures used to select and assign children to different groups in the experiments. Differential selection can be controlled by randomly selecting the sample and then randomly selecting assigning the selected subjects to different experimental groups.

Experimental mortality, or attrition, is when subjects leave the experiment before it is over. If they leave for reasons related to the experiment itself (for example, "Treatment A" may be too difficult), then between-group differences may be affected by persons leaving the experiment. For example, because only the slower students left the experiment,"Treatment A" has more bright students left in it than the other groups. Between-group differences may be due to group differences, not treatment differences. Mortality can be controlled by checking to see if the subjects who have left the experiment are significantly different from those who remained in the study.

Selection-maturation interaction means that certain types of students (selection) may be more prone to the maturation effect. For example, hyperactive children are more likely than nonhyperactive children to experience fatigue during a treatment. Selection-maturation can be controlled by random selection and assignment and by equalizing the amount of time of each group's treatment.

Examples of Research Designs

The purpose of this section is to illustrate the way in which certain designs control for or fail to control for threats to internal validity. Campbell and Stanley provided a very thorough discussion of the threats to the internal validity of 12 research designs.

The first example, the one-group pretest-post-test design is an example with many threats to internal validity. The design of the study involves, first, a group of children being selected and assigned, not randomly, to one experimental group. The group is then given a pretest (O). The pretest is given to provide information on the group before the experimental treatment is administered. Next, the group receives the treatment (X). Following the treatment a post-test (O) is administered to determine children's status after the treatment. This research design can be graphically represented, following Campbell and Stanley, as O X O.

With this design, however, there are a number of extraneous factors that could be responsible for pre- and post-test score differences. We examine this experiment in terms of each of the eight threats to internal validity. First, history could be affecting results. Many events, other than the treatment, occurring between the pre- and post-test could have been responsible for differences in scores. If the pretest was given on a Tuesday and the post-test on a Friday, differences in scores may have been due to children's eagerly anticipating enjoying the weekend; as a result, they were not attentive on the post-test. Similarly, maturation, such as boredom with the task over the experimental period, could affect performance.

Regarding testing and regression, simultaneously, changes in pre- and post-test scores may have been due to either children becoming "test-wise" after the pretest (testing) or regressing toward the mean on the post-test. That is, if they scored at an extreme on the pretest, they would have scored closer to the mean on the post-test. The regression effects are less clear in this design than the testing effects, however.

Instrumentation may affect results because the way in which children are measured may change from pre- to post-test. For example, observer fatigue during the second observation may cause inaccurate scoring of the post-test.

Selection and morality are not problems. Regarding selection, because there is only one group, differential assignment to groups cannot affect results. Similarly, with mortality, because there is only one group, mortality cannot affect one group differently than another.

This brief discussion of the one-group pretest-post-test design should point out the weaknesses of such an approach. Results obtained with this design actually raise more questions than they answer; because of this, we question using such an approach.

In the next experimental design to be discussed, the pretest-post-test control group design, we can eliminate all threats to internal validity by adding two procedures to the inadequate one-group pretest-post-test design: random assignment to groups and two different experimental groups. In this design all children are randomly (R) assigned to one of two groups. This means that all subjects have an equal chance to be in either group. All subjects are given both pre- and post-test (O) but only one group receives an experimental treatment (X). The other group is the control group. That is, it has all the same experiences as the experimental groups except for the experimental treatment. Thus, an important first step in conducting an experiment is the random assignment of subjects to conditions. This design has been graphically represented by Campbell and Stanley as:

ROXO

ROO

In this design, neither history, maturation, nor testing differentially affects results: Both groups should have equally mature students and the passage of time should affect them equally. In addition, children in both groups experience the same pre- and post-test. Instrumentation is controlled when we control intrasession, or within session, history, particularly when students respond to standardized written tests or observers are randomly assigned to make post-test observations.

Regression is not a problem with this design because both groups experience both pre- and post-test; thus, regression should affect them equally. As a result, no between-group differences due to regression should occur.

Selection is controlled because students are randomly assigned to groups. Different types of students (*e.g.*, motivated *vs.* not motivated) should be equally distributed between groups because of the randomization. Mortality should be checked. When students leave the experiment, the researcher should check to see if more students leave one group (*e.g.*, the treatment group) than the other. In addition, the type of students leaving should be checked. Is one particular type of student (*e.g.*, bright) leaving?

This brief discussion of two experimental designs should make clear the importance of both randomization and control groups. By incorporating these two procedures into a weak design, we made it much stronger.

External Validity

Experimenters are typically most concerned with the internal validity of experiments. A premium is placed on knowing that results are due to specified experimental manipulations, not extraneous factors. The concern with external validity is often given less prominence. External validity is concerned with the extent to which the experimental results can be "generalized" outside of the experimental setting. For example, can an experiment involving middle-class children attending a university preschool be generalized to a group of lower socioeconomic status (LESS) Head Start children?

Campbell and Stanley discussed four possible threats to the external validity of experiments. The reactive or interactive effect of testing poses a threat to external validity. That is, occurrence of a pretest may sensitize subjects to the upcoming experimental treatment. As such, the pretest may make the subject more or less susceptible to the experimental treatment. The use of the pretest with the experimental group may mean that the results of the treatment are not generalizable (or applicable) to the unpretested population at large.

Selection biases interacting with experimental treatments also effect external validity. This means that certain types of subjects chosen for an experiment may be more or less susceptible to an experimental treatment than others. For example, in a study where preschool children were trained to engage in thematic-fantasy play, it was found that the training was more effective with brighter preschoolers than it was with less bright children. This result suggests that the type of subjects chosen often affects results. These results can only be generalized to a population similar to the population used in the experiment.

Reactive effects to experimental arrangements is a threat to external validity. In short, people, especially children, behave differently in an experimental laboratory than in a more familiar, less contrived settings. Indeed, the mere presence of an observer in a familiar setting causes children to act differently than if they were not being observed. The best example is probably from the infancy literature. It is well known that infants' exploratory behaviour decreases when they are put in a strange situation. As a result, children may behave one way during an experiment but very differently when the same treatment is used in a more familiar context.

The last threat to external validity discussed by Campbell and Stanley is interference due to multiple treatments. This means that if experiments are designed in which children are given more than one treatment, the effects of the previous treatments may be maintained. As a result, we can only generalize to those groups having the same series of multiple treatments.Generalizability, or the extent to which we can generalize results from one experiment to the population we have sampled from, is an important aspect of the external validity of experiments. Bracht and Glass discussed two general categories related to the generalizability of experimental results. They are population validity and ecological validity. Population validity is concerned with the ability to generalize from the experimental subjects (kindergartners in Clarke County, GA) to the population at large. Ecological validity is concerned with the extent to which experimental results can be generalized to other environmental conditions. Bracht and Glass have expanded Campbell and Stanley threats to external validity by adding:

1. Explicit description of the experimental treatment is necessary so that others can try to replicate the results in similar and different conditions.
2. Novelty and disruptive effects suggests that changes in behaviour may be merely due to a change in routine (*e.g.*, having a different colour reading book) rather than to the content of the experimental treatment (*e.g.*, a new reading series).
3. The Hawthorne Effect suggests that subjects act differently merely because they have been given special attention, such as treatment.
4. Experimenter effects means that a treatment is more or less effective because of the personality of a particular experimenter.

In short, factors influencing the external validity of experiments are related to the interpret ability of the experimental results outside of the experimental setting. It should be noted, however, that use of a no-treatment control group (*i.e.*, a group that is similar to the experimental group, but gets no special treatment at), compared to a control group that gets a placebo, does not generally result in a Hawthorne Effect.

Ideally, experiments should be designed that minimize threats to both external and internal validity. As previously noted, those advocating the use of the experimental approach often are more concerned with internal than with external validity. One experimental design that does minimize threats to internal and external validity is the post-test-only control group design:

RXO

RO

Note that in this design both randomization and multiple groups are used, but pretests are not. All threats to internal validity are controlled and the testing threat to external validity is also controlled. Issues of ecological validity, however, still need to be addressed.

Ecological Validity

Ecologically valid experiments seem to take the best from the two worlds of experimental and naturalistic research. Following Bronfenbrenner conception, ecologically valid experiments involve observing children in their natural habitat, such as a preschool classroom, and designing an analogue experimental situation. The designing of the experimental analogue should be such that children are in a similar environment as their classroom. Similarity involves similar physical props (*e.g.*, toys), social configurations (*e.g.*, number and gender of playmates), and mental-demand characteristics (*e.g.*, children are assigned by teachers to play in certain areas at certain times). Comparisons should be made between the same or similar children in both the natural and experimental environments. Similarity of results documents ecological validity. An example of such a study was conducted by A. D. Pellegrini and Perlmutter. The play behaviour of preschool children was observed while they were in the classroom. Based on these observations, it was determined that children played in same-gender dyads, without adults. Further, the attractiveness of play props was determined for boys and girls. An experimental analogue to the classroom was designed whereby the children played in same-gender dyads with the same toys. Children were expected to play with both male and female preference toys. This regimen was not unlike that made by teachers in their requiring children to interact with a variety of play results in the classroom. The results were such that children's play was similar in both contexts. Consequently, the experiment was ecologically valid.

The value of such an approach is that we can make causal statements about the effects of toys (due to the experimental manipulations), while simultaneously knowing that children play in like ways in their natural environments. For educational researchers ecologically valid experiments are a necessity, not a luxury. We need to know that an experimental results effect children's real experiences and can be generalized to classrooms. It is of some interest knowing that children can behave in an experiment in a certain way. We need to know how they actually behave in their everyday context.

Experimental Approach Evaluated: Advantages and Disadvantages

As we have discussed throughout this chapter the real advantage of the experimental approach is its controlled nature. This control of threats to internal validity allows the researcher to begin to make cause-effect statements about certain sets of variables. The awareness of causal relations among variables is necessary in order to understand the nature of the phenomena being examined. The objective nature of experiments, along with other empirical forms of inquiry, is also advantageous. The explicit description of experimental methods and results allows other researchers to attempt to replicate and interpret previous experiments. As noted earlier, objectivity is not the sole property of experiments; it characterizes all good scientific research.

There are also disadvantages to the experimental approach. The controlled nature of experiments is often inversely related to the experiment's external validity. That is, the more controlled an experiment is the less it approximates real-world conditions. The behaviours elicited in experimental situations may be characteristic only of those settings, not characteristic of behaviour in analogous real-world situations. As Bronfenbrenner noted, the study of human development is becoming the study of children in strange situations for brief periods of times. Further, in most applied settings we often cannot meet the assumptions of laboratory experiments. For example, the director of children's programmes in a local museum cannot assume that all children will react to a set of exhibits the way one or two groups have reacted. It may be that the children in the first two groups are very different than the groups to follow; thus, results from the first two groups is not generalizable to either groups. In this case, the educational coordinator will have to make connections between specific samples of children and the effects of certain exhibits.

Remediation of Weaknesses

How do we remediate the problems of the experimental approach? There are at least two possible answers. The first may be by the utilization of field experiments. This methodology is particularly important for the study of school children. The work of P. K. Smith and Connolly is particularly important here. These researchers used field experiments to systematically manipulate aspects of the school environment and the curriculum content.

A second possibility is in line with Bronfenbrenner notion of ecological validity and recent approaches to cross-cultural psychology described earlier. In order to understand children, we should observe them in a number of different contexts, both natural and experimental. For example, in order to understand the way children play with toys we should observe them in school, in the laboratory, and at home. Our choice of laboratory analogues should be grounded in meaningful and familiar contexts.

Conclusions

In this chapter we have examined one way to study children. The use of the experimental method is questioned by a number of researchers who rightly noted that humans are different form chemical compounds. They recommended more naturalistic approaches to child study. Experimentalists, on the other hand, often point their fingers at naturalistic researchers and scorn their "unscientific" or "soft" approaches. Such dichotomous, often hostile, camps exist today in some aspects of child study. This my-paradigm-is-better-than-your-paradigm attitude in child study is counterproductive at best and vicious at worst. If we have learned anything in our discussion of different methodologies, it should be that, first, different methods are used to answer different questions. Second, we should view experimental and naturalistic contexts as different contexts in which we can study children. Indeed, children should be studied in both. If we find that children act in the same way in both contexts we can be sure of the reliability of that finding. The description of context specific behaviour, however, is also important. Children are expected to behave very differently in different situations, so it is important to describe the behaviour eliciting properties of different contexts. In short, we recommend a multimethodological approach to child study.

5

Language Development in Child

Introduction

Language is clearly influenced by environmental factors, as indicated by the fact that although all normal children acquire language over the preschool years in much the same way all over the world, the language they learn to speak is dependent on what is spoken around them. Language is thus a characteristic that is highly affected both by humans' general biological inheritance and by the uniqueness of the environments in which they grow up.

This chapter is about the development of language, the principal mode of human communication. Although a few nonhuman primates have shown simple language abilities, none has approached the level found in all normal humans. Language enables individuals to communicate on a daily basis, but it also does much more.

Language allows us to share the experience of others without having to be there ourselves. We listen to the firsthand reports of others and gain information about events happening in other parts of the world without travelling there. We read the conclusions others have reached after a lifetime of experience and absorb the knowledge without living that lifetime.

What Makes a Communication System a Language?

Everyone knows what language is, yet differentiating language from other types of communication systems is something that linguists argue about. There are a number of features of language, however, that we think all, or most, linguistics and psycholinguists can agree on, and these include arbitrariness, productivity, semanticity, displacement, and duality. We define each of these briefly and then discuss different *aspects* of language, including phonology, morphology, syntax, semantics, and pragmatics.

Features of Language

1. **Arbitrariness** refers to the fact that a word is not inherently related to the concept it represents. For example, the fact that English refers to the orb in the nighttime sky as the moon and the brighter orb in the daytime sky as the sun is totally arbitrary. There is nothing about the features of these heavenly bodies that dictates their names. The exception to this, of course, are onomatopoeia words (for example, the choo choo sound resembles the sound a train makes and thus conveys the meaning of a train).
2. **Productivity** refers to the fact that speakers can combine a finite set of words to produce an infinite set of sentences. True language is creative, and speakers and listeners can produce and comprehend sentences that have never been uttered before. Language is not a limited set of utterances to be memorized. Rather, although the number of words of a language may be finite, these words can be put together via a system of rules (syntax, or grammar) to produce an infinite number of proper sentences.
3. **Semanticity** refers to the fact that language can represent events, ideas, actions, and objects symbolically.
4. **Displacement** refers the fact that what one speaks about need not be limited to the immediate context. Rather, one can talk about the past or the future, or events that are occurring a great distance from and out of the immediate perception of the speaker and listeners. All other animal communication

systems deal with the here and now (with the possible exception of bees, whose dances seem to communicate the location of flowers some distance from the hive).

5. **Duality** refers to the fact that language is represented at two levels: phonology, the actual sound that a speaker produces, and the underlying abstract, meaning of language, reflected by the syntax (rules of putting words together) as well as semantics (meaning of those words and concepts).

The concept of duality implies that there are at least two different aspects of language, and in fact there are at least five different aspects: phonology, morphology, syntax, semantics, and pragmatics, and they all develop.

Aspects of Language

Phonology refers to the sounds of a language. The sounds infants and children make are limited by their physical structures (tongue, mouth, position of larynx in their throat), and, not surprisingly, the sounds that infants and children are able to produce change over time.

Related to the *production* of speech sounds is the perception of speech sounds. The basic units of speech are called to as *phonemes*. There is evidence that infants come into the word with the ability to perceive most, if not all, of the phonemes found in all human languages, suggesting substantial biological preparation for infants to learn language.

How can one tell if babies can perceive phonemes, or more importantly can discriminate one phoneme form another? One procedure relies on infants *habituating*, or decreasing responses to, a repeated stimulus. Phonemes such as "ba" and "pa" can be arranged along a continuum, so that the difference between hearing a "ba" sound and hearing a "pa" sound is gradual. Despite the lack of an absolute physical distinction between the "pa" and "ba" sounds, Englishspeaking adults "hear" the difference at a certain point on this continuum. Eimas and his colleagues presented infants with one "physical" example of the "ba/pa" continuum until they habituated to it, in this case by decreasing the rate at which they sucked on a pacifier. After habituating to this one example, infants were presented with other sounds at different points on the "ba/

pa" continuum. If they perceived the new sound as being from the same phonemic category as the old one (for example, both "ba" sounds), they should continue to habituate to this new sound (that is, decrease their sucking). This is because even though the sound is physically different from the one they heard before, it is just another example of the sound they had just heard repeatedly (that is, just another "ba"). If, however, the new sound is perceived as a member of another phonemic category ("pa" instead of "ba," for example), they should increase their sucking rate (or *dishabituate*). One- and 4-month-old infants generally behaved on this task as if they classified the phonemes "ba" and "pa" the same way that older children and adults do. That is, young infants seem to categorize language sounds the same way as language-experienced speakers of a culture do, despite the fact that the physical distinction (that is, the acoustic signals) distinguishing these two sounds would seem to be arbitrary.

Although infants can discriminate among the sounds of language at birth, or shortly thereafter, they eventually learn to distinguish the particular the sounds of their native tongue and have a difficult time telling the difference between many phonemes in other languages by as young as 6 months of age. For example, Japanese speakers have a difficult time distinguishing between the English "l" and "r" sounds, as adult English speakers have difficulty discriminating between phonemic contrasts that occur in Japanese or Czech but not in English. Yet research indicates that infants are able to discriminate foreign speech sounds that their parents cannot, whereas some sound discriminations are made only with experience. Such research findings suggest that infants can make some phonemic discriminations that adults speakers of their language cannot make, but with time lose the ability to discriminate sounds that are not heard in their mother tongue.

It is worth noting here that infants have some language experience before they are born. Sound gets through the abdominal wall, and fetuses are able to hear the voices of their mothers and other people months before birth. There is evidence, for example, that babies prefer their mothers' voices shortly after birth, that they will prefer immediately after birth to listen to a story their mother had read out loud during the last weeks of pregnancy and that newborns prefer to listen to the language their mother speaks rather than a foreign language, all suggesting that infants are learning something about the sound of language beginning before birth.

Morphology refers to the structure of something, and in the case of language morphology refers to the structure of words. Although we may think that the word is the smallest unit of meaning in spoken language, that isn't always so. In English, for example, we add sounds to words to make them plural (add an s) or past tense (add an *ed*), and these word endings are also units of meaning. The smallest unit of meaning in a language is called a *morpheme*, and they come in two types. *Free morphemes* can stand alone as a word, such as "dog," "chase," or "happy." *Bound morphemes* cannot stand alone but are attached to free morphemes. They convey meaning by changing the free morpheme they are attached to. These include the rules for making nouns plural (add an s), past tense (add an *ed*), forming the present progressive (add an ing), as well a prefixes (*un*happy) and suffixes (happi*ness*).

One clever way of assessing young children's knowledge of the rules of morphology is the "wug test". Children are shown a picture of a novel object and told the name of this object (*e.g.*, "This is a wug."). Children are then shown two of these creatures and told, "Now there are two______." The correct response, of course, is "wugs." Using this and related techniques, children's knowledge of the regular rules of plurals, past tense (*e.g.*, "This man knows how to rick. Yesterday he ______."), and the present progressive ("This man is ______.") can be evaluated.

Syntax is the knowledge of sentence formation, or grammatical rules—rules for how words are combined into phrases and sentences and how sentences are transformed into other sentences. A competent speaker of a language can identify and create variations of a single sentence, each having different meanings. For example, the sentence, "The boy rode the horse," can be made negative ("The boy didn't ride the horse"), transformed to pose a question ("Did the boy ride the horse?"), or expressed in the passive voice ("The horse was ridden by the boy"). To do this requires a knowledge of the underlying structure, or syntax, of language. This knowledge need not be explicit, that is, available to conscious awareness. Few of us could state explicitly the rules by which we put words together to form sentences, but nonetheless, we are all linguistic experts when it comes to actual performance. Because we understand how English sentences are formed, we can recognize grammatical sentences (that is, sentences with proper syntax) even is they contain nonsense words. For example, the sentence "The grup was surfosed under his multex" is meaningless because "grup," "surfosed," and "multex" are all nonsense words. Yet, because you are an expert at English syntax, you know that "grup" is the subject of the sentence and some animate (and masculine) being, "surfosed" is a verb, specifically an action that was done to the "grup," and a "multex" is something (a noun) possessed by the "grup," possibly a body part. Not bad for nonsense.

Perhaps the primary focus of people who have studied language development has been the acquisition of syntax. How is it that children are able to make sense of the language they hear around them and come up with the rules for forming proper sentences in their mother tongue? Although there is a wide variety of syntactic rules in the over 4,000 languages that are currently spoken on Earth, there are some underlying similarities that psycholinguists have discovered. What has amazed most people who have studied language development is the complexity of language and the fact that children seem to master the basic syntax of their native tongue before they turn 5. They learn language easily despite the fact that the speech that surrounds them is full of errors. That is, the language that children hear is "degenerate," or imperfect. Somehow, children take the imperfect language that surrounds them and weave a theory of language (that is, syntax) that corresponds to that which their parents speaks. This, among other evidence, has caused many to propose that the learning of syntax has a strongly innate basis to it. (see the later section on nativist theories). Anyone who has tried to learn the syntax of a foreign language as an adult has an appreciation of the difficulty of this task, yet in the span of several years children acquire language (that is, syntax), despite the fact that other aspects of their cognitive skills are seriously immature.

Semantics refers to meaning, specifically the meaning of language terms. "Meaning" here, however, refers to more than just a simple definition. Words refer to concepts or objects, but are also related to other concepts or objects. For example, children must learn not only that "dog" refers to a four-legged family pet called Spot, but to other perceptually similar creatures, who themselves are members of the larger group of "mammals" and "animals." They must also learn that the word "dog" does not refer to horses, goats, or pigs, and that it may be related to other objects such as cats and fire hydrants, although not in the same way it is related to animals.

Often times, the errors children make in using words provides us with a good indication of their level of semantic development. For example, children often make *overextensions* – using a word like "dog" to refer to objects that are not dogs, such as cats, horses, and cows. Overextensions indicate that children's boundary for what constitutes a semantic category is too large (in this case, all four-footed, hairy animals). At other times, children will make *underextensions* for example, claiming that only their pet Spot is a "dog" and that other canines must go by another name. Underextensions indicate that children's boundary for a category is too narrow. Over the course of development, children learn to categorize words and concepts as adults in their culture do, although this process continues throughout life and it is likely that none of us has exactly the same meaning, or mental representation, for all common concepts used in our native language.

Perhaps the most obvious indication of semantic development is a child's vocabulary. Children go from three or four words in their vocabularies at age 1 to about 10,000 words by age 6. In fact, most changes in language development beyond the age of about 5 are not in syntax or phonology, but in semantics in the form of vocabulary growth.

Pragmatics relate to the use of language in social context, or the ability to use language to get things done in the world. It refers to knowledge about how language can be used and adjusted to fit different circumstances, such as using different tones when speaking to small children versus adults, and using more formal words when speaking to teachers and grandparents than to same-age friends. Knowing the phonology, morphology, syntax, and semantics of language does one little good in communicating unless one can use language appropriately in a social context.

Grice specified several conversational principles that children must learn. Messages should have the right *quantity* of information. For example, in administering an exam, an instructor might say to students, "Write your name at the top of the page." It would be inappropriate in this context to provide much more information, such as "Take a pencil, holding it so the graphite portion is pointed downward; pressing it against the top of the 8½ x 11 -inch paper, move the pencil so that the markings spell your name." Similarly, a message such as "Write name," would be a bit too ambiguous in this context. Children are more likely to provide too little as opposed to too much information in their attempts at communicating.

Messages must also have the proper *quality* of information, particularly that they be truthful. Exceptions are when one is joking or being sarcastic, and such situations are usually determined by the context or tone of voice.

Messages must be *relevant*, that is pertinent to the present context. If, in response to the request to "Write your name on the top of the page," a student were to ask, "Will it rain today?", something is amiss. The question is irrelevant to the context. Finally, there is a *manner* in which conversations occur. Speakers take turns and present their arguments in a coherent fashion.

None of us perfectly follows these conversational principles (our everyday language is filled with errors in syntax, semantics, and pragmatics), but children must learn the "how-tos" of conversation if they are to be taken seriously as conversation partners. All types of language knowledge (phonology, morphology, syntax, semantics, and pragmatics) are combined in a package called *communicative competence*. Generally, as children or, indeed, adults participate in varied context, they become communicatively more competent.

Different Theoretical Perspectives of Language Development

Although philosophers have long been interested in questions of language development, in-depth scientific study did not begin until the 1950s. Since that time, however, children's language development has been one of the most popular research topics for developmental psychologists.

Behavioural Theories

The earliest historical mention of language learning was in the fourth century a.d., when the philosopher St. Augustine wrote in his autobiography that he remembered learning language as a very young child. Adults around him, he recalled, would point to objects and repeat the names for them, and after many repetitions he learned the language.

St. Augustine's view of language acquisition essentially prevailed for 16 centuries, anticipating the behavioural theories of the early and mid-1900s. Behaviourists held that language, like any other behaviour, is learned by instruction, practice, imitation, conditioning, and reinforcement. According to this theory, children learn the meanings of words as St. Augustine described by associating them with certain objects or events that are present when the words are used. Other learning occurs by operant conditioning, they theorized, when parents reward their children for saying words correctly and punish or ignore them when they say words incorrectly.

In most of their research, the early behaviourists focused on *words,* not communication or grammatical structure. Moreover, they emphasized the parents as models of and reinforcers for language. The behaviourists actually paid relatively little attention to children, who for generations had been producing perfectly understandable original sentences and phrases they could not have possibly learned through conditioning and imitation, such as "all-gone sticky" to announce that their hands have been washed.

Many claims of the behaviourists have not stood the test of time. For example, although words can be learned via conditioning principles in the laboratory, there is little evidence that such structured techniques are used by parents at home; yet almost all children are fluent in their native language before they reach school age. Other research has shown that parents seldom comment to children about the grammatical correctness of their spoken messages, only the meaningfulness of them; and although new words are obviously learned by imitation, new grammatical forms (such as plurals or the past tense) are typically not imitated until children are able to produce them spontaneously. All this makes it very unlikely that a behavioural theory of language development is adequate.

Nativist Theories

With the many shortcomings of the behavioural approach, the stage was set for a revolution. According to Chomsky the study of language acquisition, learning theory was dead. In its place he offered a bold new theory. Children don't learn language the same way they learn to tie shoelaces; they learn language because it is a natural biological function of the human species. Language, he argued, was analogous to eating: we may exhibit different outward signs of these natural functions—eating rice and beans *versus* animal protein, or speaking English *versus* French—but the underlying structures of digestion and language are inborn.

Chomsky proposed that we acquire our native language via a language acquisition device (LAD) that is presumably located in the brain and programmemed to recognize the deep structure the underlying universal grammar of any language. Once the child is exposed to a sample of his or her native tongue, the LAD sorts out the rules of grammar and proper usage automatically and the child is able to produce well-formed sentences regardless of his or her knowledge of the world or communication experience. What people actually speak the outward manifestation of language Chomsky referred to as surface structure.

With Chomsky's revolution came an increased interest in language development and new ways of looking at old problems. In the late 1960s and early 1970s, the focus turned from the *structure* of language to the *function* of language. Developmental psychologists discovered the riches that the study of language development had to offer and became some of the first practitioners of the new discipline of *developmental psycholinguistics*. For example, R. Brown and his colleagues did extensive work charting in detail the development of three children (Adam, Eve, and Sarah) from their first words through the early preschool years.

Chomsky's theory provided the major theoretical impetus for much of the research during this time. The linguistic approach, as practiced both today and in the decades immediately following the publication of Chomsky's theory, is focused on the language children learn to speak, not on the children themselves. Adherents of the linguistic approach believe that every language has a structure a set of rules that all who speak that language understand, whether or not they are able to express them formally. As children gain experience with the language being spoken around them, they discover those rules for themselves. And once those basic rules are mastered, children can substitute words and create an endless number of sentences.

Most developmental psycholinguists following the Chomsky line believe that humans are biologically destined to use language. They offer as evidence the fact that all humans use language and that it develops similarly in all cultures and with very little or no formal training.

Our understanding of language development was greatly enriched by Chomsky's theory. Liberated from the stranglehold of behaviourism, researchers were free to study language development in terms other than learning curves and acquisition rates. They could look at what the child was intending to express and why one word was learned more easily than another. The focus shifted to what the child was learning and why, not how quickly it was being learned.

But Chomsky's view was indeed a radical one, as extreme in one direction as learning theory had been in another. And although researchers had become dissatisfied with the behavioural approach, they had questions about the new biological approach as well. One researcher, George Miller, summed up the situation nicely: "Now we have two theories of language acquisition, one *impossible* and one *miraculous*". As research on language acquisition progressed through the 1970s and 1980s, so did disagreement concerning how best to approach the topic. In fact, one researcher stated that by the end of the 1980s, language development was considered by some to be "the most contentious topic in developmental literature".

Research following the Chomsky tradition is thriving today, but so is research from many different perspectives. Many developmental psychologists now take an interactivist approach, looking not just at the structure of a child's developing language, but also at the cognitive and social factors that influence language development and, conversely, at the role that language plays in cognitive and social development.

Social Interactive Theories

Few theorists take either of the extreme positions exemplified by the behaviourist and nativist perspectives of language development. Most recognize that language development can best be understood as an interaction between a biologically prepared child and the language environment in which he or she grows up. It would be a misrepresentation to state that there is only one interactive perspective, but the one we feel is most relevant to our concerns is one that proposes that a child's social environment plays a significant in his or her acquisition of language.

Social Interactive approaches view the child's cognitive structures and social needs as interacting with the objects, people, and events in the environment to develop language. New language abilities, in turn, help develop new social and cognitive skills. This interactive perspective is well illustrated in the theorizing of Bruner, who set out to fill the gap between "the miraculous and the impossible." He rejected the idea that language is encountered willy-nilly by the child and that the innate language acquisition device abstracts rules from this shower of spoken language. Instead, Bruner believes that language is carefully presented to children by the people around them. Not only is the content selected for the child's current abilities, but the presentation is executed to provide the best possible chance of learning. We illustrate how we believe this interactive process of language acquisition takes place by describing in the sections below how infants and children, in interaction with others, acquire their first language.

How Children Acquire Language

Children gradually acquire their native language over the course of the preschool years. It would be a mistake, however, to think that language development begins only with a child's first words. As we saw earlier, infants can perceive and tell the difference between phonemes shortly after birth or before. They also communicate effectively with their parents months before they speak their first words, and how parents respond and talk to their preverbal infants also have some consequences on children's developing communicative competence.

Early Nonlanguage Communication

Babies come into the world with a variety of abilities such as sucking, grasping, and turning their heads toward a nipple and away from a blanket covering their faces. They are also born with the ability to communicate with others to make their needs known and to establish the foundation of lifelong attachment bonds.

These and other early, well-formed abilities are not selected by chance; they are so vital to our survival that they must be present at birth. In some cases, such as sucking and head turning, the survival value is obvious. But early communication ability is also of crucial importance to human survival and development.

Adults' Speech to Infants. Communication implies an interaction between individuals, and researchers have investigated the role that adults, especially mothers, play in early nonlanguage communication. Anyone who observes adults interacting with a baby will quickly realize that the adult end of the interaction involves a peculiar form of speech commonly known as "baby talk." ("Hello, Ben! How is the big boy today? Huh? How is Mama's big boy today? Did you go for a walk? Did you? Did you go for a walk with Daddy? Did you see the ducks? Did you?).

Gelman and Shatz studied the way mothers talked to their infants and found certain commonalities: high-pitched voices, short phrases, lots of questions, many repetitions, and exaggerated emphasis. This style has been termed *infant-directed* (or *child-directed*) *speech*, and is found in many cultures, in both men and women, and in children as young as 4 years. (Infant-directed speech has also been referred to as "motherese," although research has shown that it is also practiced by fathers, babysitters, older siblings, and elderly gentlemen in supermarkets.)

Although not all cultures talk to babies in the same exaggerated way as American mothers frequently do, some aspects of infant-directed speech may be universal. Several researchers have suggested that the special intonation patterns that mothers use with infants may have initially evolved as a means for the mother to control her infant's emotional state and to communicate her emotions to the infant. Such nonverbal communication plays an important role in developing a secure attachment between mother and infant, and, according to Locke, "Spoken language piggybacks on this open channel, taking advantage of mother-infant attachment by embedding new information in the same stream of cues". Although a secure attachment is not necessary for children to develop language, there is evidence that maltreated toddlers have significant delays in language acquisition.

How do adults and older children know infant-directed speech? How have they learned what words to present to this particular infant and how to present them? Bruner suggested that people have a learning device in their brains that takes cues from a young child and interacts with the child's language acquisition device. Bruner suggests calling this the *language acquisition support system* (LASS).

One reason why people may use infant-directed speech with infants and young children is because that is the way babies expect and "want" to be spoken to. Infants show a preference for infant-directed speech. Four-month-old babies who have been taught to turn their heads to one side or the other to select which of two tapes they will listen to prefer tapes of infant-directed speech over conventional speech. Using other techniques, Cooper and Aslin reported a preference for infant-directed speech by 1-monthold infants. The results of these and other studies suggest that the auditory system of newborns is prepared to process certain types of language, and that the singsong speech adults often direct to babies is no accident, but reflects the type of language infants most readily discriminate and attend to.

Infants not only seem to prefer to listen to infant-directed speech, can but apparently discriminate between language sounds better when they are spoken in infant-directed as opposed to adult-directed speech. For example, 1- to 4-month-old infants were able to tell the difference between similar three-syllable sounds (such as "marana" *vs.* "malana") if they were spoken in an exaggerated style so that the middle syllable was accepted (ma-ra-na and ma-la-na) as in infant-directed speech. They could not tell the difference between such syllables when they were spoken in normal adult speech.

Infants' Social Vocalization. If a mother talks to her 3-month-old baby, the behaviour most likely to occur in the next 10 seconds is baby's vocalization. The second most likely behaviour is baby's smile. During the first 6 months, infants vocalize along with speaking adults. By 7 or 8 months, babies will take turns vocalizing with an adult.

Language sounds in the form of cooing and laughter begin at 2 to 4 months and increase to 9 to 12 months, when they decline and one-word utterances begin. Sounds made during babbling vary widely, including sounds heard in the baby's native language and sounds that are not. Babbling sounds change with age. All of this caused some early theorists to conclude from diary studies that babbling served as an exotic smorgasbord of universal language sounds from which infants selected those they heard in the language being spoken around them, while gradually eliminating those they didn't hear. This popular theory is still cited today by some, but more recent research findings have not supported the early diary studies' data. Babbling does not contain all the sounds found in human language, only a small subset. The developmental changes in infants' language sounds over the first 6 months reflect anatomic changes in the vocal apparatus more than approximations toward the sounds of one's native language.

Stark and Stoel-Gammon and Menn described the developmental stages of infants' babbling as follows:

Stage 1: Reflexive vocalizations (birth to 2 months). These include cries, coughs, and the sounds associated with feeding and breathing, such as burps. They may make a few vowel sounds, but the vocal tract of these young infants closely resembles that of nonhuman primates; their tongue fills their oral cavity and their larynx is high in their neck (which permits them to breath and swallow simultaneously). This arrangement limits greatly the range of sounds an infant can produce.

Stage 2: Cooing and laughter (2 to 4 months). Infants now begin to make pleasant noises, especially during social interaction. These are mostly vowel sounds such as "oooh" and are termed cooing because they resemble the sounds made by pigeons. A few of the sounds will also contain some consonants such as g and k. Crying decreases and takes distinct forms that convey meaning to caregivers discomfort, call and request. Sustained laughter appears.

Stage 3: Vocal play (4 to 6 months). This ia a transition between cooing and true babbling. Infants begin to utter single syllables with prolonged vowel or consonant sounds, including both very loud and very soft sounds.

Stage 4: True babbling (6 months and older). True babbling sounds appear, such as "bababa" and "nanana." Consonant-vowel patterns are repeated, and playful variations of pitch disappear. This type of vocalization is not just a response to caregiver's social interaction, but often occurs when no one is present. The feedback infants get from hearing their own babbling is important. This is demonstrated by the fact that deaf babies, although going through the first three stages, do not engage in true babbling at this time.

Stage 5: Jargon (10 months and older). Babbling consists of many nonrepeated consonant-vowel patterns. Jargon babbling is strings of sound filled with a variety of intonations and rhythms to sound like meaningful speech. Babies now often sound as if they are carrying on their end of a conversation, with the intonations sometimes reflecting questions or explanations, but their "words" are only babble sounds.

It has been suggested, however, that babbling plays a more important role in language development than just a poor attempt at spoken words. Babbling may serve as a way to relate socially with family members long before the cognitive system is able to appreciate the intricacies of language that certain sounds made in certain orders symbolize certain specific ideas.

Evidence for this is that although *sounds* of babbling don't gradually come to approximate speech, the *intonation* of babbling does. Infants begin to "converse" in many ways that do not involve words, but rather the conventions of speech. They develop the ability to take turns, match the speaker's tone of voice, pause between strings of syllables, end phrases with upward or downward inflections and match the pitch of adults speaking to them higher for mother, lower for father.

The Second Year (12 to 24 Months)

Children show the beginnings of true language ability around the age of 10 to 13 months. It is at this time that they speak their first words that can be understood by family members and that consistently have the same meaning for example, saying "dada" frequently to refer to the male parent and not to request a cookie or address the family cat.

Over the next 6 months or so, children increase their vocabularies a few words at a time, but their speech consists of one-word expressions. Nouns account for the single largest category of children's early words, many referring to familiar people, toys, and food, although their pronunciation of these words is often dissimilar to those of adults.

Not only are young children's initial pronunciations of words often at odds from those of adults, but so also is their meaning. As we mentioned earlier, young children often *overextend* the meaning of words, using a word to denote things it should not (for example, using "doggie" to describe any furry mammal, including cats and horses). Overextensions often produce corrections from adults and thus can be viewed as a method for acquiring new information. In the example of a child overextending "doggie," the parent might respond, "That's not a *doggie*, it's a *kitty*". The adult might also add other information, such as "We have a doggie at home, don't we? But this one is a kitty." Or "Doggies say 'woof-woof,' don't they? Kitties say 'meow.' Can you say that?" Thus, children's lack of knowledge and immature response can be adaptive here, leading to getting more information from their parents.

Although toddlers are greatly limited in their ability to express themselves through language (*productive language*), they can understand substantially more (receptive language). This includes not only words, but also some rather complex sentences. For example, Hirsh-Pasek and Golinkoff found that 16- to 18-month-old infants, most of whom could produce "sentences" no longer than one word, were able to tell the difference between sentences such as "Where is Big Bird washing Cookie Monster?" and "Where is Cookie Monster washing Big Bird?" This trend toward receptive language being more advanced than productive language is true not only for children in the one-word stage of language development, but also for older children and adults.

Around 18 to 24 months, toddlers begin putting the few dozen words they know into short, usually two-word sentences or phrases. Children obviously talk about things that are familiar to them, including actions ("Timmy hit!"), possessions ("my ball"), location ("mommy kitchen"), recurrence ("more cookie"; "daddy again"), and nonexistence.

If toddlers' communication were restricted to these two-word utterences, they may have a difficult time getting understood. However, these beginning language users supplement their simple sentences and single words with gestures and intonations. For example, "MOMMY!" can be a clear cry of distress, whereas "Mommy?" can be ther initiation of a light conversation. Add a little hand waving and an empty cup and "Mommy" becomes a request for a drink refill. And coming from behind a chairback, "Mommy" can be the beginning of a round of peek-a-boo. Sometimes toddlers are even more obvious. For instance, one 18-month-old would get his mother's attention by climbing up next to her on the sofa, putting one hand on each of her cheeks, and turning her face toward his as he finally said "Cookie?" Another 2-year-old communicated to her mother that she did *not* want any more milk by giving a negative head shake as she was saying "More milk."

In their short tenure as language users, 2-year-olds have also learned pragmatics adjusting language to circumstances. They watch their listener for signs that they are being understood. They know they must beclose to their listener in order to be heard and that if they are not close, they must speak louder.

The Preschool Years (2 to 5)

Sometimes usually between their second and third birthdays and by the time they're ready for kindergarten, children's productive language leaps from two-word phrases to adult-level proficiency. We can think of no other cognitive accomplishment that is so complicated and yet acquired so well in such a short period of time. And perhaps especially impressive is the fact that children master the syntax of their mother tongue with little if any formal instruction but normal social interaction with adults and older children.

Children increase the number of words they know and use and the length of the sentences they speak. Children's vocabulary increases drastically over the preschool years. It has been estimated that children learn an average of a dozen new words a day between 2 and 5 years of age, and that they know between 8,000 and 10,000 words by the time they start school.

As children start to lenthen their sentences, they do so by using words that convey the most meaning and omitting the "little" words that make language easy to understand but that are not absolutely necessary for comprehension. For example, a child may say "I jump pool" or "Al me go store?" rather than "I'm going to jump into the pool" or "May Al and I go to the store?" When heard in context, the meaning of these truncated sentences are relatively straightforward. Children are economical in their word choice, using only the concrete and high-information words that are most important in conveying meaning. Such speech has been described as *telegraphic*, in that it is accomplished much as telegrams were written, including only the high-content words and leaving out all the ifs, ands and buts.

Researchers have found that the reliable increases with age in the length of their utterances shown by preschool age children is a good indication of early linguistic development, and this is measured by a child's *mean length of utterances* (MLU). MLU is measured by counting the number of *morphemes*, or meaningful language units, in children's speech. These include both the *free morphemes* that can stand by themselves (such as "hat," "walk," and "pretty"), and *bound morphemes* that are attached to a word's beginning or ending (such as un-,*-s*, *-ing*, and *-ed*). The relation between a child's linguistic sophistication and MLU is quite high, at least for MLUs up to 3.0.

Overregularization. Many of the morphemes children learn are word endings. For example, 2- and 3-year-old children learn that adding an -s to the end of a word makes it plural and adding an *-ed* makes a verb past tense. Once children learn these rules, they tend to apply them even when it is not correct to do so. This is referred to as *overregularization*. For example, once children learn the *-ed* rule, they often apply it incorrectly to words they previously used properly, such as *teached, goed* (or *wented*), and *comed* (or *camed*). Children who have been saying *teeth, mice,* and *cups of sugar* may suddenly and consistently switch to *tooths* or *teeths, mouses* or *mices,* and *cup of sugars*. They have learned a rule for regular words and generalize it to irregular words.

This can be assessed by using the "wug" test developed by Berko described earlier. Research has found that children begin to overregularize words typically around 20 months and continue to do so until about their third birthday, when they are more likely to use the irregular forms of verbs and nouns properly. This phenomenon is not limited to children learning English, but has been found in a wide variety of language, suggesting that children around the world approach the problem of language acquisition in a similar way.

Negatives. Children do not need language to express a negative. An emphatic shaking of the head is often enough to express the concept "no" or "no way." When children start to express negative ideas linguistically, they do so by negating an entire phrase by putting a negative word such as "no" or "nor" at the beginning. For instance, children may say, "No go store," or "Not Daddy do it." They may sometimes add the negative to the end of a sentence, as in

"Wear sweater no". Note that children who negate sentences in this way are also speaking telegraphically and have relatively short MLUs.

Following this stage, the negative term is moved inside the sentence and put next to the main verb, for example, "I no do it" or "We no run." In the final period, children learn to use auxiliaries much as adults do and as reflected in sentences such as, "I don't want to go," and "You can't have this." Obviously, these later forms are associated with longer sentences.

Questions. Questions also show a regular pattern of development in most children. Children's earliest questions are posed by adding a raised intonation at the end of declarative sentences, such as "Heidi go outside, Daddy?" or "Go soon?" This is a legitimate form of a *yes/no question* that adults often use.

More sophisticated questions involve use of "wh" words, such as *where, what, which, when, who, why*, and *how*. Proper use of "wh" questions involves inverting the order of the subject and auxiliary, so that the declarative sentence, "You are going to town" becomes "Why are you going to town." Children's earliest "wh" questions are asked by putting a "wh" word in front of a declarative sentence, as in "What dat?" or "Why Mommy go?" They later include the auxiliary, but fail to invert the subject and the verb as in, "Why you are going to town?" or "What you are doing?" In the final stage, usually achieved by the time children start kindergarten, children are forming their questions much as adults do.

Something that all parents of toddlers and preschool teachers know is that children will sometimes ask questions, particularly "Why" questions, for which there is often no good or simple answer. Some children we know, around the age of 2, began to use "why?" and "what?" in response to many things adults said to them. One child, after being told by her father that she couldn't go outside, asked "Why?" again, and he told her about the dark clouds gathering to the west. Her third "Why?" brought an explanation of the evaporation-precipitation cycle, and by her fourth "Why?" he was sure he had a scientific genius for a daughter. His wife burst his bubble by suggesting that perhaps their daughter was just interested in listening to Daddy talk. She had learned that "why?" was a magic word that caused adults to take a deep breath and explain *something* at great length.

Another child of 2 had her mother consulting the pediatrician about possible hearing impairment because she responded "What?" after everything her parents said to her. Again, it seems this child was using a "wh" word to extend conversations. When a parent said "Where is your bunny?" she would respond with "What?" This caused the adult to elaborate: "Your bunny, you know, the pink bunny that Grandma gave you? Where is it?" A second "What?" would bring another round of adult conversation: "Did you leave your bunny in the car when we went to the store? I hope you didn't leave it in the store."

The usage of "wh" words at an early age does not indicate acquisition of the concept of questions and answers. What it does illustrate is how social needs can advance ahead of true language abilities. Preschoolers like to converse with others and seldom let minor details, suhc as lack of language ability, get in their way.

Language development continues beyond age 5, of course, but the basic syntax of early schoolage children is remarkably similar to that used by adults. Children become more proficient at using infrequent grammatical structures, such as passive sentences, and they make fewer subject/verb agreement errors (for example, saying "They were going" instead of "They was going") and errors associated with use of the proper form of pronouns (for example, "He and she went" instead of "Him and her went"). But these are subtle changes and the "poor grammar" of the school-age child rarely interferes with communication. Vocabulary increases markedly over the school years, especially vocabulary that is encountered more in print than in speech and children's understanding of the pragmatics of communication still continues to develop.

One aspect of children's developing pragmatic abilities can be seen in their ability to monitor their own speech and evaluate whether they are being understood or not. One way of assessing children's ability to monitor the effectiveness of their own speech is to look at the frequency with which they make *verbal repairs,* or correct themselves when talking to a listener. M. A. Evans looked at the verbal repairs of kindergarten and second-grade children during "show and tell" time at their schools. She found that second graders made significantly more verbal repairs than the kindergarten children. Following is an example of a story told by a second-grade girl that includes several verbal repairs:

We went to – uh me and Don went to Aunt Judy's. And and uh my brother came down on Fri – Friday night, Uh there was a acc came on the train, And there was an accident. And they thought uh that uh . . . the – there was an accident with a – a van, And they thought – there was pig's blood in it, And they thought there was somebody hurt. But it was the pig.

Why should the older children make more repairs, indicative of errors, than younger children? Evans believed that it was not because the kindergarten children were the more effective communicators. The second-grade children were more aware of their speech and the need to communicate effectively. This resulted in more self-monitoring of their speech and correcting themselves, or providing additional information, when necessary to improve communication. As children get older and are able to plan their speech more carefully, the frequency of verbal repairs declines.

Language in Context

Although language seems to play an important role in how we represent the world and as a tool for thought (see the later section on language and thought), the explicit purpose of language is to communicate. Communication is a social phenomenon, and the fact that humans are social animals likely played a significant role in the evolution of language. Social factors are thus likely involved in how we use language. We have already discussed social-interactive ideas about how infants and young children acquire language, but social factors influence more than the initial acquisition of language, but also the type of language one speaks in any particular situation. Language occurs in social contexts. Social contexts are characterized as including different people, often of different social status and familiarity. Once a child learns the basic rules of a language, she must learn how to modify her speech as a function of the social situation. This can be seen as a form of pragmatics and includes children learning to be polite (saying "please" and "thank you"), as well as learning to use different language *codes*, or *registers*, in different social situations.

Speech Registers

We have already seen how children as young as 4 years of age modify their speech when talking to infants and young children. They simplify their language and use a tone or modulation of voice that serves to attract and maintain the attention of the younger child (infant-, or child-directed speech). This is a form of *speech register*. It is a distinct style of speaking that differs from the way children (and adults) talk to one another. It is used only is specific contexts (speaking to young children) and would be considered inappropriate if it were used in other contexts.

Perhaps more significant are speech registers that children learn to use in formal situations, with unfamiliar people, or both versus the speech registers that they used in informal situations with family and friends. The most obvious distinction for most children is between speech used in school with teachers (a school register) and speech used in informal social settings (a social register). Children, particularly those whose home language represents a nonstandard version of the majority language, need to differentiate these two types of speech registers and use the more formal one where appropriate if they are to get the most out of their schooling.

When the type of language children use at home differs noticeably from the language used at school, there is the potential for educational difficulties. In most cultures, families from middle-class backgrounds often speak a "standard" version of the language, one that is used in school, whereas families from lower socioeconomic backgrounds often speak a nonstandard version of the language, one that is different from that used in schools and one that is often regarded as "inferior". For example, in the United States, the most prevalent language distinction between social and school registers for native speakers is often children whose home language is described as *Black English* (or more recently as *Ebonics*).

Black English

Most of us are familiar with Black English. Although used mostly by members of the African American community, not all African Americans speak it, and many non-African Americans do, so the term can be somewhat misleading. Black English is characterized by some special rules of pronunciation and syntax. Perhaps most obvious to speakers of standard English is Black English's use of the verb "to be." It is often not conjugated as in standard English (for example, "I be" or "They be," as opposed to "I am" or "They are"), and it is sometimes not used at all in a sentence, depending on the precise meaning that is trying to be conveyed. For example, the verb "to be" may be omitted if the sentence refers to a one-time or unusual occurrence of an event, for example, "He playing ball" for a person who doesn't usually play ball. But if the sentence refers to a recurrent event, the verb "to be" is inserted in the sentences, for example, "He be playing ball," to describe a person who regularly plays ball and is playing ball right now. Black English is not an inferior linguistic form of standard English. For the most part, the two share common syntax and vocabulary, but where they differ, one is not simply a degraded form of the other. Black English is a syntactically complex form of English capable of expressing complex ideas and emotions.

However, Black English is not the language of the schools, nor of the mainstream American marketplace. This means that children speaking Black English will often be misunderstood by their teachers (who have a difficult time understanding Black English), have a difficult time reading text or understanding directions expressed in standard English, and may be unjustly judged as intellectually inferior based on they language style they use to express themselves. Research has shown that the actual language abilities of young speakers of Black English may be underestimated when tests are administered only in standard English.

Although there has been some substantial debate over the years on the costs and benefits of providing children instruction in Black English, most young speakers of Black English seem to acquire some aspects of standard English and use it in school. For example, DeStefano reported that the classroom speech of 8-to 11-year-old African American children contained more components of standard English than their speech out of school. Thus, even young elementary school children are able to switch dialects and registers, from social registers (Black English) to school registers (standard English). However, there is some evidence that many African American adolescents tend to *increase* their use of Black, compared to standard,

English, over adolescence, as use of Black English becomes an important part of their social identity.

The debate on how to educate children whose home dialect is substantially different from the dialect used by teachers and others in the school is a lively one, and we do not pretend to have an answer. It should be recognized, however, that Black English, or other regional dialects, are not inferior languages and that the language itself does not impede thought. It may impede educability, however, and the opportunity to partake fully in the American economy. Children of all social classes learn to use different registers. It may be more difficult for speakers of Black English, because the different registers are actually different dialects of the same language with some different syntactic and phonological rules. Moreover, language serves as a form of social identity, and children and adolescents may be reluctant to give up their language style merely for the sake of doing well in school. The ideal, seemingly, would be for children to master both dialects and have the flexibility to switch between them as the situation demands. These different dialects then truly become different registers, to be used when and where appropriate.

Second-language Learning

Learning to use different registers is something that most children readily learn to do, although this may be a bit more difficult then the social register is substantially different from the school register, as is the case for speakers of Black English. However, fewer children learn to speak different languages, but when they do they show sensitivity to social context, just as they do when using different registers. For example, young children who speak two languages usually use each language in specific contexts one language for use at home and church and another for use at school. Second and third languages are a fact of life for children in some parts of the world, such as areas of Europe, for instance, where there may be several "official" languages in a single country. There is only one dominant language in the United States, but the influx of immigrants over the past decade has increased the number of children in schools who do not speak English as a first language. By understanding the way in which successful learners of English have mastered the language, we should be able to design educational environments to optimize instruction for children who are learning English as a second language.

Acculturation and Second-Language Learning

Several theorists have proposed that second-language learning is associated with the extent to which children are, or wish to become, integrated within the new culture. This *acculturation hypothesis* holds "that learners will acquire the target language only to the degree to which they acculturate". For example, R. C. Gardner and Lambert proposed that there are two types of motivation for learning a second language: integrative and instrumental. *Integrative motivation* refers to a person's desire to learn the second language so that he or she can more easily associate with members of the majority culture. *Instrumental motivation* refers to a person's desire to learn the second language for more utilitarian purposes, such as getting a job. Gardner and Lambert found that people expressing integrative motivation were more successful at mastering a second language. In more recent research, J. S. Johnson and Newport reported that the only factors other than age of arrival to the United States that predicted Korean and Chinese immigrants' eventual language proficiency in English were self-consciousness and degree of American identification, both factors that would seem to be related to degree of acculturation.But how do children who speak one language go about the process of learning a second language? The work of Fillmore is particularly relevant here. Generally, she has suggested that children develop a second language by putting themselves in social contexts that will facilitate the process of learning that language. She observed five children (5 to 7 years old) in school settings of second-language users and outlined the cognitive and social strategies that nonnative speakers of English used to learn English. These strategies are listed in the order in which they were used:

1. First, successful learners attempted to establish *social relations with native speakers*. In essence, the children were using the native speakers to provide them with the "input" to learn the language.
2. The first cognitive strategy used by the children was *to assume that what was being talked about in a specific situation was relevant to the situation at hand*. Children used the linguistic routines

that were specific to these contexts in similar situations; for example, when recess ends, children may, "Let's line up." Being exposed to this utterance and the context of recess ending and lining up should result in comprehension and production of the appropriate utterance in the appropriate context.

3.&4. The second social strategy children used to learn the language was to *give the impression that they could speak the language*. In attempting to do so, the nonnative speaker had to use the second cognitive strategy: *use some expressions that you understand*. Children often began by using *routines* and formulaic expressions like "Yah," "What's happening!" and "Gimme" to participate in groups. The use of this type of strategy allows children to continue to participate in groups so that they may continue to learn the language. Such formulaic expressions allow children to use aspects of the second language long before they have mastered them.

5. The third cognitive strategy was for nonnative speakers to look for and *use recurring parts in the formulaic expressions they knew*. To do this, nonnative speakers must first notice how parts of the expression vary with the changes in situations, and then notice which parts of the expression resemble the parts of the meaning of the utterances known by them. By doing so, nonnative speakers can determine the meaning of the constituents of expression. For example, if the word *hungry* appears in a number of different phrases that are used in the presence of food, the nonnative speaker could deduce that *hungry* is related to eating.

6. The fourth cognitive strategy is to *make the most of what you've got*. Children use most frequently those strategies that they have mastered. This strategy may involve the overgeneralized use of a term, such as *sangwish* (sic) to refer to all food.

7. The fifth cognitive strategy is: *Work on the big things and save the details for later*. Successful learners of a second language used major constituents first and only later tried to sort out the grammatical details of the expression; they used phrases that they had already mastered to help them construct novel utterances.

8. The third social strategy used was to *count on friends*. Second-language users needed the help of someone else if they were

to learn the new language effectively. Friends had the belief that the nonnative speaking children could learn the new language. By doing so, they continued to interact with the language learner, often simplifying their speech in the process.

We have seen that children learn a new language most effectively when they have the desire to communicate with others and become part of the culture represented by the new language. Children are viewed as active learners who are motivated to learn new language forms by a desire to communicate ideas that they cannot express to others with their current linguistic repertoire. Fillmore work also shows that learning a second language is not just a "linguistic" problem, but is affected by a child's cognitive and social skills and the presence of a supportive social environment of peers. Although the effect of the interaction of social, motivational, and linguistic factors is most obvious in the learning of a second language, it is also true for the acquisition of a child's first language. Language is acquired in a social context, be it home or school, or with parents or with peers, and we must be mindful of these social and emotional factors when trying to explain language development.

Role of Age in Learning a Second Language

Our earlier discussion concerned young children learning a second language. Would learning be easier if children were older or younger than the 5-to 7-year olds studied by Fillmore? The answer is obvious here: Younger is better when it comes to learning a second language. People who learn a second language only as adults rarely become proficient in that language. This is seen both in phonology ("foreign" accents) and syntax.

It is easy to spot almost anyone who learned a second language as an adult. Even if they are articulate, well-educated, and have an impressive vocabulary, they almost always have a noticeable accent. Research has confirmed this. Oyama studied Italian immigrants in the United States and assessed their accents as a function of (a) their age of arrival to the United States, and (b) how long they had resided in the United States. Only the first factor, age of arrival, and thus age at which they were first exposed to English, predicted the degree of their accents.

Perhaps more subtle is syntax. Presumably, people who live in a country for many years will eventually master "like a native" the syntax of a language, even if they retain an accent. This was tested in research by J. S. Johnson and Newport, who examined second-language learning as a function of age. They tested 46 native Chinese or Korean speakers who had emigrated to the United States and learned English as a second language. The age of people at time of arrival in the United States ranged from 3 to 39 years, and they had lived in the United States between 3 and 26 years when they were tested.

J. S. Johnson and Newport reported that their subjects' grammatical proficiency in English was related to the age when language training began:

> People who learned their second language early in childhood showed greater proficiency as adults than people who learned later in childhood. Such a result might not be so surprising if it concerned only people's pronunciation of words (phonology), but these data are for *syntax*, and indicate that it is the age at which one starts the second language, and not necessarily how long one has been speaking it, that determines eventual proficiency in a second language.

Benefits of Bilingualism

Second-language learning is obviously necessary for children immigrating to a new country, but is it advisable for children from the majority culture to learn a second language? For better or worse, Americans have been able to function well in the modern world learning only English. The rest of the educated world learns English in order to speak to us. But with mass communications and an economy that is truly worldwide, learning a second language may make some sense. Is there any evidence of cognitive benefits or detriments of learning a second language, beyond the ability to converse in two tongues?

Researchers in the early part of this century noted that bilingual immigrants to the United States fared less well on a host of intellectual tasks than monolingual natives. They interpreted these results as indicating that it was the two languages of the new immigrants and not their lower socioeconomic status that was responsible for their intellectual deficits and argued strongly against teaching children a second language. Later research turned this interpretation on its head, however. Peal and Lambert assessed Canadian children who were fluent in both French and English and found that bilinguals performed better on a series of cognitive tests than monolinguals from the same social class. Other research has confirmed these early findings. Ben-Zeev proposed that bilingual children develop an ability to seek out the language rules and evaluate which are required for the circumstances. In general, these children may develop a keener sense of *metalinguistic awareness*, or a knowledge of how languages work.

On the downside, children who acquire two languages at once may show some slowed development in each language. Thus, although speaking two languages proficiently may be better than speaking one, it is likely not true that it is as easy to learn two languages as it is to learn one. However, it is true that if two languages are going to be learned, the earlier the better. The obvious pedagogical implications for this is that we should introduce children to a second language (whether it be English of Japanese) early and not wait for formal instruction to begin after the language-learning process becomes laborious.

Critical Period for Learning Language

We would not be thought to be making a profound statement if we were to say that adults learn most things more easily than children. Children's cognitive limitations make it impossible for them to learn some things and others are learned only after much repetition. Yet, as we've just seen in our description of second-language learning, language seems to be an exception. Children are better at acquiring both first and second languages than are adults, and this has caused some people to propose that children are especially prepared by biology to learn language and that there is a critical period beyond which language acquisition becomes difficult.

Locke stated that there are four types of evidence for a critical period for language acquisition. First, there is the evidence we cited earlier concerning the relation between age and second-language learning. Eventual proficiency of both phonology and syntax is greater the younger children begin learning the second language.

Second, there are cases of people who were socially deprived or isolated early in life and who, as a result, are able to develop only a tenuous mastery of syntax.

A third source of evidence comes from differences in proficiency in sign language in the deaf as a function when children were first exposed to sign language. The logic here is much the same as that in the J. S. Johnson and Newport study, except that now sign language is the first, not the second language, for these people. Newport reported findings very similar to those of J. S. Johnson and Newport: the earlier children were exposed to Sign Language, the greater their eventual proficiency.

A final source of evidence comes from recovery of language function as a result of brain damage. There are specific areas of the brain that are devoted to processing language (further evidence of the special biological basis for language). When these areas are damaged early in life, other areas of the brain can take over their function and eventual language proficiency can be nearly normal. Recovery of language function after brain damage is reduced with age, and there is little recovery when damage occurs in adolescence or later.

It is clear that the cognitive system of the young child is especially suited for language learning, of both a first and second language. This ability is gradually lost over childhood, and although adults are able to acquire a second language, they rarely attain the same proficiency that is achieved when language is acquired in childhood. This is evidence for the presence of a critical, or more appropriately, a sensitive, period for the acquisition of language. The window of opportunity seems to be relatively wide, however. But if children have not acquired a first language by adolescence, they may never fully acquire one; and if language instruction in a second language is delayed much past childhood, it is unlikely that phonological or syntactic proficiency will ever be attained.

Language and Thought

When people think about thinking, they usually do so in terms of language. For most people, thought without language is unthinkable. Although language is not our only means of thought, it is certainly the basis for much of our cognitive processing.

The connection between language and thought is not a constant one but develops over childhood. Bruner argued that preschool children, although possessing language, represent their world primarily in terms of images. Not until the early school years do children begin to use language as a tool for thought. K. Nelson has similarly proposed that the children's acquisition of language over the preschool years transforms their thought, permitting them to classify objects into culturally defined categories, represent events in terms of narratives that can be remembered and communicated to others, and develop a sense of self and knowledge of other's minds that is so critical in human social and intellectual life. In the section that follows, we focus on the role of private speech in young children's thinking, a phenomenon that characterizes the preschool child. Although the role of language on children's developing thought is an important factor, we believe that this brief section will introduce readers to some of the key issues and behaviours surrounding this important area.

The developmental relationship between language and thought was investigated earlier in this century by Vygotsky. He believed that thought and speech have different roots in development and that the two are initially independent. However, with development, thought and speech merge: thought becomes verbal, and speech becomes rational.

Vygotsky was particularly interested in the role of *egocentric*, or *private speech*, on children's thought. Private speech is overt language that is carried out with apparent satisfaction, even though it does not communicate. It can be observed when children are alone or in social settings.

Examples of private speech are the collective monologues described by Piaget. In collective monologues, two (or more) children will be talking about some common activity, but not necessarily talking to one another. Take, for example, the "conversation" of two 5-year-old boys overheard not long ago. Michael described how his ghostcatcher was going to drive his ATV over to Jimmy and catch some ghosts. Jimmy commented that his ghostcatcher had been slimed and he had to hurry back to the fire station (ghostcatcher headquarters). The conversation continued for some time, with both boys moving their toys and describing their actions; but what one boy said appeared to have little to do with what the other said or did.

Vygotsky believed language serves to guide children's behaviour (and thus their thought), but young children cannot yet use language covertly, "in their heads." In order to guide their own behaviour through language, they must talk out loud to themselves. With development, children become able to use inner speech. In other words, private speech serves as a cognitive self-guidance system and then goes "underground" as covert verbal thought.

In contrast to Vygotsky's view of the role of private speech in cognitive development is that of Piaget, who believed that the egocentric speech of preschoolers reflects their general egocentric perspective of the world. As children become increasingly able to decenter their cognition and perception and see the point of view of another, private speech decreases. For Piaget, private speech plays no functional role in cognitive development but is merely symptomatic of ongoing mental activity.

Most research that has been done to examine the relationship between private speech and thought support Vygotsky's position. For example, children's performance on school-type tasks often improves when accompanied by private speech and children are more apt to talk to themselves on difficult as opposed to easy problems or after making errors. Also, brighter preschool children use more private speech to guide their problem solving than less bright preschoolers, although this pattern is reversed for older children. This suggests that private speech peaks early in brighter children and persists in older children after it has gone "underground" as covert verbal thought for the brighter older students. And private speech does indeed "go underground," progressing from words and phrases, to whispers and mutterings, to inner speech. There is also evidence that preschool children are generally unaware that inner speech is even possible. Rather, they tend to believe that when a person is "thinking" he is *cannot* be simultaneously talking to himself. Moreover, when prompted to use inner speech (for example, "Silently think about how your name sounds"), preschool children are just as likely to say that they had a picture of their name in their head while thinking than to say that they said their name in their head.

Vygotsky was apparently right about the role that private speech plays in young children's cognitive development. Preschool children who talk to themselves are most likely using their overt language to guide their problem solving. Older children resort to overt, private speech when the faced with difficult problems, such as a thorny math assignment. And adults, including the authors of this book, sometime read out loud when trying to make sense of a particularly difficult passage. These findings also indicate that language, either spoken out loud or quietly "in one's head," is a powerful tool, not just for communicating with others, but for thought.

6

Assessment of Parent-Child Relationship

Introduction

The parent-child relationship provides the primary context for the development of the child's sense of self and self in relation to others, that is, the child's beliefs about what can be expected in relationships. Lieberman and Zeanah underscore the importance of the early mother-child relationship when they suggest that "the infant-mother relationship has the power to promote mental health or serve as the genesis of psychopathology in the young child". Understanding the quality of the parent-infant relationship within which the infant or young child is developing plays an important role in the assessment of social and emotional functioning and in formulating a diagnostic profile for infants and young children. Cicchetti asserts that "disorders in infancy are best conceptualized as relational psychopathologies, that is, as consequences of dysfunction in the parent-child environment system". The Committee on the Family of the Group for Advancement of Psychiatry has argued that, in general, important and common relationship conditions can exist independent of severe individual psychopathology, and that these conditions should be described in relational terms, with specific diagnostic criteria. Furthermore, the Practice Parameters for the Psychiatric Assessment of Infants and

Toddlers developed in USA, by the American Academy of Child and Adolescent Psychiatry recommend a "developmental, relational, and multidimensional" approach to assessment of psychiatric disturbances in infants and toddlers. More recently, a research agenda for the proposed *Diagnostic and Statistical Manual of Mental Disorders,* calls for a three-part approach to assessing relationship disorders including: "1) standardized procedures for evoking and observing interactions within the dyad; 2) questionnaires for each member to delineate his or her individual perceptions of the relationship; and 3) a structured clinical interview to supplement questionnaires and observations and integrate additional clinical information".

In the field of infant mental health, the parent-infant relationship is often the focus of therapeutic work. Thus, it is important to conceptualize primary relationships as entities to be assessed and, when indicated, diagnosed. Including assessment of the parent-child relationship as part of the digms that share evaluation process can inform and focus intervention approaches.

Parent-child relationship problems are characterized by perceptions, attitudes, behaviours, and affects of either the parent, the child, or both that result in disturbed parent-child interactions. If disturbances in the parent-child relationship interfere with the functioning of the child or parent and continue over a period of time, a diagnosis of a relationship disorder may be warranted. An assessment of the affective and behavioural quality of the parent-child interaction can reveal significant relationship difficulties. If the relational disturbance has a long duration and/or high intensity, the disturbance may be evidenced by the served that infants who did not formse parents' perceptions of the child or the meaning they ascribe to their child or their child's behaviour and can affect the nature of parental involvement with the child.

It describes domains of functioning for assessing the parent, child, and dyad that may contribute to relational disturbances. Although "parent" is used throughout the chapter, another significant caregiver who holds a parenting role may be substituted as needed, such as a grandparent or foster parent. This chapter also describes structured evaluation procedures for evaluating parent-child relationships, cultural considerations, and relational diagnoses for infants and young child projects qualities of the parent and implications for treatment. Finally, considerations for future research are recommended, linking assessment research to practice.

Conceptual and Theoretical Foundations

Using a relational approach to assessment integrates theoretical application of developmental and psychiatric disciplines. Foundations for assessing child mental health at the parent-child relational level can be supported by several compatible theoretical paradigms that share prioritization of the importance of early experience and context in examining development. Foundational contributions of the following perspectives are reviewed: attachment/ ethological theory, psychodynamic/object relations theory, social learning theory, family systems theory, and multiple systems theories, including bioecological and transactional approaches.

Attachment/Ethological Theory

John Bowlby conceptualized the parentchild relationship as an *attachment behavioural system* that represents the foundations of the child's psychological development. Bowlby observed that infants who did not form securely attached, intimate relationships with a primary caregiver often developed psychological and behavioural problems. Drawing on ethological theory, Bowlby posited that infants produce behaviours to elicit protective and sustaining behaviour from caregivers. Infants cry when hungry and coo to attract attention. Later, babies maintain proximity to their parents and turn to parents frequently for assistance and approval, as well as for confirmation of safety. When a parent responds quickly and appropriately to the child's cues, the child learns to rely on the support of the parent. This "secure attachment" allows the child to develop a sense of efficacy, as the child feels safe to explore the world.

According to attachment theory, the child constructs "internal working models," or mental and emotional representations of these early parent-child interactions. The child projects qualities of the parent-child relationship onto other relationships. Beliefs about the self, about the relationship, and about the world are categorized, much as other cognitive and emotional data might be. For example, the child may internalize "I am lovable" or conversely "I am not lovable" as a result of these interactions. These internalizations have been linked with developing social cognition and social competence. Indicators of relationship quality are found in the behaviour of the child, the caregiver, and the dyad, and in narratives describing these relationships.

Psychodynamic/Object Relations Theory

Freudian psychoanalytic theory provides a perspective for understanding how an individual's developmental trajectory, including personality structure, may be shaped by the quality of the early parent-child relationships one experiences. This theory posits that the seeds of personality are sewn during children's early interactions with their parents and suggests that unresolved intrapsychic conflicts that arise from how early stages of child development are negotiated or experienced can lead to neurotic symptoms in adulthood. Anna Freud described the quality of the early mother-infant relationship as paramount to the child's subsequent psychological development. When a mother consistently reads her infant's cues and sensitively responds to her child's physical and emotional needs, providing an "auxiliary ego" for the young child, her infant feels satisfied. With the infant's needs gratified, the infant turns his or her emotional interests from the self to the proximal environment, which includes the mother. When the infant initiates expressions of affection toward the mother and she responds in kind, the pair form an emotional bond. These early relational patterns characterized by emotional reciprocity become the template for the young child's future relationships and are likely to foster a healthy progression along developmental lines through subsequent developmental stages. In contrast, the "rejecting mother, " described as being incapable of or unwilling to identify and respond to her infant's needs, has been associated with subsequent developmental psychopathology in the child.

Spitz, Mahler, Winnicott and others have suggested that the abilities of theiors that are human being to establish healthy social relations are acquired early in the mother-child relationship. Winnicott described the parent-child relationship as a psychological "holding environment" for the developing child. The assumption is made that if this relationship is disturbed, the tend to respond to him primarily whe child will lack the adaptive abilities necessary to effectively interact with the environment. A negative behaviour. A sense of effectance and competence is the result of the ongoing experience of interacting with an empathic, consistent, and responsive caregiver who helps the child to understand and structure his or her world.

Object relations theory represents a more contemporary view of psychodynamic theory. The "object" of the infant's desire is the mother. This early relationship becomes the template for future relationships. Mahler, through extensive observations of infants, toddlers, and mothers, proposed stages of early development in which the relationship between the infant and the mother progresses from an undifferentiated state during the first few weeks of the infant's life to a close symbiotic relationship, to attempts at separation and rapprochement or an exploration of the environment and touching base with the parent for "emotional refueling, " to a psychological state of individuation when the child is about 3 years old. According to this model, the parent's feelings of rejection, ambivalence, and inability to help the toddler to complete this early developmental task can contribute to borderline or narcissistic personality organization, in which the individual lacks a consolidated sense of self as separate from others. Winnicott emphasized the importance of "mutuality" in the early parent-infant relationship as "setting the emotional tone of interpersonal experiences and their intrapsychic colouring throughout life" and suggested that the child who experiences inconsistent or unpredictable care becomes "a reaction to impingements from the environment. "

Social Learning Theory

Bandura theorized that social behaviours are learned either through direct experience with subsequent reinforcement of those behaviours or through observing others modeling certain behaviours that are rewarded. Behaviors that are contingently rewarded continue while behaviours that are ignored cease to be performed. The parentchild relationship becomes the primary environmental influence shaping the child's behaviour. Thus, for example, the toddler whose parents tend to respond to him primarily when he is hitting his younger brother is likely to continue this negative behaviour. Although the parent's reprimands may seem like a negative consequence, for the child this is still experienced as parental attention.

Bandura later incorporated the concept of self-efficacy as a motivational factor in the development of behavioural patterns. Children who believe that they are capable of performing certain tasks are more likely to attempt those tasks and perform them successfully. This sense of efficacy may be derived from previous experience in which the behaviours have been reinforced by parental encouragement or a history of successfully accomplished tasks.

Based upon the tenets of social learning theory, Patterson elucidated a pattern of "coercive" parent-child interactions that lead to the development of conduct disorders in children and antisocial behaviour in adulthood. This model con-teracting during an evaluation may inform the clisists of a pattern of escalating negative interactions between the child and parent associated with the parent's attempt to set limits, a particularly salient issue during toddlerhood. For example, a parent gives the child a directive to do or not to do something; the child attempts to avoid the directive by engaging in negative behaviour such as noncompliance or tantrums; the parent responds with criticism or threats; the child returns with an increase in the negative behaviour; the parent increases the threats. This interaction often ends in the child receiving physical punishment. The parent in this scenario unwittingly reinforces the child's negative behaviour.

Another social learning theory of parenting and its influence on child development is that of noted that warm parental support incorporates behaviours that convey supportive presence, acceptance, positive affect, sensitivity, and responsiveness to the child's needs and are generally thought to enhance children's positive social and emotional development.

Family Systems Theory

Family systems theories, such as structural family therapy, offer a framework for assessing parentchild interactions. According to this theory, aa family consists of parental and child subsystems that function interdependently as a single unit. The parental subsystem possesses the responsibility of caring for and raising those within the child subsystem. Within a healthy system, parents establish family rules and behavioural expectations that maintain clear boundaries between the parental and child subsystems in a way that meets the socioemotional needs of all members. Pathology occurs when there is a disturbance in the family system. For example, when a parent's capacity to meet the needs of the children is compromised by physical or mental illness, one of the children, usually the oldest child, may assume parental responsibilities, which may result in ambiguous boundaries or cross-generational alliances, as well as conflicts within and/or across subsystems. This is observable even in 2–or 3–year-olds who become focused on their parents' emotional states. Thus, observations of the whole family interacting during an evaluation may inform the clinician about patterns of interactions that preclude the optimal functioning of the family system.

Multiple Systems Theories

Contemporary theories have extended consideration of the child's developmental milieu to include multiple synergistic systems. Transactional systems theory and bioecological systems theory are two complementary models that support a relational approach to clinical assessment and treatment in infant mental health. In transactional theory, development depends on the complex interdependent interactions of the child, parent, and environment over time. Development is dynamic, and children's mental and emotional health depend upon multiple factors, including nutrition, responsive caregiving, parental mental health, safety of neighbourhoods, and quality schooling.

Similarly, Bronfenbrenner elaborate on the interaction of the individual child with multiple environmental systems. In bioecological systems theory, nested hierarchical systems both influence and are influenced by the developing child. However, it is the proximal processes, or the daily interactions of life, that bear the most importance for development. For the infant, daily activities with the parent are most influential. Bronfenbrenner contends that the quality of these proximal processes matters more than any individual contribution of the child (*e.g.*, temperament, medical condition) or parent (*e.g.*, pathology, education) alone. The degree to which the infant and parent can contribute to and participate in high-quality proximal processes predicts the adjustment of the child and dyad.

Reasons for Looking at Relationships

In the context of normal development, the parent-child relationship plays a critical role in the infant's emergent behavioural and emotional regulation. Recent research integrating neurobiology and attachment suggests that the infant brain develops in response to regulating social interactions with a caregiver, engaging in a circular feedback system of increasingly complex interactions. These developing regulatory processes are influential in the infant's developing attachment and subsequent sense of self and social competence outside of the parent-child relationship.

An early caregiving environment characterized by physical safety, satisfaction of physiological needs, empathic responsiveness, mutual enjoyment, learning opportunities, and age-appropriate limit setting helps the child develop a consolidated sense of self and prepares the child for future social interactions. A supportive parent-child relationship has been found to serve as a buffer for children living in stressful urban environments. A parent-child relationship that fails to meet the child's needs may place the child at risk for developmental delays, emotional dysregulation, behaviour problems, and psychopathology later in life. For example, Carlson found that disturbances in the early parent-child relationship, specifically disorganized attachment behaviour identified in infants ages 12 or 18 months, were associated with behaviour problems and psychopathology during middle childhood and the adolescent years. Lyons-Ruth, Easterbrooks, and Cibelli reported that the manner in which fants who demonstrated disorganized insecure attachment behaviours at 18 months had externalizing behaviour problems at the age of 7 years, while infants with avoidant insecure attachment behaviours showed internalizing behaviours at age 7 years. Research has also shown that interventions directed toward at-risk parent-child relationships can decrease maternal depression, improve the child's cognitive development and emotional regulation and improve mothers' perceptions of their infants' adaptability and reinforcement value, as well as increasing maternal positive affect and verbalization with infants.

Contributions of Parent

Empirical studies of parenting and attachment theory underscore the importance of examining the context within which the child is developing when evaluating the young child's mental health. The quality of the parent-child relationship or *optimal parental care* provides for the infant's physical and emotional needs as well as sensorimotor stimulation and physiological and emotional regulation. The mother's ability to demonstrate affection has been linked to enhanced infant development and involvement with mother and other caretakers. Maternal contingent reinforcement of an infant's signals has been found to be important to the development of the infant's sense of effectance and competence. From her study of infantmother interaction in the home, Clarke-Stewart described quality maternal care, which results in optimal, secure attachment, as socially responsive and affectionate but not necessarily excessively physical. Apparently, while holding and physical contact can be very important in the early months of life, this type of contact can become restrictive as the child matures. Maternal attention must be paid to the infant's changing developmental needs, such as readiness and need for autonomy. Sander suggests that the manner in which these developmental issues are negotiated is extremely important in determining the continuing nature of the relationship.

From her observation in the home and experimental studies in the lab, Ainsworth suggested the following five variables as most important to a high-quality parent-infant relationship: (1) responding sensitively and empathically to the infant's signals; (2) providing frequent physical contact; (3) allowing the infant freedom to explore; (4) helping the infant derive a sense of consequence of his or her actions; and (5) engaging in mutually enjoyable and reciprocal activities. Through these early interactions, not only does the mother teach the child about the self and the self in relation to others, but also the quality of this early interaction allows for optimal development in capacities for organization, linguistic and problem-solving skills and cognitive abilities.

In addition to the mother's provision of nurturant, responsive care, developmental psychologists such as Bruner and Vygotsky view the adult's role as important for communicating and translating the culture for the young child. The structure, modeling, and focused joint attention with the child allows the child to first observe and then internalize the adult's approaches, communication, and problem-solving strategies. This process of *scaffolding* leads to the growth and development of higher mental processes and attentional abilities. Through focusing, encouraging, and assisting, parents provide a "zone of proximal development" in which young children can do more than is possible independently, thus helping them learn what they can do.

Disturbed Parenting

The grave effects of maternal deprivation or disturbed parenting on a child's personality and ling tellect are well documented. Children of parents with psychiatric disorders may experience a type of deprivation. Psychiatric hospitalizations require long separations between mothers and young children, and psychotic symptoms may also serve to separate mother and child.

Several factors that may influence a parent's contribution to the early parent-child relationship are the parent's expectations, values, and atti-child vulner able to emotional and behavioural dystudes toward the infant's or child's needs, the parent's own history of being cared for, and perception of the self as a parent. These are further influenced by the parent's personality and level of cognitive development. If a mother is under pressure of urgent and unsatisfied needs of her own, she will tend to behave inconsistently, being influenced by fluctuating moods or needs. The mother who is functioning at a lower cognitive level, either due to genetic endowment, environmental deprivation, or psychotic delusions may not be able to perceive her child as a separate individual. She is not able to attribute a level of complexity to the child's behaviour. Sameroff speculates that "the cognitive level from which the mother viewed the child was another complicating factor in the manner in which early differences get translated into later deviancies". For example, the cognitively impaired mother who approaches her infant from a sensorimotor perspective might demand that her own physical needs be met. Beckwith suggests that if the mother's needs for success or effectance are not met, either because the infant is not alert due to prematurity or a medical condition or because the infant has a challenging temperament and is difficult to comfort, the mother may become distant and negativistic. Because she may feel rejected, she may turn around and reject her child. This process has been implicated in nonorganic failure to thrive and child neglect and abuse.

Numerous studies have documented adverse effects of maternal depression on mother-infant interactions, although the mechanisms are still in need of theoretical and empirical elucidation. Women who are depressed have been characterized as either withdrawn or rough, insensitive, and intrusive in their handling and care of their infants. Depressed mothers have been found to more often mirror the negative affective expressions or behaviours of their infants than their positive affective states. Maternal depression disrupts the process of mutual regulation, including motherinfant interaction and intersubjective experiences that contribute to the child's social-emotional and internal working models, thereby leaving the child vulnerable to emotional and behavioural dysregulation. Maternal depression also has been found to be a risk factor for delays in cognitive development, and it increases risk for subsequent major depression and behavioural problems. Infants of depressed mothers have been found to exhibit more dysregulated behaviour and to be more difficult to read. Cohn and Tronick noted that infants as young as 3 months exhibited heightened distress levels, increased protests, and gaze aversion in response to observations of their mother's still-faced simulated depression. Maternal depression has been associated with insecure attachments in 1 year-old infants, cognitivelinguistic delays in preschool children and depressive mood and behavioural problems in young children. However, the quality of mother-child interactions, specifically maternal sensitivity, was found to mediate the association between chronicity of maternal depressive symptoms and child outcomes.

More recently, a meta-analysis of six studies examining the effects of maternal depression on infant-mother attachment concluded that maternal depression was significantly associated with insecure infant-mother attachment. Lyons-Ruth and colleagues identified two specific patterns of behaviour among depressed mothers interacting with their infants that seem to be associated with disorganized attachment behaviours in infant-mother interactions. Some mothers display "hostile, selfreferential" interactions characterized by rough or intrusive handling of the infant, while other report that their mothers show a "helpless, fearful" pattern marked by withdrawn or less involved interactions with their infants.

Contributions of Child

Thomas, Chess and Birch suggest that constitutional variability in children has tremendous influence on parents' attitudes and caretaking styles. Infants' arousal level, rhythm, response threshold, capacities, and weaknesses play important roles in shaping parents' perceptions about and feelings toward their infant. The parent and the child influence each other's ability or desire to relate. Therefore, problems in the early parentinfant relationship may develop when there is a mismatch in the goodness of fit between parent and child. For example, an active infant with a high need for stimulation may become frustrated and irritable in the care of a parent whose rhythm or tempo is much slower.

An infant's temperament, specifically mood, emotional reactivity, and behavioural regulation, all impact the quality of the child's participation in the parent-child relationship. The term "difficult" was coined by Chess and Thomas to describe a cluster of child temperament characteristics that challenged caregivers. Infants who exhibit these difficult behaviours were more likely to (1) elicit less sensitive parenting and (2) require more sophisticated parenting skills. Therefore, infants requiring the most skilled parenting may, in fact, elicit parenting that fails to meet their greater needs.

The interaction of child temperament and parenting style has been examined in studies of parental limit-setting. Kochanska reported that fearful toddlers tended to develop better social conscience over time when mothers used gentle discipline (psychological and deemphasizing power) as compared with children whose mothers used negative discipline (coercive and/or angry). On the other hand, Arcus in her work with Kagan found that inhibited children had more favorable outcomes when parents used stronger forms of limit setting. Parents who report that their children are temperamentally fearful or reactive to limit setting also describe the parenting process as less pleasurable. Thus, certain infant temperament characteristics are associated with risk for relational disturbance.

Gender may affect the parent's responses to the infant. Six-month-old boys have been found to be more emotionally reactive (expressing both more positive and negative affect) than girls. Girls tend to show more curiosity and capacity for self-soothing than boys. Mother-son dyadic interactions have been found to be more organized than mother-daughter interactions. However, boys may be more vulnerable than girls to the negative consequences associated with maternal depression on cognitive development.

Medical Conditions

Children with chronic illnesses are two to three times more likely to experience emotional maladjustment or behavioural disturbances than their healthy peers and the risk for psychopathology seems to increase with the severity of the disability. A series of studies have implicated chronic illness as a potential risk factor for parent-child relationship disturbances and subsequent emotional and behavioural problems in childhood. The findings showed that children diagnosed in infancy with congenital heart disease and cystic fibrosis demonstrated higher rates of insecure attachments at 12 to 18 months as compared with a healthy comparison group. Insecure-avoidant attachment behaviours in preschool children with cystic fibrosis were associated with poor nutritional status and poor growth. Other researchers have documented that mothers of children with asthma tended to view their children as more demanding, less reinforcing, and less acceptable than mothers who had healthy children. The mothers of children with asthma also reported higher levels of parenting stress and tended to demonstrate more rejecting, overprotective, or overindulgent parenting styles as compared with mothers in the control sample, underscoring the potential risk to the parent-child relationship when a serious illness is diagnosed.

Premature birth has been recognized as a risk to the quality of the parent-child relationship for over 40 years. Several pathways accounting for these relational problems have been proposed. Infants who are born prematurely have been found to have a higher incidence of attentional problems and difficult temperaments than peers who were born at term. It appears as though multiple risk factors (*e.g.*, negative emotionality and health problems) may increase the likelihood that an infant will experience lower quality parent-child interactions. More recently there has been recognition that parent-child attachment is influenced by a complex interaction of both parent and child variables. Poehlmann and Fiese reported that the premature birth of a child was found to be a moderating factor for maternal depressive symptoms and the quality of the mother-infant relationship. Premature infant birth in combination with maternal depression was predictive of insecure attachment behaviours in infants at 12 months. Other research has shown that the mother's representations of her infant were more predictive of the presence of secure infant attachment behaviours at 19 months than the child's health history, which included prematurity and intracranial hemorrhage. However, the presence of neurological impairments in infants was associated with a specific insecure attachment, that is, disorganized attachment, in children.

Assessment of the Parent-Child Relationship

The goal of this assessment is to obtain a comprehensive picture of the parent-child relationship within its sociocultural context. The findings from such an assessment can assist the clinician in formulating an intervention plan and in evaluating progress during the therapeutic process. Sources of information should include the parents and other primary caregivers, the child, the extended family when indicated, day care providers, and the pediatrician. If the family is involved in other services, such as social services or mental health services, information should also be obtained from these collateral sources. The University of Wisconsin Parent- Infant and Early Childhood Clinic's relational assessment model involves a diagnostic evaluation that uses a multimodal approach and actively involves the parents through interviews, observations, and parent report assessment instruments. Observations of parent-child interactions are conducted across developmentally salient situations. Assessment procedures are structured to address particular domains appropriate to the child's level of development. For example, infants need emotionally available parents who are capable of reading their cues and responding in a sensitive and timely fashion, whereas toddlers need caregiving that is respectful of their emerging autonomy and provides cognitive and emotional scaffolding, clear expectations, consistent limit setting, and assistance in managing transitions and with affective and behavioural regulation. Note that an observation of interactions should be considered to be just "one snapshot in time" while the parent-child relationship represents the child's and parent's "sense and quality of connectedness" over time and across settings. The parent's mood and parenting capacities, the family's stress, and the family's access to and need of social supports and resources should also be evaluated as part of the parent-child relationship assessment.

Interview with Parents

Developing a therapeutic alliance with the parents is critical to the assessment process. Taking a collaborative approach with parents throughout the assessment may build such an alliance. At the onset of the interview, parents should be asked about their concerns about their child and what they would like to get out of the assessment. By empathically listening to parents' experiences of their child and their struggles in parenting, the clinician can begin a parallel therapeutic process with the parents that may have a positive effect on their relationship with their child. Several elements of the parent interview that are particularly salient to an assessment of the parent-child relationship include the following:

1. Demystify the assessment process by explaining the multimodal nature of the assessment procedures and the parents' significant role in the assessment process.
2. Ask parents what information and assistance they would like to receive from the assessment.
3. Provide a safe, comfortable, developmentally appropriate environment for children and parents. Ideally, all members of the family household as defined by the parents should attend the initial evaluation. Having the whole family present provides the clinician information about family dynamics, including sibling relationships and cross-generational alliances.
4. Assess the parents' optimal parenting capacities across several developmentally salient situations (*e.g.*, routine tasks of daily living such as feeding, limit-setting, play, separation/ reunion).
5. Involve the parents in assessing their child's regulatory capacities and behaviours and their capacity to see their child as a separate individual by observing the child together and discussing what you and they are observing.
6. Learn the parents' perspectives and meaning of the child and his or her behaviours by asking parents to describe their child and their impressions about the source or cause of the presenting problem.

7. Include a perinatal history about the pregnancy, labor, and delivery. This time represents the critical beginnings of the child's relationship with each parent. An unplanned or symptomatic pregnancy or a complicated labor or delivery may have profound implications for the parentchild relationship. Ask open-ended questions (*e.g.*, "What was the pregnancy like for you?") to allow parents to share those aspects of the experience that are important to them.
8. Involve parents in assessing their relationship by reviewing a videotape of the parent and child interacting together. Help them focus on strengths as well as on reading their child's cues. "Wonder along with" the parents about who their child reminds them of in general and when the problem behaviour is present. This information may help to elucidate parents' projections of negative intentionality attributed to their child.
9. Assess the sociocultural context of the parent-child relationship, respecting and appreciating the family's beliefs and values. Recognize the parents as the experts in their personal sociocultural environment and ask them to educate you about their life experiences and worldviews. Seek additional consultation from cultural experts to address the clinician's cultural knowledge deficits or biases.
10. Provide parents feedback about the assessment findings with a caring attitude, void of judgment about the parents or their parenting style. This approach will facilitate a therapeutic joining with the parents vital to the development of a collaborative treatment plan.

Observations of Parent-Child Interactions

When conducting an assessment using observational methods to assess the quality of the parentchild relationship, there are several key points to remember:

1. Note the intensity, frequency, and duration of the affect and behaviour between parent and child. This information may differentiate normal interactions from pathological interactions and assist the clinician in determining the seriousness of a relationship problem. For example, the DC: 0–3 Axis II system uses this information to classify the

relationship problem as "a perturbation, a disturbance or a disorder".

2. Assess the quality of interaction within the context of the situation. For example, differentiate parental directives or conversation related to structured tasks from those intended to join with or engage the child in a mutually enjoyable social interaction.
3. Consider parents' responses relative to the child's age and developmental level. Examples of reading cues and responding sensitively include a mother who adjusts the way she holds her infant after noticing the child's discomfort in a particular position or the father who responds to his toddler tugging at his arm by touching, talking to, or picking up his child.
4. When the child engages in negative testing or oppositional behaviour, note whether the parent responds to the child in a way that suggests he or she experiences the child's behaviour as resistant or "bad."
5. Note whether the rapidity and regularity with which the parent responds to the child helps the child feel that his or her actions have an effect on the parent.
6. Differentiate a genuine sense of "connectedness" from "going through the motions." An emotionally connected parent is aware of and involved with the child even when not actively interacting with the child. The parent is attentive to the child, subtly monitoring the child with an empathic awareness of the child's emotional state. Connectedness may also include seeing the child as a separate individual.
7. Assess the parent's capacity to reflect the child's affect and/or behaviour through echoing (with infants), gazing, confirmation of affect, behaviour, approval, encouragement, and praise, as well as labeling of the child's internal feeling states. This process of "mirroring" represents the parent's emotional availability and affective attunement to the infant or young child.
8. Assess the parent's capacity for "scaffolding" by looking at the amount and way in which the parent gains, helps to focus, and sustains the child's attention to the relevant aspects of

the situation. Scaffolding is a process in which parents recognize their child's developmental capacities and provide a physical and socioemotional environment that gives the child an opportunity to expand his or her capacities. Just as a metal scaffold allows construction workers to build taller buildings, parents' emotional and cognitive scaffolding helps their child reach higher levels of cognitive, social, and motor skills as well as emotional and behavioural regulation. Scaffolding with a younger infant may be manifested by protective caregiving. With an older child, this process may include assistance such as teaching, demonstrating, stating expectations clearly, and setting limits with a sensitivity to the child's affective and cognitive status.

9. After the observations, ask the parents how typical the interaction was. If the parents indicate that it was different from usual, inquire about how it was different and what attributions parents make about the differences. For example, parents may state that the child was much more cooperative than usual and that they rarely have the opportunity to play with their child one on one. Such information informs the diagnostic process and the planning for therapeutic intervention.
10. Observe from the child's perspective as well. Ask the question, "If I were this child, what would I see/experience when I look up at my mother or father?"

A systematic approach to assessing parent-child interactions is central to identifying the areas of strength as well as areas of concern that may contribute to disturbances in the parent-child dyad. Researchers have identified specific characteristics of the child, the parent, and the parent-child interaction that deserve attention during a relational assessment. The Parent-Child Early Relational Assessment (PCERA), a method that incorporates both an objective assessment of strengths and areas of concern across situations and a subjective component that involves parents in assessing their relationship with their child and the meaning of their child's behaviour through video replay interview, is described below. This is followed by descriptions of several other empirically validated methods for assessing the quality of the parent-child relationship.

Parent-child Early Relational Assessment

The PCERA attempts to capture the child's experience of the parent, the parent's experience of the child, the affective and behavioural characteristics that each bring to the interaction, and the quality or tone of the relationship. The PCERA may be used as part of an initial diagnostic evaluation to formulate relationship issues and focus intervention efforts, for monitoring progress in therapy and to assess outcomes inlation treatment efficacy studies. The quality of the parent-child relationship is assessed from videotaped observations of the child interacting with the parent during four 5 minute segments that include feeding, structured task, free play, and separation/reunion. The rating scales are based on empirical developmental studies and attachment, psychodynamic, and Soviet cognitive-linguistic theories and informed by clinical observations of those aspects of functioning seen as important for differentiating parents experiencing difficulty in parenting from well-functioning parents. The PCERA identifies areas of strength and areas of concern in the parent, the child, and the dyad. Relational profiles may be developed for use in focusing clinical intervention efforts, programme evaluation, and research with families at risk for early relational disturbances. Ratings are made on a 5-point Likert scale for 29 domains of parental functioning, 30 domains of child functioning, and 8 of dyadic functioning. The amount, duration, and intensity of affect and behaviour exhibited by the parent, the child, and the dyad are rated:

1. Items assess aspects of parental behaviour and affect including parental positive and negative affect, mood, sensitivity and contingent responsivity to child's cues, flexibility/rigidity, and capacity to structure and mediate the environment, genuine connectedness, mirroring, and creativity/resourcefulness.
2. Child items include positive and negative affect, somber/serious mood, irritability, social initiative and responsiveness, interest/gaze aversion, assertion/aggressivity, persistence, impulsivity, and emotional regulation, important aspects of infant functioning vulnerable to stress and family functioning.
3. Dyadic items include mutual enjoyment, tension, reciprocity, and joint attention.

The parent, child, and dyadic scales were initially developed on an NIMH-funded clinical intervention project studying maternal psychiatric disorders and the quality of the mother-child relationship. The PCERA has been further developed for use with normative and other at-risk populations.

Clark, Goodman and Brumley found that PCERA scores differentiate patterns of mothers with depression and mothers with schizophrenic disorders from well-functioning mothers. Both construct and predictive validity have been established. PCERA ratings of early mother-infant interactions have been correlated with both concurrent measures of child temperament and behaviour and parenting stress and with later quality of mother-child interactions and security of attachment behaviours at 12 months and has been found to document change following therapeutic intervention.

Each of the four situations in the PCERA provides a window for understanding what has been shared in the parent-child relationship. Each situation is experienced differently, with some eliciting conflictual feelings and others allowing for feelings of competence in the parenting role. After the procedure has been explained to parents, written consent is obtained for videotaping. The clinician explains that the videotaping is for the family's benefit so that the parent and clinician can view the tape together in a reflective manner during a subsequent session. Parents also are told, "We understand that this is just a snapshot of one point in time. We'll be interested in your sharing with us how it [the interaction] is like or different from how things usually go." The videotaping procedure involves placing the camera at a 45–degree angle to the parent and child, who are seated together at a small table, and using a medium shot to capture the facial expressions of the parent and the child.

During the feeding situation, the parent and young child are provided a snack of juice, raisins, and crackers and told, "We are interested in seeing you and [child's name] during feeding or a snack time together. Please be with [child's name] as you usually would." If the mother is breastfeeding, she is asked if she is comfortable being videotaped during a feeding. If she is not comfortable or if the infant is bottle fed, parents are asked to bring a bottle. The feeding situation allows for an assessment of the parent's capacity for nurturing and social interaction as well as sensitivity to the child's cues and need for regulation. The child's readability, affect regulation, social initiative, and responsivity during feeding may also be assessed. Comfort, tension, and regulation of the dyad in this situation is observed.

The instructions and nature of the structured task are determined by the age of the child. For example, parents of infants under 7 months are asked to change their baby's diaper and attempt to get the baby interested in shaking a rattle. Parents of children between 8 and 12 months are given two cups and a toy and asked to hide a toy under one cup and alternately hide it under the second cup within the child's sight and have the child try to find it. At 8 to 12 months, they are also told, if time permits, to read a book together. For children 13 months and older, they are asked to build a tower of three cubes and have the child do the same. With a child of 19 months and older, the task includes building a tower with more cubes and having the child make a design with coloured blocks that matches the block design cards. This task is always a little difficult for the child to complete on his or her own. This situation allows for an assessment of the parents' capacity to structure and mediate the environment according to the child's developmental and individual needs. Some of the tasks tap the child's emerging abilities and require adult cognitive scaffolding and emotional availability in order for the child to complete the task successfully. The child's attentional skills, persistence, and interest in complying with parental expectations in a structured situation are observed. The dyad's capacity for joint attention to an activity, reciprocity in negotiations, and mutuality may be assessed.

The introduction to the free play situation explains, "This is a free play time for you and your child. You or [child's name] may choose the toy or toys that you would like to play with together." These toys may include rattles, plastic keys, a cloth diaper or small blanket (for peek-aboo), a busy box, two toy telephones, a ball, two small stuffed animals or puppets, a doll and bottle, small cars/ trucks, and bristle blocks. The free play allows for an assessment of the parents' capacity to be playful with and enjoy their child, to facilitate their child's capacity for exploratory and representational play. In addition, the dyad's capacity for social interaction, mutuality, and reciprocity can be observed.

At the end of the instructions for the free play, parents also are given instructions for the separation/reunion episode. They are told, "We'd also like to see how things go for [child's name] when you leave the room. After 5 minutes of play I'll knock on the door but won't come in. Let [child's name] know that you're going to be leaving the room for a few minutes. Then please come stand outside the room for a few minutes with me." This situation allows assessment of the parents' ability and level of comfort in preparing the child for a brief separation. The child's capacity for self-regulation and quality of mood and exploratory play during the parents' absence is assessed. The dyad's quality of affect and engagement at reunion may also be observed.

Confirmatory factor analyses of 12-month free play interactions revealed eight subscales: Parent Subscale I, Parental Positive Affective Involvement and Verbalization; Parent Subscale II, Parental Negative Affect and Behavior; Parent Subscale III, Parental Intrusiveness, Insensitivity, and Inconsistency; Infant Subscale IV, Infant Positive Affect, Communicative and Social Skills; Infant Subscale V, Infant Quality of Play, Interest, and Attentional Skills; Infant Subscale VI, Infant Dysregulation and Irritability; Dyadic Subscale VII, Dyadic Mutuality and Reciprocity; Dyadic Subscale VIII, Dyadic Disorganization and Tension. Internal consistency of factors, interrater reliability, and predictive and discriminant validity have been established for the PCERA in a number of studies with normative and high-risk populations. Training is recommended.

A video replay session, in which brief segments of the videotaped interactions are played back and viewed with the parents, is an important part of the assessment process. In a semistructured interview, the parents' perceptions, attitudes, and goals during the interactions with the child are assessed. Objective assessments often fail to answer questions about what parents are experiencing with the infant/child. The video replay interview allows parents to share what they were seeing, doing, and feeling in relation to the child and their perceptions of the child and themselves as parents. By "wondering along with the parents" about their perceptions, attitudes, and feelings about their child, the clinician can gain insights about parents' phenomenological experience of the parent-child relationship that influence their behavioural interactions with the child. Before the tape is replayed, parents are asked, "How was this interaction like or different from how things usually go at home for you and [child's name]?" "What was the most enjoyable part of this session for you?" "What part was the most difficult or did you like the least?" "Do you have any questions or comments about the taping?" During the replay, the clinician encourages the parents to share their subjective perception of the child's behaviour and of themselves in the parenting role.

First, the meaning of the child to the parent is assessed by stopping the tape at a point when the child's face can be seen clearly on the screen. The clinician asks the parents, "I wonder who [child's name] looks like or reminds you of [physical features, temperament, behaviour]?" "How did you select your child's name?" "How would you describe that person?" Then, parents' capacity to read their child's cues may be assessed by stopping the tape at a point when the parent is not responding to the child's cues, misinterpret cues, or has difficulty responding empathically. In addition, parents' capacity for reflective functioning is assessed, that is, the ability to reflect upon the internal affective experience of their child and themselves. The clinician asks parents, "How were you feeling during that interaction?" "What do you think was going on for your child?" "What do you imagine your child may have been feeling then?" This process helps the clinician to assess parents' capacity to see the child as a separate individual and their ability to empathically read their child's cues. Parents' capacity for reflective functioning, that is, their ability to reflect upon the internal affective experience of their child and themselves, is assessed. In addition, the clinician can also help parents to expand their perceptions of their child and his or her behaviour and increase their ways of being with their child by wondering with them about alternative explanations for the child's behaviour.

To assess the reinforcement value of the child and parents' sense of competence in the parenting role, the clinician stops the tape at a point when parent and child are experiencing a mutually satisfying interaction and asks, "How do you think [child's name] felt at that moment?" Then the clinician asks parents what they think they did to elicit this positive response. The clinician offers additional observations that amplify parents' strengths in reading their child's needs and responding in a developmentally sensitive manner. Additional questions in this video replay interview to inform the clinician about parents' experience of parenting this child include, "How would you describe yourself as a parent?" "In general, what have you found most difficult or frustrating about being a parent?" "What have you found most enjoyable about being a parent?" "When do you feel best, or that you have done well as a parent?" "Did becoming a parent change you as a person in any way? How?"

Finally, it is extremely valuable to obtain a relational history from each parent to better understand their own template of being parented, or, their internal working model of relationships. The following questions may be asked during the video replay session or at a subsequent session: "How would you compare yourself to your own parents?" "What do you remember about being parented by your mother or father when you were young?" "What words would you use to describe your mother or father? Please give specific examples of these. " "How was discipline handled in your family?" "Who was available/ responsive to you?" "Who kept you safe, physically and emotionally (or did not)?"

Review of Other Parent- Child Interaction Assessment Methods

The still-face procedure was developed to assess the synchronous nature of parent-child interactions. In the still-face procedure, a parent is instructed to withdraw from interacting with the infant (by making a still or affectless facial expression) for a short period of time. The infant's affective and regulatory responses to the parent's affective withdrawal are observed. Based on the infant's response, judgments are made regarding the infant's typical affective responding and history of experience with the parent. The Still-Face evaluates the reciprocity and achievement of mutual goals of mother-infant interactions, which are central to the infant's sense of well-being. These interactional goals include initiation of interaction, mutual orientation greetings, exchange of affect, and mutual disengagement.

According to Cohn and Tronick, face-to-face interactions between parents and children are regulated mutually, with parent and child each contributing to the interaction. Infants learn to adjust their own affective and regulatory states to match those of the parent, and vice versa. Ideally, over time, these exchanges become increasingly synchronous, with each member reading and responding to the other's cues. In less than ideal circumstances, the parent may not participate successfully in the affective interchange, and may send poorly matched emotional and reactive messages to the child. The child may respond by engaging in regulation that is more self-directed than relational, finding comfort in sucking, turning away, and rocking. While the domains assessed have relevance for clinical intervention, the StillFace procedure is primarily a research paradigm.

Nursing Child Assessment Satellite Training

The Nursing Child Assessment Satellite Training (NCAST) Teaching and Feeding Scales assess mother and child behaviours on 149 variables: 76 in the Feeding Scale and 73 in the Teaching Scale. Designed for use with infants and yhoung children up to 36 months of age, the NCAST scales have been widely used with infants at risk due to such circumstances as prematurity, failure to thrive, and maltreatment. The NCAST has also been used to measure the quality of mother and child interactions in samples of children with developmental delays and social-economic disadvantages. During feeding and teaching activities, the absence or presence of behaviours are rated, indicating the mother's sensitivity to the child's cues, responsiveness to the child's distress, and ability to foster of social-emotional and cognitive growth.

Half of the items in each scale tap into the dyad's capacity for reciprocity and contingent responsiveness, considered central to learning developmental tasks. Children's behaviours are rated for clarity and responsiveness to the caregiver. The teaching scales are more strongly correlated with cognitive development than the feeding scales, and have predictive validity when examining children's language and cognitive outcomes at 3 and 5 years of age. Although the domains of parental functioning in the NCAST are central to positive parent-child interactions and early childhood social-emotional development, use of the NCAST scales in mental health settings may be limited by presence/absence ratings, reducing the possibility of measuring incremental change with therapeutic intervention. Training is recommended.

HOME Inventory for Families of Infants and Toddlers

The HOME Inventory for Families of Infants and Toddlers was developed to examine the quality of stimulation and interaction in the young child's home environment. In particular, the measure focuses on cognitive and social-emotional stimulation with materials and the quality of parent-child interaction. The protocol is completed by a single observer interview in the child's home. The observer-interviewer asks the parent questions and observes aspects of the setting and parent-child interaction. The interview is not standardized, to allow parents to feel more at ease in the process. The assessment needs to be administered while the child is awake and at least one parent is available. The HOME takes approximately an hour to administer, and items are scored "yes" or "no."

While the HOME was not standardized on a diverse sample, subsequent use with varied samples has established its utility with children and families from a variety of backgrounds. The HOME correlates substantially with measures of cognitive development and has sufficient test-retest reliability. Strengths of this assessment include its ease with the child. The teaching activities are of use and predictive validity of cognitive development.

Emotional Availability Scales

The Emotional Availability Scales (EAS), assesses the emotional availability of the parent for the child, and the child for the parent. Parental sensitivity, structuring, nonintrusiveness, and nonhostility are assessed in the context of a parentinfant interaction. Children are observed for their responsiveness and involvement with parents. The EAS uses global ratings, taking the context into account, to make clinical judgments about the quality of behavioural interactions.

Contemporary theory sets forth two main adaptive roles for emotion: approach/avoidance motivation and signaling intent/communication. Regulation is needed to optimize emotional functioning. Emotional availability emerged as a relationship construct, in which members of dyadic interchange (*e.g.*, parent and child) engage in reciprocal interactions, which, ideally, become smoother over time. The EAS has been found to be associated with security of attachment.

Clinical Problem-Solving Procedure

The Clinical Problem-Solving Procedure, developed by Crowell and Feldman, is based on the "tool-use task". Crowell asserts that mental health problems are not found "within the infant". In examining parent-child interaction problems, she cites several essential elements: It is important that the behaviour of the parent and child be observed directly, and that the child's age and developmental level be taken into account. The assessment needs to be short and simple, with an uncomplicated scoring scheme. Finally, it should allow parental match to child developmental level to be observed, and the activities should reflect everyday life. The Crowell procedure consists of nine episodes consisting of free play, cleanup, bubbles, four teaching tasks, separation, and reunion. In this procedure adapted for infants, the parent is given a variety of common toys and activities and instructed to play with the child. The teaching activities are increasingly difficult, and the last two are technically beyond the child's developmental capacities.

Strange Situation

The Strange Situation (SS) was developed by Ainsworth to assess the quality of the security of the child's attachment to the parent, and its use as a reliable research instrument is widely accepted. However, as a clinical assessment tool, the SS has several limitations. The SS makes its determination of attachment security entirely from the child's behaviour, primarily from the child's behaviour during reunion with the mother. Additionally, because the SS capitalizes on fear of strangers, which becomes salient at about 6 months of age, use of the SS is limited to the end of the child's first year and about halfway through the second year. While the concept of the SS is to activate the attachment system using a moderately stressful situation, for some children the scenario is very stressful, possibly highlighting differences in temperamental proneness to distress and not solely attachment. For others, who have been in large-group day care from an early age, being left by the parent and the introduction of a stranger may not be novel at all and thus not experienced as very stressful.

Parenting Stress Index

The Parenting Stress Index (PSI) is a 120–item, self-report inventory measuring the parent's per-richness of perception, openness to change, coception of specific areas of stress in the parentinfant relationship. The PSI measures variables of stress within the child domain, parent domain, and other life circumstances domain. Child domain subscales include measuring to what extent the child is experienced as acceptable, reinforcing, demanding, adaptable, unhappy, and distractible/hyperactive. Parent domain subscales measure to what extent the parent feels stress associated with attachment to the child, feeling competent in the parenting role, restricted in roles, depressed, socially isolated, healthy, and satisfied with the spousal relationship. The other life circumstances domain assigns a stress value to situations such as divorce, changes in income, and pregnancy. Except for the Life Stress Scale, items are scored on a 5–point scale (from 1 = strongly agree to 5 = strongly disagree). For the other life circumstances items, the respondent simply indicates whether a specific life event has occurred within the past 12 months. A total stress score is calculated by combining the scores from the child and parent domains. Scores within the clinical range on the Attachment Scale indicate that the parent may not feel emotionally connected to the child or that the parent has difficulty reading the child's cues and meeting his or her needs. The other subscales provide additional information about child and parent factors that may contribute to disturbances in the parent-child relationship.

Working Model of the Child Interview

The Working Model of the Child Interview systematically examines parental perceptions of their infant. An hour-long interview, the WMCI has been found to be correlated with the child's behaviour in the Strange Situation and with mother-child interactive behaviour and has been adapted for use in clinical settings. Narrative features emerge that are considered to be clinical indices of the nature of the parents' experience of the child. These include richness of perception, openness to change, coherence, intensity of involvement, caregiving sensitivity, acceptance/rejection, infant difficulty, and fear of loss. The parents' affective tone and organization of the narrative are also considered and are classified as either balanced, disengaged, or distorted.

The Insightfulness Assessment

The Insightfulness Assessment evaluates parents' capacity to empathically understand their children's internal experiences of the world. The IA involves videotaping the child and parent during a play activity. Subsequently the parent views segments of the videotape during an interview designed to assess his or her perspective about the child. Transcribed interviews are coded using 10 scales: insight into child's motives, openness, complexity in description of child, maintenance of focus on child, richness of description of child, coherence of thought, acceptance, anger, worry, and separateness from child. The scales provide the basis for 4 classifications: Positively Insightful, One-Sided, Disengaged, and Mixed. Although IA is a relatively new instrument, there is growing evidence to support its validity and re-logical defenses but also to young children's beliability in differentiating securely attached parent-child dyads from insecurely attached dyads. Mothers classified as Positively Insightful have been associated with securely attached children while mothers identified as One-Sided tended to have insecure/ambivalent children and mothers in the Mixed classification had children with insecure/disorganized attachment patterns. Furthermore, these classifications have been found to be independent of parental educational level. Finally, change in parental classification from noninsightful to insightful has been associated with improvement in preschool children's behaviour following a therapeutic treatment programme.

Adult Attachment Interview

The Adult Attachment Interview is a semistructured hourlong interview method consisting of 18 questions used to classify a parent's state of mind with grossly path logical care spect to attachment. Parents are asked to describe their salient early childhood relationship experiences, and to give five adjectives that best describe their relationship with each parent, then specific memories to support each adjective. Hesse describes the central task on this interview to be "producing and reflecting upon memories related to attachment while simultaneously maintaining coherent discourse with the interviewer". The narrative is classified as either secure/autonomous, dismissive, preoccupied, or unresolved/ disorganized. Parents' attachment classifications on the AAI have been found to be associated with their child's attachment behaviour with that parent. Training in the coding of the AAI is required.

Diagnosis of Relational Disorders

Understanding the quality of the parent-infant relationship is an important part of developing a diagnostic profile for infants and young children. The primary relationships of infants and young children contribute not only to the development of children's personality and structure of psychological defenses but also to young children's beliefs about what is possible to expect in relationships with others.

The *DSM-IV* and Medical Diagnoses

The *Diagnostic and Statistical Manual of Mental Disorders*, a multiaxial classification system developed to assist clinicians and researchers in the identification, study, and/or treatment of individuals with mental health problems, includes Axis I, clinical disorders; Axis II, personality disorders (used only for adult clients) and/or mental retardation (developmental delays in children); Axis III, general medical conditions; Axis IV, psychosocial and environmental stresses; and Axis V, global assessment of functioning. Several Axis I diagnoses address disturbances in the parent-child relationship. Reactive attachment disorder is defined as "markedly disturbed and developmentally inappropriate social relationships in most contexts that begins before age 5 years and is associated with grossly pathological care". The two subtypes include inhibited type and disinhibited type. The *DSM-IV* also describes rumination disorder as recurrent vomiting and feeding or eating disorder of infancy and early childhood as failure to eat adequate amounts of food without physiological causes; both are associated with lack of environmental stimulation and/or child neglect that constitute a disturbance in the parent-child relationship. Other *DSM-IV* diagnoses that may be associated with problems in the early parent-child relationship include separation anxiety, sleep disorders, oppositional defiant disorder, and expressive language disorder, as well as the V code of a parent-child relational problem. Although not found in the *DSM-IV* system, the medical diagnosis of a nonorganic failure to thrive has been associated with a disturbance in the parent-child relationship. This disorder is usually recognized by the child's pediatrician when a child who shows no other signs of illness demonstrates poor growth patterns that cannot be accounted for by parental growth patterns or further medical testing. Such patterns have been associated with caregiver deprivation and neglect. These children often manifest other signs of child neglect or maltreatment such as poor hygiene and/or frequent accidental injuries. Although these systems vary in their classification, each system describes a disturbance in the balance between the child's proximity seeking and exploration of the environment.

DC: 0–3

The *Diagnostic Classification of Mental Health and Developmental Disorders of Infancy and Early Childhood* (DC: 0–3; Zero to Three) is a multiaxial classification system designed to provide clinicians and researchers a diagnostic profile of an infant's or young child's functioning within the context of his or her caregiving environment. The axes include Axis I, primary classification; Axis II, relationship classification; Axis III, physical, neurological, developmental, and mental health disorders or conditions described in other classification systems; Axis IV, psychosocial stress; and Axis V, functional emotional developmental level.

Axis II describes parent-child relationship disorders as perceptions, attitudes, behaviours, and affects of the parent, the child, or both that result in disturbed interactions in a specific parent-child relationship. The parent may relate to the infant from the beginning in light of his or her own personality dynamics, including projections and defenses. These may interact with distinct infant characteristics and lead to relationship difficulties or disorders.

Diagnoses of relationship disturbances or disorders should be based not only on observed behaviour but also on the parent's subjective experience of the child as expressed during a clinical interview. Where there are difficulties in the relationship, the intensity, frequency, and duration of the disturbance are the factors that guide the clinician to classify the relationship problem as a perturbation, a disturbance, or a disorder. Within the DC: 0–3 system, Axis II is used only to diagnose significant relationship difficulties. Infants with a primary diagnosis (Axis I) need not have a relationship diagnosis (Axis II). The relationship axis does not address the full range of relationships, from well adapted to disordered. Some parents may have tendencies in the directions described in Axis II—toward, for example, overinvolvement or hostility. Milder forms of relationship disorders may be triggered by the child's temperament or behaviour, family dynamics, or other stresses that challenge parents' usual balance between nurturance and more problematic parental functioning. Clinicians are cautioned not to overdiagnose a relationship disorder when such milder and transient forms related to stress are observed. The clinician may want to keep the described categories in mind when they appear in milder or transient forms in order to understand the dynamics of the family and to guide intervention. Classifications include Overinvolved, Underinvolved, Anxious-Tense, Angry-Hostile, Mixed, or Abusive (Verbally Abusive, Physically Abusive, or Sexually Abusive Relationship).

The Parent-Infant Relationship Global Assessment Scale (PIR-GAS) is a rating scale used to determine the level of disturbance in a parentchild relationship on Axis II of the DC: 0–3. The PIR-GAS covers a range of parent-infant relationship quality over time and can be used to describe the strengths of a relationship as well as to capture the severity of a relational disorder. These ratings range from well-adapted (90) to grossly impaired (10). A rating below 40 includes disordered, severely disordered, and grossly impaired relationships. These qualify for a relationship diagnosis based on the severity and pervasiveness of the dyad's difficulties. At these levels, the majority of the behaviours must be in evidence in an intense, ongoing, and persistent manner. For ratings between 70 and 40, the relationship tendencies or features may be usefully described, but are not severe enough to be considered a disorder.

Three aspects of a relationship are used in deciding whether a relationship disorder is present: (1) the behavioural quality of the interaction, (2) the affective tone, and (3) the psychological involvement of the parent with the child. When a disorder exists, it is specific to a relationship. The categories of relationship disorders described in Axis II of DC: 0–3 are used only to diagnose significant relationship difficulties. The relationship axis does not address the full range of relationship quality, from well adapted to disordered. In other words, readers should be aware that an Axis II diagnostic classification is appropriate only when a clinician would rate the relationship being assessed as below 40 on the PIR-GAS.

The behavioural qualities and affective tone are required criteria for making a relational diagnosis, since these are observable and of sufficient concern to assess and treat. The quality of psychological involvement is presented to elaborate and guide the user to the possible dynamics related to childhood relatio the behaviours worthy of further exploration and treatment and is determined through an interview process with the parent, such as the ERA Video Replay Interview, the WMCI, or the AAI through identification of a parent's internal working model of relationships or "ghosts in the nursery".

Behavioural quality of the interaction is reflected in the behaviour of each member of the parent-infant dyad. The behaviour of the parent, the child, or both may be disturbed. Sensitivity or insensitivity in responding to the infant's cues, contingent or noncontingent responsivity, genuineness of involvement or concern, regulation, predictability, and the quality of structuring and mediating of the environment are parental behaviours that contribute to the quality of the interaction. Averting, avoiding, arching, lethargy, nonresponsiveness, and defiance are examples of behaviours that infants and toddlers may bring to the interaction. At times it is not clear whether the behaviours of concern are initiated or reactive. For instance, a mother or father may look depressed, uninvolved, or unresponsive with the young child. However, this may in part be a result of the unfocused gaze or other unresponsive, nonreinforcing behaviour of a medically ill infant. Disturbances in infants and young children may also appear as delays in development (language, motor, cognition, or social-emotional) and may constrict the child's interactive capacities. These delays may be both the result of and contribute to the relationship disturbance.

Affective tone refers to the emotional tone characteristic of this dyad. Intense anxious/ tense or negative affect (*e.g.*, irritable, angry, hostile) on the part of either member of the dyad or both may contribute to the characteristic affective tone of the dyad. The concern here is the dysregulating function of intense or flat affect and the uncertainty as to what may happen next that is conveyed when intense affect is present.

Psychological involvement is focused on parental attitudes and perceptions of the child (*i.e.*, the meaning of the child's behaviour to the parents). The parents' image of a caregiving relationship developed from past experiences in early childhood relationships often influences their perceptions of a particular child and what can be expected in a relationship. Disturbing or adverse past relationship experiences may result in a parent misinterpreting and projecting these feelings onto the infant; for example, the parent may misinterpret certain behaviours of the infant as demanding, negative, or attacking.

Integrating Culturally Sensitive Approaches

The integration of culturally sensitive approaches into the assessment of the parent-child relationship is critical to obtaining an accurate picture of the child in the context of his or her family, community, and larger sociocultural environment. The meaning of the child and his or her behaviour to the parents as well as the parents' response to the child will be coloured by the parents' cultural lenses. Most multicultural experts agree that culturally competent clinical assessments and interventions include examining one's own cultural beliefs and biases, acquiring knowledge about the family's culture, and developing culturally congruent clinical skills.

Conclusion

In conclusion, assessment of the parent-child relationship and, when indicated, diagnosis of a relationship disturbance or disorder is an important component, if not the centerpiece, of a clinical assessment of mental health in the infant or young child. Involving parents in the process of assessing their relationship with their child allows parents to become collaborative partners in the intervention process. Parents who take an active role in the assessment process and who feel their concerns have been heard and understood by the clinician are more likely to engage in the assessment and therapeutic process. By conducting interrelated assessments of each member of the parent-child dyad as well as the dyadic unit, the clinician obtains information that is essential to developing treatment goals and intervention strategies. Goals should be developed collaboratively with parents for the child and each parentchild relationship. When assessing the infant or young child in the context of the caregiving environment, it is critical that the process include the acquisition of information from others such as day care providers, pediatricians, parents' mental health providers, early intervention programmes, social services, alcohol and other drug addictions treatment providers, and the court system. It has been our experience that the most successful interventions involve coordination of services across settings with regular communication. Depending upon the needs of the particular dyad, focused intervention strategies may be incorporated into the therapeutic education process. Empathically listening to the parents' own struggles and reflecting their feelings and concerns enhances the therapeutic relationship between clinician and parent. Finally, assessing the quality of the parent-child relationship should be an ongoing process, because early childhood is a time of rapid change, and the needs of the parent-child dyad will change as the relationship evolves.

There is a need for universally accepted procedures for assessing relationship disorders across the life span, such as parent-infant, parenttoddler, and so on. Future research efforts should establish the validity and reliability of these methods in differentiating normative relational patterns from pathological relationship patterns as well as categorizing symptomatology and behavioural observations to define various syndromes of relationship disturbances. A universally accepted nosology will facilitate research in the etiology and developmental trajectory of the disorders as well as the effectiveness of various intervention approaches.

7

Generation of Thought in Children

Introduction

The abilities to remember the past, to impose a symbolic meaning on an object, and to be aware of what the self is doing appear in all children at remarkably similar ages. Is this concordance due to the fact that all children have similar experiences, or is it partly a consequence of the growth of specific parts of the central nervous system? Until recently most American psychologists have preferred to award most of the power to experience and have resisted the fixity implied by the elaboration of a genetic script. For example, the majority of psychologists have assumed that prior conditioning is the reason highly aroused adult rats bring their forepaws up to their whiskers. But if the forepaws of infant rat pups are surgically removed, the aroused adult animal moves the remaining stumps in ways that are consonant with the muscular actions that would lead a normal rat to rub its whiskers. Similarly, if a white crowned sparrow is raised from hatching to adulthood in complete isolation, without exposure to the singing of other birds, it will still sing a song. Although the song is not the same as the one that normally reared sparrows sing, it is a form of the normal adult song. These surprising facts suggest that the rats' whisker rubbing and the sparrows' singing originate in structures in the central nervous system whose appearance requires neither prior practice nor support from sensory input.

Many developmental psychologists believed that the child learns the language of her community by first imitating what she hears and then slowly perfecting a correct grammar and appropriate vocabulary through trial and error. This tedious argument has now been replaced by one that assumes each child is born with the potential competences to understand and to speak a language, each of which will be actualized when the brain reaches a certain level of maturity, as long as the child has been exposed to the speech of others.

Experience can either hasten or retard the time of emergence of the basic human competences: children living in extremely isolated areas of the world with minimal variety and cognitive challenges can be four, five, or even six years behind American children in the development of some of the basic strategies of thought. But these abilities will appear eventually in any environment containing people and objects, even if the people know little of what a child requires and there are no books, pencils, radios, television sets, or manufactured toys. The basic cognitive competences are best viewed as processes that are prepared to be actualized given proper experience, as a sparrow is prepared to learn the song of its species when it reaches a certain stage of growth at about ten days of age and is exposed to its song during the next forty days. Consider just a few fundamental members of the class of prepared competences.

The conviction that the world contains discrete objects that exist over time is an obvious candidate. The five-month-old becomes visibly upset if he continues to reach for what appears to him due to an arrangement of mirrors to be an object, but feels nothing. If the child did not expect to feel an object, he would not become surprised and subsequently distressed. By eighteen months, children will, after lifting a cloth and finding no object, search persistently for the toy they have watched being hidden under that cloth moments earlier for they know the object must be somewhere.

Second, by their fourth birthday, children appreciate that the appearance of an object may not reveal its true identity. They know that most of the time an object can be recognized at a distance by a few salient, frequently occurring qualities, but that, on occasion, a salient feature can be misleading. If a four-year-old sees a smoothly polished white stone that resembles an egg, he will say it is an egg.

But after being allowed to feel the object and bang it on a table, he will acknowledge that the object really is a stone.

The idea that a change in the position or the appearance of an object must have been produced by a preceding event is a third idea the mind is prepared to invent. Two-year-olds who see a broken cup or a distorted mask of a face will ask, "Who broke it?" or, "Who hit him?" They would pose these questions only if they believed that the distortion had been caused by a prior event. Children learn quickly which of the many events prior to an outcome is its likely cause. In one experiment, four-year-olds were shown a box containing two inclines. Each child saw a ball roll down one of the inclines and a light "roll" down the other; both the ball and the light traversed their inclines and passed out of sight simultaneously. A second or two later, a jack-in-the box popped up from a box to the right of both inclines, and the child was asked what made the jack-in-the-box appear. The children's answers indicated that they regarded the ball, and not the light, as the cause of the appearance of the jack-in-the-box.

Fourth, the child's mind finds it easy to treat one event as representative of another that is, to have a symbolic attitude toward events. A three-year-old assumes that a schematic outline of a house can stand for the real object, and that a vocal utterance can refer to a real event in the world. When a father who is feeding a child says, "Milk," the one-year-old assumes that the pattern of sound refers to the cup and/or its liquid contents and is not a random event having no relation to the real world. This talent may be especially elaborated in humans, for, despite great patience, David and Anne Premack had difficulty teaching a chimpanzee to treat a picture of an apple as equivalent to a real apple or to recognize an eye as part of a face.

A category is a fifth idea the child is prepared to create. The three-year-old is addicted to treating all objects that share dimensions as if they were related to each other. He will spontaneously pick out four small red blocks from a large array of objects with varied shapes and colours and, after placing them on a separate part of the carpet, will smile. Children will treat the larger of two square pieces of plain wood as representative of an adult and the smaller as representative of a child, simply because of the shared dimension of relative size. And, despite the fact that very few parents point out the similarity in form between a crescent moon and a thin sliver of lemon peel, a majority of children insist on calling the latter a moon. Children quickly learn to distinguish among the basic categories of physical objects (like people and balls) and among dynamic events (like running and eating) and, within physical objects, among animals, plants, and nonliving objects. Children also create categories for qualities, features, or dimensions of both objects and events. They appreciate that dirtiness is a likely quality of a blouse, size a quality of cars, and sweetness a quality of food. Five-year-old children know, therefore, that the qualities *heary, shiny,* and *upside-down* are used only to describe objects like chairs or cars, not events, and will tell an adult that "it's silly" to use those words to describe a party, a game, or a motor trip. The fact that the words for objects (usually nouns), events (usually verbs), and dimensions (usually adjectives and adverbs) appear in the child's speech in the second and third years is taken as evidence for their primacy in the child's conceptualization of experience.

As the child creates categories, she is disposed to invent their complement. Soon after learning the meaning of *up,* the child learns the meaning of *down;* after learning the meaning of *high,* she learns the meaning of *low;* after *good,* she develops the meaning of bad. The appreciation of opposites is comprehended too early and too easily to be the product of painstaking instruction.

Finally, the idea that a current state of affairs can be reversed in thought or action and a prior state reconstructed seems to be an intrinsic quality of human mental life. One four-year-old asked his mother if a person who dies can get another person's bones and become alive again. As we shall see, Piaget nominated this competence as the most essential in his theory of cognitive development.

Although intuition suggests that a three-year-old who has been locked in a dark, objectless room for three years would not display these competences after only a few months of recovery in a natural environment, it is important to note that monkeys raised under such deprived conditions from the opening months of life have, after their initial fearfulness subsided, shown many of the abilities displayed by normally reared monkeys.

The function of experience is to provide the conditions that actualize the universal competences and to supply information for new structures. Many cognitive processes, like the life functions, are inherent and not learned in any simple sense. By providing targets for the child to act upon, experience creates opportunities to form new structures, as the seed needs soil, water, and sunshine to initiate the photosynthetic events that will produce flowers.

The Paradox of Piaget: One would expect a theorist who believed that the development of cognitive processes follows a universal sequence to award the balance of power to maturation rather than to the child's active experience. But Piaget, who remains a central figure in cognitive development, argued for half a century that, because all children act in and on the world in similar ways, their experiences should produce a sequence of cognitive victories that are the same in all children.

It is helpful in understanding Piaget to appreciate, first, that he regarded himself as a philosopher, and not as a child psychologist, for he was concerned more with the grounds for holding a belief than with the belief itself. That is, children and adults regard many of their ideas as true, but they are usually not aware of why they treat a particular belief as correct. People base their beliefs on four different foundations: actual direct experience (a stone falls to the ground if thrown); a statement of authority (the earth is round and one of many planets); intuition, which combines experience, emotion, and the statements of authority to create premises (children are basically born good and become corrupted with experience); and logic (a statement cannot be both true and false simultaneously).

Piaget believed that a major change in cognitive development occurs after six or seven years when the child begins to use logic more often and intuition less often as the basis for beliefs about the physical world. Thus, both the eight-year-old and the five-yearold may intuitively sense that there is more water in a tall, thin cylinder than in a flat dish in which the water rested moments earlier. But the older child subdues the intuition with a recently acquired rule that states that the amount of water in a vessel must remain the same if the only change is in the shape of the container holding it.

Second, Piaget was a pragmatist. He believed that knowledge has a purpose, which is to aid adaptation to the puzzles encountered in the world. Thought is to serve action. Hence, Piaget concentrated on the cognitive processes activated when the child is solving problems, and he was relatively indifferent to perception, fantasy, and dreaming because these functions seem to have little to do with problem solving.

Third, Piaget assumed that the child is cognitively active and inventive, acquiring knowledge initially through manipulation of objects and later of ideas. The child is always trying to construct a more coherent understanding of events. Although people and objects provoke the child to do mental work, even in the absence of these external pressures the child is continually integrating what he knows and making sense of discrepant experience. As a result, children arrive at insights without the help of adult tutoring. The seven-year-old appreciates that a set of sticks of different lengths can be arranged in a series according to their length, even if he never has witnessed that particular arrangement or has been told about it by friend or parent. The realization that objects can be placed in a series in accord with their magnitude on a physical dimension is one of many private discoveries that accompanies intellectual growth.

The next two assumptions are related. Cognitive growth is supposed to be both gradual and connected. New structures grow slowly over a period of years, and the structural products of the earlier stages are contained in those of the latter. Thus, the fourteen-month-old's ability to open and close his hands in imitation of an adult performing the same act is part of a continuous growth sequence that begins with the grasp reflex of the newborn.

The central cognitive process in Piagetian theory is the operation, whose essential quality is reversibility. An operation, created from actions with objects, permits the child to reverse a state of affairs in action or thought. The ability mentally to divide six stones into subgroups of various sizes (3 and 3, 4 and 2, 5 and 1) and to recombine them into a single set of six is an operation. So is the ability to plan mentally a sequence of actions that takes one from home to school and then back to the beginning of the sequence.

Margaret Donaldson provides a nice example of the ability to reverse an action in mind. Suppose someone were careless enough to let an expensive Ming vase fall and shatter. What has happened is irreversible, for the vase will never be the same again. However, it is possible to reverse the series of events in one's mind, return to the moment before the vase fell, and to restore the vase to its prior state of integrity.

Unlike many investigators who are concerned with the accumulation of static knowledge contained in categories and rules, Piaget was concerned with *process* that is, with the acquisition of ways to transform knowledge. Caricature exaggerates but conveys the contrast. Many theorists have regarded cognitive growth as the acquisition and elaboration of schemata, words, concepts, and rules. These knowledge elements, added one by one to the repertoire, permit increasingly accurate and efficient mental work. By contrast, Piaget went to the other extreme, awarding centrality to processes and implying that use of these processes would generate the basic knowledge. If an evolutionist were Piagetian, he would talk primarily about the changes in breathing, eating, and reproduction, rather than the changes in the anatomical parts that participate in these functions.

The use of cognitive structures is monitored by two complementary processes Piaget calls *assimilation* and *accommodation*. The child who, in balancing the two, attains a successful solution to a problem is in a state of equilibrium. The process by which equilibrium is reached is called *equilibration*. The key tension in every problem is the initial preference for using knowledge and abilities that have worked in the past, pitted against the recognition that old habits are not adequate and must be altered. Imagine an experienced suffer on an unusually windy day who finds himself riding a wave whose force and speed are greater than any he has experienced. While retaining the posture he has always used, the suffer makes subtle and novel muscle adjustments in order to maintain his balance. When the balance between his usual posture and the new one permits him to ride out the wave successfully, our suffer is in a state of equilibrium. Piaget insists that equilibration is not merely descriptive, but an idea that is necessary to explain cognitive change, for inherent in the state is a change in structure.

Although Piaget's writings have had a major impact on our study of the child and put cognitive processes at the center of psychological inquiry, there are some critical vulnerabilities in the system. First, Piaget failed to provide strong principles to explain the transition from one stage of development to the next. The stages he called *sensory-motor, concrete operational,* and *formal operational* are essentially descriptive, akin to saying that tadpoles become frogs but unable to state the processes that permit the metamorphosis. The mechanisms of assimilation, accommodation, and equilibration are simply too general to explain why a seven-year- old, but not a five-year-old, realizes that changing the shape of a clay ball does not alter the quantity of clay.

Second, Piagetian ideas are not relevant to many important aspects of cognitive functioning. Language provides an example. Some two-year-old children use and understand terms such as *you, is, like,* and *why* words that have little relation to overt actions. But Piaget argued that action schemes form the basis of the knowledge possessed by the two-year-old who has just emerged from the sensory-motor stage of development, and thus implied that the intellectual growth of a normally endowed infant who cannot use his arms or legs will be slower than normal. However, the cognitive growth of children born without limbs or with paralyzed arms and legs is normal in most ways.

Third, many children possess some competences long before Piaget said they should. For example, Piaget suggested that preschool children cannot solve problems involving relative dimensions such as *larger* or *darker*. However, two-year-old children can think relationally about the relative dimension of size when it refers to a familiar comparison such as adults and children. In one study children between eighteen and twenty-three months were shown a small and a large piece of wood. The examiner said, "I have a baby and a daddy. Which one is the baby [or the daddy]?" Over half of the children correctly pointed to the smaller piece of wood for the baby and to the larger one for the daddy. The examiner then showed each child a new pair of wooden forms of different sizes. Now the smaller piece of wood was larger than the original large piece that had been assigned to the adult. Again, over half of the two-year-old children consistently treated the larger of the two pieces of wood, regardless of its absolute size, as the adult and the smaller of the two as the child.

Perhaps one of the most basic criticisms of Piaget's ideas is that he assumed that many of the principles of Western logic and mathematics are demanded by each person's everyday experience in the world. Such a claim demands a universal logic that is not always realized. In Western logic, the affirmative statement, "The sky is blue," is equivalent to a double negative, "It is not true that the sky is not blue." Yet, in a logical system used in one form of Indian philosophy, these two statements do not have the same meaning.

Piaget, like Immanuel Kant, believed that the combination of the structure of the human mind applied to experience will yield the basic operations. Scholars who favor this view often use the discovery of number as an example, noting that it is easy for the child to discover that when one adds one stone to a second stone there are two stones, and that the number is independent of the specific stones being combined and of whether one counts them from left to right or from right to left. But it is also common for a child to see one drop of water fall on a second drop and yield one drop rather than two. In this case the addition of objects does not yield an increase in their number. Now it is less obvious that the basic principles of arithmetic are given by experience. The logical principle of transitivity states that if A is greater than B on some dimension and B is greater than C, then A must be greater than C. But experience teaches that if school A beats school B in football and B beats C, it is still possible for C to beat A. Past experience is again a poor guide to a logical rule. Piaget claimed that the past experiences of all seven-year-olds should lead them to conclude that if a ball of clay is flattened, it should still have the same amount of clay. Yet, experience teaches that a little bit of material is always left on the examiner's hand when she changes its shape; and a few children insist, rightly, that the new piece of clay must have less substance because of these tiny losses. Thus, it is not obvious that the logic we learn to apply to information originates in and is totally dependent upon active encounters with the world.

Further, not all scholars have shared Piaget's premise that the function of knowledge is action. In John Locke's famous seventeenth-century essay, understanding and a sense of knowing are the primary purposes of knowledge. Correspondingly, Locke made perception and reasoning, rather than action, the mode by which knowledge is gained. Indeed, Piaget regarded as unreliable and immature the very knowledge that Locke viewed as most certain.

Finally, it remains a puzzle why Piaget minimized the role of maturation in early intellectual growth. Even though he acknowledged that the child is born with important sensory-motor actions and processes, making a purely environmental interpretation of intellectual development impossible, he wanted to award to biology as little fixed influence as possible. "Hereditary transmission," he wrote late in life, "seems to play only a limited role in the development of cognitive functions". A similar assumption is present in a debate the twenty-year-old Piaget had with a Polish taxonomist regarding the bases for variation among species of freshwater snail. In sharp disagreement with his older colleague, Piaget minimized mutation and maximized the influence of the environment by proposing that the structures of the snail are transformed gradually through their interaction with the environment. Such a theoretical position may rest on an idealistic premise regarding the way evolution ought to proceed, for the twenty-one-year-old Piaget wrote to Romain Rolland that morality was to be based on science. In this sense, Piaget shares with contemporary social scientists who hold an egalitarian ethos the desire to make encounter with the environment rather than biological events which are less controllable – the most influential sculptor of growth.

Selection of Terms

The selection of constructs is one of the most important tasks of any science. Major progress in physiology, for example, followed the realization in the early nineteenth century that the cell and not the organ was the more fundamental biological unit. What are the basic units in thought? What level of construct will be theoretically most useful to describe uniformities and variation in cognitive function? Is it best to use general constructs, like *intelligence*; moderately general ones, like *spatial ability*; or highly specific ones, like the *ability to remember faces?*

For a long time, most Western psychologists and philosophers have favoured positing a single term or a few terms to summarize a person's ability to process experience, recall knowledge, and solve problems accurately and quickly, regardless of the domain or the way a problem is posed. There are obvious differences between older and younger children, as well as among children of the same age, in depth of knowledge and in speed and quality of problem solution. These impressive differences, some of which are stable over time, lead Western theorists to prefer a single term to summarize a person's quality of cognitive functioning. The most popular English word for this characteristic is *intelligence*. This term may seem helpful in everyday conversation, for it seems to save us from listing all the processes and structures involved in a correct, efficient performance in a specific context; but *intelligence* is not theoretically useful for two reasons. First, rather than being defined by its constituent processes or the individual's history, the term is usually defined in terms of the final outcome of a host of independent processes. The error is clarified by an analogy from evolutionary biology.

Because the clam has survived for a longer time than the dinosaur, it might be regarded as biologically more fit, even though the latter has a more complex central nervous system. But the dinosaur vanished not because of any inherent flaw in its constitution, but rather because chance produced changes in ecology that the clam managed to escape. Thus, to claim that clams are more fit than dinosaurs only restates the fact of differential survival due to chance events; it does not explain much about the qualities of clams *qua* clams. Similarly, to state that differences among children in school test scores are due to different levels of intelligence does not explain the reasons for those differences.

A better reason to be skeptical about the utility of the idea of intelligence is that children and adults are not uniform in their quality of thought across different problems. There is so much specificity in cognitive functioning that it is a serious distortion to average a set of uneven performances on a variety of problems and to regard the average as theoretically useful. Several years ago, my colleagues and I studied a group of twelve-year-old boys who were reading at third-grade level, and a second group of boys of the same age who were reading at sixth- or seventh-grade level. The group who read well had slightly higher I.Q. scores than those who were reading so poorly. But when the reading-disabled group had to decide, as quickly as possible, whether a particular oral statement was true or false, many responded as quickly as the boys with good reading skills. If *intelligence* were a useful term, the better readers should have shown faster decision times than all the poor readers on most of the items.

Similarly, quality of memory for a series of unrelated photographs of objects is not related to the quality of memory for orally delivered sentences. It is not even possible to generate a principle for recognition memory that is valid for children growing up in two different cultural settings. An original black-and-white photograph of a realistic scene which had been inspected earlier was paired with a slight transformation that involved addition of an element to the scene, rearrangement of the elements, or a change in perspective. American children were much better at detecting the transformations that added an element to the scene or changed the perspective of the photograph, but they made many errors if the objects in the scene were rearranged. By contrast, Mayan Indian children living in isolated villages in northwest Guatemala were equally competent at detecting all three classes of change in the photographs and performed as well as the Americans on the scenes that either added an element or changed the perspective.

These illustrations many more are possible imply that the concept of general intelligence is not faithful to the extraordinary differences in quality of cognitive functioning among children or within any one child across a period of months. The usual reply to this argument is that factor analysis of the scores obtained in a variety of intellectual performances typically produces a first factor that involves linguistic knowledge. Because language is intimately involved in most of the problems presented to children in clinics, laboratories, or schools, scientists friendly to the notion of a unitary ability claim this fact as support for the theoretical utility of "general intelligence."

But suppose a visiting Martian who wants to learn the most important facts about the objects Americans use in their homes brings a ruler as his only measuring instrument. Our visitor measures every object he finds in a sample of one thousand homes, factor-analyzes the resulting data, finds that the first factor contains objects less than two hundred square inches in area and less than one thousand cubic inches in volume, and calls this factor "small objects." It included forks, books, oranges, bars of soap, shoes, watches, pencils, combs, ashtrays, cigarettes, and matches. These objects share no important common function not potential for harm, origin, fragility, or price, each of which is a theoretically important quality of objects. All they share is a common size, but a common size is of minimal utility in a theory of object use. The fact that language ability emerges as the first factor in an analysis of children's performances on popular intellectual tests says more about the typical selection of questions for the tests than it does about the basic nature of human talent.

It is useful to regard different classes of cognitive ability as having long developmental histories. Each emerges in a narrow context early in development; with growth, each is applied to an increasing number of contexts until it is reliably activated in most, but rarely all, relevant problem situations. The development of cognitive functions might be viewed as a series of growth functions, one for each competence, in which the proportion of relevant contexts in which a competence is activated grows with age.

The phrase "contexts in which a competence is activated" hides an important distinction that I have glossed over up to now the distinction between cognitive competence and public performance. Although these ideas seem reasonable, close analysis reveals a fuzziness to the concept of competence which deserves to be explored. One must distinguish first between the ability to use knowledge or a talent a person already possesses, and the ability to acquire a new skill or segment of knowledge. There may be no relation between these two meanings of competence. I call the former an *actual competence* and the latter a *potential competence*. A simple example of an actual competence is a person's ability to remember the name of a close friend. The competence in this case is specific "knowledge of the name of a person." This competence does not include the ability to recall the names of people in general and certainly is not as broad as the competence to remember all classes of verbal information.

Similarly, a three-year-old who cannot count six objects that is, say aloud, "one, two, three, four, five, six" nonetheless will indicate that an error has been committed if the examiner makes a puppet omit a number or reports the same number twice while counting the same six objects. A three year-old has the competence to recognize the number sequence one through six but apparently does not have the competence to execute it. Although some psychologists are likely to say that this child has the actual competence to count to six but simply did not display it, other scientists will use the failure in performance to infer an incomplete or absent competence. But it is not always clear which actual or potential competence is to blame for a performance failure. When a child or an adult fails a problem let us say that a child cannot recall a list of six unrelated words we do not know whether the poor performance is due to failure to use an actual competence (the child knows and registers the names but is not motivated to recall them) or to a flaw in the potential competence to register lists of unrelated words. The latter could be due to not knowing the meanings of some of the words, to not knowing how to rehearse them, to not being able to focus attention, or to a host of other cognitive deficits that could produce the same flawed performance.

But suppose, through careful experimentation, we are able to locate the exact nature of the fragile competence. How general a name should we give it? Let us assume that we determine that the inferior performance is due to an imperfection in the potential competence to focus attention on the words as they were being read. It is unlikely that this person would be unable to pay attention to all verbal information on all occasions, and just as unlikely that the impaired competence is limited to this particular set of words. Elimination of these two admittedly extreme alternatives leaves an enormous space in which to find the best description of the person's "lack of competence."

This hypothetical example contains the essence of the controversy surrounding the word *competence*. Some psychologists prefer to move toward enlarging the domain of the competence; others wish to narrow it. Because the data are ambiguous, it is a matter of taste which level is preferred. I favor a restricted conception because, as I noted earlier, nature is usually very particular. Mayan Indian eight-year-olds living in the northwest highlands of Guatemala have great difficulty remembering a series of words or pictures. Despite many trials and a patient tester, the children cannot recall more than three or four words when, after each series is mastered, an additional word is added to the series just memorized. American children of the same age can remember a series of twelve words under the same testing procedure. Thus Mayan children seem to lack the potential competence to register and retrieve verbal information across half a dozen different memory tasks. The consistency of this performance would tempt most psychologists to regard the competence failure as being broad in scope. Yet when these same children were required to learn to associate a series of different geometric designs with different meaningful words, they learned them quickly and efficiently. Apparently there was something about this particular task that was friendly to their abilities.

The importance of the context is revealed in studies of discrimination in animals. Most scientists study discrimination by placing the animal in an ecologically unnatural setting. The animal is restrained in a small cage sitting in front of two geometric forms. The experimenter baits one of the forms with food; and if the animal uncovers the correct object, it gets the food. Under these conditions, monkeys learn to discriminate the form that covers the food from the one that does not but they only do so after many, many trials, implying that the discrimination is difficult. But if the testing situation is altered to resemble more closely the natural setting in which the animals live, the discrimination can be learned in one trial. Groups of marmosets tested in a situation in which they were not constrained learned, in a single trial, to discriminate the object that contained the food from objects that did not.

Each structural unit in nature has a specific set of potential competences. The ovary secretes estrogen, not a variety of steroid hormones; finch have a potential competence to learn the song of their species, not the song of the cuckoo. Children do differ in their potential competence to acquire many specific skills and domains of knowledge. But given the meager evidence, it is probably wise at this stage of psychological understanding to conceive of that competence as applying to limited, rather than broad, domains, whether the competence is adding ed to a verb to indicate past tense or being able to add numbers.

A great deal of scientific advance turns out to be discovery of the limits of a process that had been overextended. Pasteur and Jenner found that specific forms of life spoil wine and produce human illness effects that had been attributed to broad forces. Rejection of transplanted organs by a host has been attributed, until recently, to properties inherent in the entire organ that is placed in the host. It now appears that the rejection of the organ is due specifically to white blood cells and not to the entire organ. It is likely that currently popular potential competences—like intelligence or even spatial, verbal, musical, and mathematical ability are much too broad, and that future research will reveal their proper, limited sphere of operation.

A serious, and as yet unresolved, problem that makes it difficult to infer an actual or a potential competence from a child's performance arises from the child's occasional misunderstanding of a problem posed by an adult. Most of the facts about cognitive development are based on the child's answers to problems posed by an examiner. Often the child interprets a question in a way that differs from the intention of the interrogator, and the answer that is correct from the child's subjective perspective is judged incorrect by the examiner. Consider the following example.

A four-year-old child is shown an array containing four toy garages and three toy cars. Each of the cars is in a garage, leaving one garage empty. The examiner asks the child, "Are all the cars in a garage?" The young child typically says, "No," and the examiner concludes that the child does not know the meaning of all. But if the examiner first asks a systematic series of questions about only three cars and then repeats the test question, the child will answer correctly. In the first instance, the child assumes that if there are four garages, there must be four cars. Why would someone build a garage if there is no car for it? The child infers that there is a missing car somewhere, and therefore it cannot be true that all the cars are in the garages. The child understands the meaning of *all* perfectly well but brings to the problem an assumption the examiner did not expect.

Each question indeed, every communication from one person to another contains hidden understandings between speaker and listener who share a common culture. Because children must learn the assumptions held by adults who ask questions, the improved cognitive performance with age is due, in part, to a change in a special competence namely, the child's learning the adult's hidden intentions. But unfortunately, psychologists often conclude, incorrectly, that the child does not possess the knowledge or ability to solve the problem posed.

It is useful, therefore, to distinguish between the publicly observed solution, on the one hand, and, on the other, an actual competence that may not be realized, or a potential competence to acquire the skill requisite for a problem. But how shall we describe the competences that change over development, if we reject broad terms like *intelligence or spatial ability?* Because mental processes are poorly understood, it is helpful to compare the mind to a more familiar object and thought to a better-known process. Before William Harvey's discoveries of the relation of the heart to the circulatory system, the heart was compared to a furnace, and breathing to the familiar relation between the bellows and the flames in a fireplace. Indeed, seventeenth-century naturalists believed that the primary reason for breathing was to prevent the heart from overheating. Modern psychology holds two different conceptions of thought: one takes the computer as the model; the other uses the most recent findings of neurochemistry and neurophysiology. Each conception provides some helpful insight; each is limiting.

The computer model currently assumes that symbolic propositions are among the most basic units of thought, because it is relatively easy to programme computers to accept and manipulate propositions. The scholar feeds the computer sets of sentences, together with rules for manipulating them and for judging the acceptability of new propositions. The computer is so talented with propositions that it can beat a chess master and hold a meaningful conversation with an adult. However, there are two serious limitations on its utility for modeling and eventually elucidating human cognitive processes: first, it does not make certain errors that most adults make; and second, it does not handle well nonsymbolic information that cannot be represented as a spatial image. The second flaw is serious, for all the infant's knowledge is nonsymbolic, and a great deal of adult knowledge is composed of remnants of scenes, melodies, tastes, smells, and feelings. It is not yet possible to programme a computer to recall the unpleasant feeling that leads a person to avoid offering an answer to a difficult question because of yesterday's humiliation.

The biological model originates in the small points of connection between neurons called synapses. Modern neurophysiologists tell us that all information that will be stored as knowledge must squeeze through many millions of the narrow, moist synaptic clefts lying between individual neurons. In this tiny world, it is difficult to think of entities as large as propositions being transferred from nerve cell to nerve cell. The synapse forces the theorist to think in terms of much smaller units, especially dimensions like the frequency of black/white gratings or the changes in sound energy and frequency that differentiate the end of the last word of a sentence from the first syllable of the next. Thus, psychologists must choose between a behemoth that gobbles up propositions and a minuscule hydra that digests tiny bits of energy. Since neither picture seems to fit one's everyday experience of hearing a voice and recognizing at once that it belongs to a friend, we lack an intuitively attractive model that might serve as a heuristic guide for a description of human thought. Further, unlike the earlier chapters on connectedness, morality, and emotions, for which sound evidence is sparse, the greater accumulation of facts on the growth of thought permits a richer commentary on the current state of scholarship. As an initial framework, I have decided to adopt the useful and popular division between structures and their functions and shall describe the varied cognitive processes as acting upon relevant units of knowledge, as the processes of mutation, reproductive isolation, and natural selection act upon generations of individual organisms to create new species.

The basic units of cognition are still undetermined. The present consensus is that they are schemata, images, concepts, and propositions. The analogy to varied classes of cells in biology and to electrons, protons, and neutrons in physics is obvious. An alternative strategy is to posit patterns of associations as the basic units, with schemata, images, concepts, and propositions linked to each other with different probabilities of association, depending upon the incentive event that elicited the pattern. The many shapes of a set of charged iron filings that are altered depending upon where an iron magnet is placed can be used as a metaphor. In this conception, the pattern is basic. The smaller units do not exist alone, but are always part of a larger pattern.

Meaning is defined by the pattern elicited by an incentive event. Thus, the meaning of the "smell of coffee" is contained in a pattern of schemata, categories, and propositions elicited by the fragrance. The sight of coffee elicits a different pattern, and reading the word coffee in a book elicits yet a third pattern. Each of the different signs of *coffee* has a different meaning because it generates a different pattern. This idea clarifies the definition of meaning, makes the basic cognitive units dynamic, emphasizes the links among schemata, concepts, and propositions, and, finally, distinguishes between objective and subjective meanings.

Because all the available evidence treats the smaller units as basic, I shall accommodate to that historical fact and treat them as primary in the discussion that follows. However, in evaluating the evidence, the reader should bear in mind that the meaning of a construct depends on the source of its evidence. For the distinction between what one believes and the bases for the belief is especially relevant to all of the scholarship on cognition. The majority of scientific studies on perception, memory, and reasoning in adults involve American college students. In America eighteen-year-olds are as representative of humans as laboratory-reared white rats are representative of vertebrates or mammals. Indeed, a major theoretical advance occurred when psychologists recognized that many of the principles based on studies of white rats did not apply to other animal species.

Of equal significance is the fact that investigations of cognition in children or college students typically involve relatively unique conditions that do not occur outside the laboratory. For example, in many investigations of verbal memory, the psychologist presents the subject with a set of unrelated words say twenty to thirty of equal familiarity, and usually finds that subjects more often remember the first and last words than words in the middle of the list. But rarely, if ever, does a person encounter a list of totally unrelated, but equally familiar ideas. Most of the time experiences and ideas are symbolically connected to each other, and some are always more familiar or emotionally more salient than others. Under these more natural conditions, the person typically remembers the more salient information, even if it is in the middle of a long but unitary episode. I recently asked a large group of mothers to listen to a four-hundred-word essay on the advantages and disadvantages of a restrictive or a permissive regimen in raising children.

The first sentence of the essay said that experts do not agree on the best way to train children; the last sentence said that parents should try to be relaxed and consistent. A minority of mothers remembered these ideas. But a sentence in the middle of the essay said that if parents do not punish disobedience, children may get into trouble as adolescents. Over three fourths of the mothers remembered that idea, presumably because it mattered emotionally to them.

Perhaps the most significant application of the warning to reflect upon the source of a presumed fact is found in studies that use, as the basis for inference, a child's verbal answers to questions. A child's verbal replies to questions engage a special domain of cognition. Even though a five-year-old cannot tell an examiner the meaning of the "equality of two numbers," the same child is able to match five buttons in one row with an equal number of buttons in another row, suggesting that, at one level, she knows the meaning of equality. This is not a trivial issue or a semantic quibble. An observer who watched me drive my car to work would infer correctly that I behave as if I believe the earth is flat. But an observer who asked me why the hours of daylight decrease in autumn would infer correctly from my verbal reply that I believe the earth is round. The two inferences are not inconsistent. Thus, as I survey what is known about the development of human thought, the reader should take into account the exact conditions that generated the scientific knowledge.

Cognitive Processes

Perception and Schemata

A child looks out the window and sees variations in shapes of trees, colours of houses, heights of people, and speeds of cars and from this mosaic extracts information in the form of schemata. The child's ability, after turning away from the scene, to know what was and was not outside is mediated by his schemata for the scene.

The schema is the infant's first cognitive unit and contributes to cognitive units that develop later. The schema is an abstract representation of the distinctive features or dimensions of an event. Like a cartoonist's caricature, it preserves in a unique pattern the defining and distinguishing aspects of the event.

Schemata exist in all modalities auditory, olfactory, tactile, taste, and visual. The ability to recognize a melody, the fragrance of a rose, the feel of velvet, or the taste of an apple is possible because one has created a schema for each of these experiences. In all these examples, however, the schema represents the pattern of physical qualities in the original event; the schema is not a symbolic or linguistic representation. Further, the schema is to be contrasted with an image, which is a consciously elaborated representation created from the schema. Because conscious mental effort is required to generate an image from the more abstract schemata, the young infant probably has no images, only schemata. Although subjective experience provides commanding support for the existence of images, laboratory data, too, require the invention of this idea. If a person, asked to decide whether "a cat has claws," tries to evoke a mental image of the cat, it will take longer to make the decision than if the person were deciding according to conceptual knowledge.

The fact that schemata are constructed from events does not validate Locke's suggestion that all knowledge originates in sense experience. For the mind invents schemata that have never been witnessed, like the place where the sun goes in the evening. Although many cognitive inventions wind their way back to some event, implying that the schematic representation is an elemental unit, the mind also contains structures like infinity, quark, and spirit that have minimal reference to experienced events.

A major controversy surrounding the schema is whether the mind creates an idealized "average" from all prior exposures to a particular class of events called a schematic prototype; or whether the mind holds in separate schemata all the exemplars ever experienced, even while it extracts features common to all. The former process is more likely for several reasons. First, a three-year-old who has seen fish, but never a picture of one, will correctly name a schematic illustration, even though the child has never before encountered the few lines that suggest a fish.

More convincing support for the existence of a prototype is found in a five-year-old's ability to know the style in which he draws. In one study, five-year-old children were asked to draw four objects on separate pieces of paper a man, a flower, a tree, and a bird. An artist then examined the four drawings made by each child, attending to four stylistic qualities that children consistently apply across their drawings: the amount of space the child covers on the paper, the pressure of the penciled strokes, the use of straight or curved lines, and the amount of detail. The artist then drew two objects that the child had not drawn before a dog and a house—but each drawing was in that particular child's style. Each child was then shown four drawings, three in the drawing style of other children and one in the child's own style. A significant proportion of these five-year-olds were able to select the drawing that was done in their style. Because it is unlikely that these children had ever drawn the particular dog or house that they identified as their own, it appears that they had unself-consciously abstracted from all of their prior artistic products a prototypic schema that represented their unique style.

Creation of the Schema: The features of a schema are determined, in part, by their physical salience, by the probability of their being a part of a particular event, and always by their uniqueness relative to related events. For example, children and adults from different cultures, even those that have no word for the colour red, remember best the crimson typically printed on Christmas cards and regard that shade as the best representation of the category red. Eyes, mouth, and nose are always part of a person, while a hat and a jacket occur far less often: thus, the former qualities will be more definitive components of the schema for a human being than will the latter. But eyes, nose, and mouth, despite equal frequency of occurrence, are not of equal significance. The eyes are more essential for an infant's schema of a person in part, because of the physical contrast of the darker iris against the white sclera (note that in trying to disguise a person's face, newspapers block out the eyes and not the mouth).

Each prototypic schema shares some qualities with selected other schemata. The qualities that most effectively differentiate two schemata that share many features will be salient. Birds have both eyes and beaks, but the beak is the more distinctive feature because it differentiates birds from other animals that have eyes, not because the beak is physically more salient than the eyes. The mind simultaneously assesses (1) the frequency of correlated features, (2) their physical salience, and (3) their relative uniqueness with respect to "related" qualities in other events. The features that meet all three criteria are likely to be most distinctive for the prototype. Thus, the perceptual quality of "hardness" is distinctive for stones because there are so many objects in the world that are soft. If all objects were of equal hardness this quality would not be perceived and would not be included in the schematic representation for stones. Hardness is not an inherent characteristic of stones; it derives its distinctiveness because the mind implicitly compares the feel of the surface of stones to the feel of other surfaces.

The salience of the features of an event also varies with the person's intention, especially whether the purpose is to identify an event or to discriminate it from another. We use size to differentiate a blueberry from a huckleberry, but colour and shape to identify the fruit. A boy in a forest trying to determine whether a moving object is a bear or a man searches for a critical feature, like clothing or fur. But the same boy on a dark street in a large city hearing footsteps behind him would want to know if the source of the sound was a man, a woman, or a child it is unlikely to be a bear. Now the presence of clothes would not be critical in identifying the figure, and the child would probably search for characteristics in the footsteps. More benignly, if a child wonders whether a stranger is going to hug or kiss her, she will attend to the position of the stranger's hands and arms. If she wonders whether the stranger likes her, she will attend to his face and voice. Thus, identification of an event and discrimination of one event from another often rely on different qualities. What is it? and Is it X or Y? are questions requiring different evidence for their answers.

These two queries are also applied to private experience. If I feel a rapid beating of my heart, I ask, "Am I afraid?" and use the increased cardiac rate as the distinctive feature to identify my state. However, if I ask, "Am I afraid or angry?" the increased heart rate is insufficient, and I must consult other qualities. The increase in heart rate is a distinctive identifying feature of the schema for fear, but not informative if I must decide whether my state is fear or anger. Less frequently we address a conjunctive question to experience. If, upon seeing an object lying on the ground, I ask, "Is it a dead bird?" I look for features that define both birdness and loss of life. Finally, people occasionally wonder about other qualities, like the consequences of an event. They ask of an object, "Is it about to move away or to attack?" The signs of the future action require attention to yet another set of features. Thus, each private question identity, disjunction, conjunction, and "if then" often require attention to different features of an event. The schematic prototypes hold in potential readiness a variety of features that may be consulted for specific questions.

The specific problem a child is trying to solve creates a mental set that determines the features selected for attention. A nice example of the role of mental set on perception involves a procedure, often used by neurologists, called the *face-hands test*. The child, whose eyes are closed, is touched simultaneously on one check and on the opposite hand and asked to indicate where he has been touched. Typically, children under six years of age report that they were touched on the face, but fail to acknowledge that their hand was also stimulated. Some neurologists believe that the failure to report the latter touch indicates an immaturity of the central nervous system. But the younger child's failure to mention the hand is due simply to a mental set that leads her to expect that she will be touched only in one place. If before the test question the examiner says, "Sometimes I'm going to touch you only on the check, sometimes I'm going to touch you only on the hand, and sometimes I'm going to try to fool you and touch you in two places," the young child reports accurately being touched on both hand and cheek. Simply preparing the young child for the possibility of two loci of stimulation changes the pattern of performance completely.

Permanence of Schemata: Do schemata vanish? This question is part of a larger issue regarding the materialistic bases of schemata and the permanence of knowledge. Even though biologists tell us that, after fulfilling their function, some material features in the developing embryo disappear, and that proteins are continually being replaced, psychologists have been reluctant to acknowledge that schemata might disappear. They have wanted to believe that any knowledge, once registered in the brain, is stored permanently, even if it cannot be recalled or recognized and despite the recent discovery that synapses, which are likely to be the structural lattice providing form to particular experience, are continually being eliminated or replaced.

In one investigation, two-and-a-half-year-olds were shown a series of slides, some of which illustrated unusual scenes (a woman with no head, a man with four arms). When these children were ten years old, they were shown some pairs of pictures, one of which was the scene they had seen seven and one-half years earlier, the other a new one; and they were asked to guess which picture they might have seen when younger. No child did better than chance. Although some psychologists might contend that the original schemata were present but not activated in this situation (a reasonable reply), these results imply that the original schemata might have vanished because they were not renewed.

The attractiveness of assuming the permanent stability of schemata may rest on presuppositions and contained in Plato's argument for hidden, indestructible structures that form the foundation of experience and permit individuals to know the good and to act upon it. Knowledge is an ethical good in the West, the foundation of morality and of scientific advance. It may be uncomfortable to acknowledge that such sacredness might quietly disappear simply with the passage of time.

Inference and Categories

As the child enters the second year, *inference*, the amplifier of knowledge, takes information extracted from experience and "blows it up" into concepts and principles, permitting children and adults to categorize the present, anticipate the future, and interpret the past. In inference, the mind makes a leap, and, by classifying an event as belonging to a category or a related sequence of events, adds information to the original experience. A three-year-old asks his mother, "Where does the sun go when it goes into the ground at night?" The child's experience has taught him that all objects that move have a resting place, permanent or temporary. Because the sun appears to be an object that moves, the child infers that it, too, must have a place to rest. Categories and propositions are two units often involved in inference; I shall consider categories first.

Categories: Children's representations of events do not contain every detail of an original experience. Hence, a serious theoretical problem arises when the second encounter with an event is a discriminated transformation of the original. What does the mind do with the related, but different, experience? It might create a representation of the second event which has the same status as the first, even though the mind detects a relation between the two. This suggestion may seem counterintuitive, but adults can recognize correctly many unfamiliar faces, scenes, or words seen only once. Despite a high degree of similarity among events, the mind is able to keep representations sufficiently separate to permit remarkably accurate recognition.

A second possibility is that the mind creates an additional representation that combines parts of the multiple experiences in an emergent cognitive structure reflecting the features shared across similar events. This product, which many psychologists and philosophers call a *concept* or a *category*, is a representation both of the features and of the relations among the features that are common to a set of discriminably different events. My colleague, prefers the term *idea*.

The spontaneous sorting behaviour of two-year-olds requires us to attribute to the young child the ability to represent qualities common to a set of different objects. When a child playing with twenty physically different toys confidently removes an oblong yellow banana and a spherical cluster of purple grapes, we have to explain why those two objects were selected from the larger array of equally attractive toys. One reasonable hypothesis is that the child knows that the two objects share the qualities that define the category "edible things." Because the meaning of a construct often depends upon the procedures that generated the motivating data, it is reassuring that a second procedure also provides information indicating that the child stores representations of common qualities. For the child will show an increase in attention, more vigorous sucking of a nipple, or a decrease in heart rate to an example from a category that is different from the one that has been experienced over the last few minutes.

The classes of shared features that constitute a category include:

1. Perceptually available qualities like form, hue, pattern, movement, pitch, loudness, and taste. It is likely that perceptually based features dominate the categories of young infants.
2. Functional qualities that include the potential actions of objects, the actions imposed on them by others, and their potential uses by people or animals. The essential quality of chairs is that "people can sit on them."

3. Mental states evoked by events. The features of a concept need not be public but can refer to internal feeling states or ideas. The exemplars that belong to the concept hobby or game do not share any external qualities. But even though stamp collecting and tennis have no obvious common characteristic to which one can "point," they do share a private attitude toward the activity.
4. Names shared by events. The fact that flies and roses are called "alive," and Zeus and Athena are called "gods," can be a sufficient basis for a child to treat both pairs as members of separate categories, even if the child does not know the biological qualities of life or the functions of gods.
5. Relations between schemata, words, or ideas such as complementarity, opposition, inclusiveness, and relative magnitude or spatial location can be the basis for categories that are typically part of similes and metaphors. A four-year-old who told her mother that cough medicine and cookies were like night and day was using the quality of opposites to group day and a sweet taste, on the one hand, and night and a sour taste, on the other.

Categories and Language: Although many concepts have an accompanying word to name some, but never all, of the shared features, and a few concepts are based only on a common name, a concept need not have a word attached to it. One-year-olds possess the concept *household furniture*, even though it is highly unlikely that infants so young know any word that captures this idea. And adults possess concepts for the silence of a forest, the tension of a city, or the special feeling of fatigue that follows an hour of strenuous exercise, each category being based on the qualities shared across similar experiences. Eve Clark notes wisely that words evoke concepts, they do not represent them. Karl Gauss said of complex numbers, "The true sense of the square root of minus one is always pressingly present in my mind but it would be difficult to grasp it in words."

Many concepts that are nonlinguistic symbols need not have words attached to them. The child of six or seven years treats dark colours as sharing a quality of unpleasantness and light colours as sharing a quality of pleasant feeling tone. Similarly, six-year-olds group together graphic illustrations that are relatively straight and unchanging:

They regard the former as more symbolic of unpleasant feelings and the latter as symbolic of pleasant emotions. Yet few six-year-olds possess a single linguistic term that effectively summarizes these symbolic categories.

Thus, some kinds of meaning do not reside only in language but are present whenever there is a relation between two psychological units, be they schemata, feeling states, categories, or words. If an infant who is frightened by a large hairy dog develops a conditioned fear reaction to all large animals with four legs, the schematic representation of this class of events has meaning for the child, even though that meaning is not linguistic in form.

The exact relation between a representation of a category and a linguistic term that attempts to capture the category remains a puzzle. As I indicated earlier, there are good reasons for doubting a faithful relation between a word or a phrase and the schematic representation it attempts to summarize. Most psychologists now acknowledge that the young child usually has a schematic category for a class of events before he learns to name it with terms like *ball*, *milk*, or *go*. But it is also likely that the child can learn a new word for a specific event and subsequently create a category. The eighteen-month-olds who learned in one trial to call a novel Styrofoam form a "zoob." When one child returned to the laboratory a month later, she asked the examiner where the "zoob" was and applied that novel word to another unfamiliar object. But it is easier for the child to learn a new word if he or she already has some representation of the relevant idea—in this case, the notion that a certain class of events has names. Two-year-olds who know one or two colour terms, and thus appreciate that colour is a namable category, more easily learn a totally new colour term than do children who know no colour words at all. An adult, unfamiliar with physics, learns a new category when the meaning of "black holes" is explained. But words have three properties that most schemata lack. First, words for categories can be nested hierarchically. The concepts *kitten*, *mammal*, *animal*, and *living thing* form such a hierarchy and permit manipulations that involve a logic unavailable to schematic categories. Second, words participate in communication and, within a language community, gain a consensual meaning that is denied to schemata which are not amenable to communication. Finally, a linguistic category may elicit more predictable associations with other linguistic terms than do nonlinguistic categories.

Dan Slobin suggests a "waiting room" as a fruitful metaphor for the idea that a schema or category is acquired first, and then waits until the child can figure out what features of this new knowledge are expressible in his or her language and how they are expressed. When that detective work is completed, the idea leaves the waiting room to join the conversing public outside. But the room is always full of impatient ideas eagerly seeking passage on a linguistic vehicle.

A second basis for a skeptical attitude toward a close relation between thought and language is apparent in English, where the preferred word order in a sentence is subject, verb, object, regardless of the salient element in the idea that is to be expressed. If a large boulder fell on a small, sleeping dog or a small pebble hit a raging dog, the description in an English sentence would be the same, "The stone hit the dog," even though the boulder is the more salient element in the first event and the dog more salient in the second. There are some languages, Turkish for example, where the speaker can change the word order so that the salient element appears early, or even first, in the sentence.

Some scientists believe that linguistic categories can affect the adult's ability to reason. For example, the Chinese language does not have an easy way to express the idea of the negation of a hypothetical event—what logicians call the *contrary-to-fact*, or *counterfactual conditional*. In Chinese, it is difficult to express such a sentence as, "If John had not arrived on time, he would never have met Mary." And Chinese students have much more difficulty than Americans in drawing conclusions from texts that contain such propositions. Similarly, the Chinese language has no easy way to make an abstract noun of an adjective or a verb, while English permits easy construction and understanding of sentences like, "Whiteness is a lovely quality," or, "Racing through life is harmful to health." Chinese adults claim such ideas are "unChinese," affirming the stereotyped supposition held by some commentators that the Chinese are not attracted to the hypothetical and the abstract.

But do speakers of English find it easy to think counterfactually or in the abstract because English contains syntactic strategies for creating new abstract nouns and counterfactuals? Or, is it that all humans are capable of dealing with both, but the language of a community either enhances or suppresses these talents. I suspect that the latter is true, and that all children probably are able to deal with many hypothetical and abstract issues, albeit in limited ways. Children from many different cultures will adopt, early in life, a pretend set and answer questions like, "Suppose you were a bear, what would you do?" or, "What would happen if all the water in the ocean dried up?" The ease with which adolescents answer these questions implies that they are able to assume a hypothetical set, although the local language can interfere with the ability to display that talent.

Why Create Categories? Two additional puzzling aspects of categories continue to provoke debate. Why do infants and children have an addictive tendency to create categories? What features are salient for particular classes of events? The first question does not permit an easy answer in the way that "Why do infants breathe?" provokes the reply, "To supply the body with oxygen." First, we do not know whether the creation of categories is exaggerated in humans or is as common in animals as it is in young children, for pigeons seem to possess a remarkable categorization ability.

Young children are prepared to detect physical and functional qualities shared by events, but it is not obvious why the child sorts objects into a group after noting their similarities. Even if we posit an innate tendency to recognize similarity among events, it is not clear why the child acts after that private cognitive process. In most cases, the child is not trying to communicate any information to another person. The categorization expends energy yet has no obvious instrumental value, gains no external prize, and is accompanied by no obvious sensory pleasure. Eighteenth-century observers thought that it represents surplus energy that is not needed for survival. The most popular view a century later was that such forms of play are practice for the future and necessary for adaptation. G. Stanley Hall suggested that such behaviour is a harmless sublimation of phylogenetically simpler instincts. But all of these explanations of "playful behaviour" rest on the premise that a self-initiated action that expends energy and involves thought must have some purpose in the future and an immediate cause in the child's energy economy.

Although it is possible that the detection of similarities is accompanied by the generation of a special state of excitement, which, in turn, provokes the child to do something appropriate, this assumption is attractive only because it satisfies the desire to postulate some cause for the behaviour. It is just as reasonable to assume that the act of grouping similar objects occurs just because it can be performed, not unlike a well-fed sea gull swooping down over a sandy spit just because the spit is there and gulls are capable of swooping.

The Weighting of Features: The different salience of the qualities defining a category remains an unsolved issue. There are heuristic, but few empirically grounded, principles to guide inquiry. Infants seem to regard similarity in relative motion, size, shape, and spatial pattern as sources of similarity in the visual mode; loudness, continuity, and frequency, in the auditory mode; pleasure and pain as sources of similarity for private feelings. These qualities guarantee that all children will draw a small set of universal inferences. But with development, the conditions that are local to a particular environment persuade older children to award salience to qualities that are ignored by children growing up in other communities.

One way to determine the differential salience of events is to see if the varied languages of the world typically attend to certain qualities while ignoring others. Although some languages indicate whether an object is singular or plural, close or far away from the agent, or capable of activity simply by adding a linguistic feature, called an inflection, to the relevant term (like a plural *s*), it is rare for languages to add an inflection that signifies an object's colour or usefulness. Similarly, it is common for languages to add inflections to verbs that designate whether the action is in the present or the past, whether one or many agents are acting, or whether the action is causal. But inflections that indicate the time of day or the emotional salience of an action are rare. These interesting facts suggest that the colour or usefulness of objects is not as salient as their location or capacity for movement, and that the number of people acting is more salient than the time of day in which the action occurs.

However, each culture also emphasizes unique qualities, and with development, the conditions that are local to a particular environment persuade older children to award salience to qualities that are ignored by children growing up in other communities. For example, children growing up in subsistence farming villages, with domesticated animals in the village and predators outside, treat the quality of being "domesticated" as a more important feature of similarity among animals than do children growing up in urban environments in the same country; the latter treat dogs, cows, foxes, and wolves as more similar than do rural youngsters.

The features of a category that are shared most often will become salient. But even among the features that always occur together, one is typically more salient than the others. The category *animal*, for example, usually includes face, limbs, and body; but two-year-olds behave as if the limbs and face possess greater salience than the body.

Thus, a concept is not a static element of knowledge but a dynamic and constantly changing one. The mind is continually working on its knowledge and detecting features shared by two events or ideas that were originally separate and unrelated. One source of support for this active view of mind comes from errors in the child's use of a word following a time when the child used the very same word correctly. One way to explain the errors is to assume that the child suddenly detects a quality shared by words that he formerly regarded as unrelated. One psychologist kept a diary of the speech of her two daughters. At two years of age, one of the girls correctly used the words *put* and *give* in her sentences. She would say, "Christy will put on her hat," or "Daddy gave my ladybug to me"; but a year later, she began to make occasional errors in which *put* was used when *give* was proper, and vice versa. She said, "You put me bread and butter," instead of, "You give me bread and butter"; and, "Give some ice in here," instead of, "Put some ice in here." One way to interpret these mistakes is to assume that, after first learning the meanings of *put* and *give*, the child realized that both involved the actions of an agent with an inanimate object. Once that shared quality was recognized, the two words became semantically closer in meaning, and thus the substitution errors occurred. Because it is unlikely that the child was taught the shared quality, it is reasonable to guess that the detection occurred unconsciously. The mind is continually working on its knowledge.

Even common linguistic concepts like *animal* change in definition, in degree of consensus, in availability for thought, and in accessibility to verbal report as the child develops. For first-grade children, the word *animal* refers primarily to mammals; for tenyear-olds, birds and insects have become part of the category.

Uniqueness also influences the salience of a quality. The features common to one set of events, but absent in a related class, are candidates for salience. Pointed ears, for example, are more salient than eyes for the category *dog* because humans do not have the former, while both humans and dogs possess the latter. Even though the majority of species of bees are solitary, not social, most texts categorize bees as social animals because the cooperation in a hive is unique in the animal world. Qualities that differentiate classes of events that share many properties often become salient-a principle in accord with E. Rosch's work on prototypes and A. Tversky's work on similarity. The mind has two simultaneous missions: to detect the qualities shared by events, while simultaneously differentiating similar events into classes that differ on a small number of qualities. Indeed, some psycholinguists believe that the acquisition of new words is best understood as an attempt to name correctly a contrast the child has detected and cannot ignore. For example, the child who has been calling all animals *dogs* feels pressed to learn and to use the word *horse* when he realizes that horses contrast with dogs with respect to size, shape, and typical location.

Propositions: When two or more linguistic concepts are related, the unit we call a *proposition* is constructed. The proposition "Autumn is nostalgic" specifies the existence of a relation between two linguistic categories. Propositions can define a category ("An opera is a musical play"), state a function or a relation between categories ("The temperature rises in the summer"), name a feature of a category ("Dogs have legs"), or state a procedural rule that is applied to categories ("The speed of a car is found by dividing the distance covered by the time").

A child faced with a problem, especially in an academic setting, typically generates solution hypotheses in the form of propositions. Two major developmental changes relevant to such propositions are: first, that children become able to perform complex cognitive manipulations on propositions; and, second, they become able to coordinate two or more propositions when solving a problem.

The ability to coordinate two or more ideas is an example of a basic principle that explains the mastery of related linguistic categories during the first half-dozen years of life. The intuitively reasonable principle states that, among a set of related linguistic categories, those that have more dimensions will be mastered later than those that have fewer. For example, three-year-olds appreciate the meaning of on before they master the meaning of *under*. Why is this so? The two ideas both involve only the relation of one object to another. On refers to the relation of one object to the surface of another, but when a shoe is *under* a table, it is also on a rug. Thus, to understand *under*, the child must deal with two ideas, eliminating one and favoring the other. Similarly, children learn the meaning of *big* before *tall* because the former refers to size in any dimension, be it height, width, depth, or volume; while *tall* specifies a particular dimension namely, height. Thus, the child must suppress information from the other spatial dimensions. Finally, children learning English generally learn to add an "s" to indicate more than one object before they correctly use forms of the verb "to be". In the case of plurals, all the child has to master is the distinction between one and many objects. But in order to know whether "am" "are," "s," "was," or "were" is the correct form the child must know at least three other factors-the number of people, the time when the action occurred, and whether the agent is the self or someone else. Cognitive difficulty varies with the number of schemata, categories, or dimensions the mind must detect, accommodate to, or coordinate. This ability seems to grow most rapidly during the years prior to puberty and, judging by the folk belief that mathematicians are most creative during their twenties and thirties, may begin to decline slowly after the third decade.

Children and adults are vulnerable to two habits that obstruct the generation of effective propositional solutions. The first is a resistance to retiring hypotheses that have been effective in the past. The three-year-old who believes that all metal objects sink in water may resist renouncing that belief in favor of the more exact rule that the density of an object relative to water will determine whether that object sinks or floats. When the situation involves personal problems with a strong emotional component, the resistance to casting aside premises about people or self that prevent an insightful solution is more common. Many young children believe that all violations should be punished, regardless of the circumstances. Hence, a five-year-old who violates a standard (steals money or tells a lie), and is undiscovered, is likely to feel uncertainty. The child has a problem because he has broken a rule and has not been punished. Hence, the rule seems invalid. But the child does not want to discard the rule and so may commit another, more obvious misdemeanour which does attract the parents' attention and, as a result, provokes punishment. This sequence allows the child to retain his original rule. Some of the most painful moments during adolescence occur when beliefs held for years regarding the wisdom of parents, the loyalty of friends, or the trustfulness of teachers are invalidated. The adolescent, with considerable regret, is forced to question a proposition that has been a loyal guide to action for a long time.

A second obstacle to the generation of good solutions is failure to detect the less salient qualities of familiar events. Children were given the following problem: A man is in a log cabin whose windows have no glass on a cold windy night. The only materials in the cabin are some glass bottles, a pot, and a pile of old newspapers. What might the person do to protect himself against the cold?

The key to the solution is to detect the relation between the most essential quality of a window that is, an extension across an open space and one of the noncritical qualities of a newspaper-namely, that it can be used to cover open spaces. Although all children may know that newspapers have that atypical characteristic, most children are unlikely to retrieve this knowledge and to use it in this context. This homely example contains a key characteristic in the generation of fruitful hypotheses. Most of the day, children and adults solve problems that are routine; the problem situation calls for ideas that are normally used in that situation. The door is stuck, so one pulls harder. The room is cold: one turns up the heat. In these an numerous other situations, one activates old rules that have work in the past and so are readily available. There is minimal thou and the reaction is almost automatic.

But in problems where the solution is not immediately obvious and thought is required, the ideas generated are typically the most reasonable or the ones that come to mind quickly. For example, if a finger is cut, and there is no Band-Aid available, one looks for a small piece of cloth and Scotch tape. The ability "to protect and absorb" is a dominant quality of both cloth and Band-Aids, and adhesion to skin is a salient quality of both Scotch tape and the adhesive normally on the Band-Aid.

Many problems require the generation of qualities that are not very representative of the event central to the solution. Children are much less likely than adults to search for these uncharacteristic features. In one study, children of different ages were shown a tall cylinder holding a few centimeters of water with a small bead floating on the surface. They were then shown a tray containing scissors, string, gum, tongs, a block, and a glass of water, and were asked to figure out how to get the bead out of the cylinder without turning the cylinder upside-down. The string and the tongs were purposely made too short to reach the bead because most children would automatically think of solving the problem that way. The problem was rigged so that the only way to solve it was to fill the cylinder with the water in the glass so that the bead would float to the top. Although all children must have seen objects float to the top of containers with liquid many times in their past experience, very few first-grade children generated that solution in this particular situation because more reasonable ideas were available, like using the string and gum or the tongs. They did not think of using the glass of water to fill the container because a glass of water is normally used for drinking. The idea of rising water levels is more characteristic of faucets on sinks or of rising rivers. The few children who regularly generate uncharacteristic qualities of events that lead to original and instructive solutions to problems are typically called *creative*.

While most intelligent children are not necessarily creative, most creative children are intelligent. But their creativity is based on three other characteristics: they have a mental set to search for the unusual; they take delight in generating novel ideas; and they are not unduly apprehensive about making mistakes. A major hallmark of the creative person is some indifference to the humiliation that can follow a mistake. This attitude gives the child freedom to attempt mental experiments that may fail and to consider high-risk solutions without worrying too much about their potential failure.

Scientists have tried to determine the personal characteristics of creative adults. One investigator asked experts in architecture to nominate the most creative architects in the country. Forty of these creative architects were compared with others who were judged very successful but not exceptionally creative. The three most important differences between the two groups were that the creative architects placed a premium on imagination and originality, enjoyed being alone and doing solitary work, and were less concerned with what others thought of their work. Creative people search for original solutions, however unpopular or unconventional.

A child's birth order is associated with his or her receptivity to original ideas. Frank Sulloway, a historian, has found that, among eminent scientists, later-born men are likely to be ideologically rebellious, while first-born men are a little more reluctant to disagree with the dominant theoretical position. The development of evolutionary theory required a willingness to oppose the strong and pervading nineteenth-century belief in the biblical story of creation. Both Darwin and his fellow discoverer of evolution, Alfred Russell Wallace, were later-borns; and only thirty-five of the ninety-eight scientists who publicly opposed Darwin or the earlier pre-Darwinian evolutionists, from 1750 to 1870, were later-borns. By contrast, only two of thirty pre-Darwinian scholars favouring evolution were first-borns. Sulloway has also examined the different revolutionary ideas promoted by Copernicus, Bacon, and Freud. Of twenty major opponents to one of these three ideas, 80 per cent were either first-borns or eldest sons; 20 per cent were later-born. Of the forty-three early proponents of one of the ideas, 84 per cent were younger sons, and only 16 per cent first-borns or eldest sons. Even though first-borns attain higher I.Q. scores than later-borns, they are less likely to invent or promote a controversial theory that places them in opposition to the ideas of the respected majority.

Memory

When psychologists say that the knowledge stored in schemata, categories, and propositions is remembered, the term *memory* is being used broadly to embrace a variety of separate processes. A three-month-old watches an orange ball move up and down on a pulley mounted against a black background, and creates a schema for this complex experience. When this infant returns a day later to see the same event, he becomes bored more quickly than an infant who is watching this event for the first time because the former child recognizes the original event. A tenyear-old is shown a series of twelve pictures of familiar objects in a particular order. The pictures are then turned over, and she is given a matching set of twelve pictures and asked to duplicate the original order. After the child performs that task successfully, the examiner takes the child's pictures away, leaving only the original twelve pictures, which are still turned over, interchanges the positions of pictures 2 and 7, gives the child's pictures back to her, and asks her to duplicate the new order. The successful performance requires a recall of information that was stored, in part, as categories.

In *recognition*, the child simply has to decide whether an event in the perceptual field was experienced in the past. In recall, the child must retrieve all the necessary information without the help of reminders. Most of the time, recognition memory is better than recall memory, with the difference between recall and recognition being more dramatic in younger than in older children. The tenyear-old who has been shown a group of twelve pictures is usually able to recall spontaneously about eight of them but is able to recognize all twelve even if they are included in a much larger set of photographs. A four-year-old will also recognize all twelve but is able to recall only two or three of the pictures.

There are three major aspects to the development of memorial competences. The first is the firmness of the registration of information. Because familiarity aids registration, and adults have more knowledge than children, adults generally register more information. Familiarity can be roughly equated with the richness of the associations, especially symbolic ones, generated by an event. There is evidence for the interesting suggestion that, after the third birthday, when growth of language is accelerating, the firmness of registration is enhanced. When adults were asked if they remembered where they were and what they were doing when they first heard the news of Smt. Indira Gandhi's assassination, those who were between four years and seven years of age at the time of the tragedy had a very good memory of that moment. However, those who were less than three years of age did not.

Registration is also facilitated if the child actively rehearses, elaborates, or recodes information. If a child and an adult are shown a circular array of eight designs for a brief period (say, a tenth of a second), and are then asked to recognize the position of any one of the designs, children do as well as adults if there is a very short delay (less than a half-second) between the original display of the designs and when they have to answer. This finding suggests that children and adults are similar in the ability to register an equally familiar event. But if the delay between seeing the circular array and being asked to respond is as long as two seconds, adults perform better than children; hence, it may be that the adults are doing something with the information during the delay that aids their later memory. They may be rehearsing, elaborating, or recoding the original information. Young children do not automatically utilize these cognitive processes that aid registration.

Children were asked, "If you wanted to phone your friend and someone told you the phone number, would it make any difference if you called right away, after you heard the number, or if you got a drink of water first?" Since kindergarten children were just as likely to say they would phone first as to reply they would get a drink of water, we infer that they did not realize that the numbers might fade from memory if they did not rehearse them. By contrast, most fifth-graders said they would make the call at once.

Just before adolescence, the typical American child seems to have consolidated many of the essential competences that facilitate recall of new information that has been presented in the immediate past. Children six to thirteen years of age were shown two pictures and asked to remember their order. A third picture was then added to the first two, a fourth to the first three, and so on until each child had to remember the order of twelve pictures. American children were able to remember all twelve by ten years of age, and some could master this task as early as age six. By contrast, most Indian children growing up in a small farming town were not able to remember all twelve pictures until they were fourteen years old, because, unlike the American children, they did not use strategies for rehearsing and organizing the information.

Strong motivation to remember can provoke use of these strategies. In one study, rural Costa-Rican nine-year-olds were first tested on six different memory tasks to evaluate the quality of their recall memory, and then trios of children with similar memory scores were assigned to one of three experimental groups a motivation group, a strategy group, and a group that had no special experience. The children in the motivation group were given memory tasks on five occasions during which they were encouraged to try as hard as they could in order to get a prize. The children assigned to the strategy group were taught a set of strategies to aid memory: to rehearse the information, to try to make up associations, to detect patterns of organization in the information, to count, and to cluster information that belonged to the same category. The children who were neither motivated nor taught a strategy were simply given memory tasks identical to the ones given to the other children. One year after the first testing, all children were retested on the same six memory tasks that had been administered a year earlier. The children who had been taught the strategies showed a significant memory gain on all tasks. But, surprisingly, the children who were motivated improved on five of the six tasks because they spontaneously invented some of the effective strategies. The advantage of being taught the strategies was greatest for a very difficult task in which the child had to remember the changes in the spatial position of some pictures. The children who were neither motivated nor taught strategies showed the least amount of improvement over the year.

Personal preoccupations also influence what is registered; hence, children of differing motivations, despite similar ability and age, will preferentially register and remember different information. For example, highly aggressive preschool girls remembered pictures illustrating aggressive scenes better than minimally aggressive girls.

A second aspect of the growth of memory involves the processes that are activated when the child tries to recall information registered in the past. The older child uses rules more systematically, including the search for a category, a time, or a place marker that acts as a clue to retrieve appropriate information. The older child seems to know something of how his or her knowledge is packaged and so gains access to it more efficiently.

A third aspect involves the psychologists' measurement of what has been registered. Progress in the study of human memory is frustrated by the fact that experiences can be registered in different structures, including schemata, categories, and propositions; but the psychologist usually probes a person's memory of an event in only one way. Adults who were asked to recall a specific personal event evoked either by an olfactory stimulus (the smell of coffee, of baby powder, or of moth balls), or by a printed word that represents each of the odors, remembered different events. The memories evoked by the actual odors were less often discussed with others and had more pleasant associations. The child who is shown a picture of three people playing on a beach may represent their clothing in schemata, but their actions in a linguistic category. If the psychologist asks the child to report verbally what is in the picture, the child may not say what the people are wearing, even though that information is represented in schemata.

Years ago I showed school-age children a series of scenes with brief exposures, initially for less than a second. They saw each scene six times at increasing durations until the last, which was visible for over one second. Each time they saw the scene, they described it; and, on the last exposure, when the picture was clear, they were asked to describe it in detail. Immediately after this verbal description, the lights in the room were put on, and each child was asked to draw the picture they had just described. It was common for some children to omit important elements in the drawing that they had mentioned moments ago in their verbal description. If I used the child's drawing to decide what he or she saw I would conclude the child did not see a particular feature of the scene. If I used the verbal recall, I would conclude that he or she had seen it.

Additionally, each method used to probe what a child registers has its own internal logic. A verbal description is monitored by a desire to use correct grammar and retain a logical relation between sentences. A drawing is constrained by the motor ability to represent the objects and their proper relation to each other. Although recognition of an experience seems to be more sensitive than recall in assessing what is in memory, this method can exaggerate what is registered, for the child might represent only part of the event, yet he is presented with the entire event. Thus, as I have noted many times, the truth value of a statement about a child's memory is limited by the method used to evaluate what has been stored.

Evaluation of an Idea

As the child grows, she more regularly evaluates the accuracy of her perceptions, the quality of her solution hypotheses, the appropriateness of a category, and the correctness of a conclusion. *Thoughtfulness* is a good term for this quality, and children differ in degree of thoughtfulness. Some children accept and report the first idea they generate, and act on it after only the briefest consideration: we call these children *impulsive*. Other children, of equal talent, devote a much longer time to evaluating the accuracy of their ideas; hence, they reject incorrect conclusions and offer a correct answer on the very first attempt; we call these children *reflective*.

This property – called *reflection-impulsivity* – is applicable only to those problem situations where the child believes an aspect of his intellectual competence is being evaluated; he holds a standard for quality of performance on the task, understands the problem, and believes he knows how to achieve its solution. Several equally attractive response alternatives must be available, but the correct answer should not be immediately obvious. Under these conditions, the child who does not want to make an error must evaluate each solution hypothesis. These children who are concerned with minimizing error take a great deal of time to search for the best solution. Those who are less concerned with error devote too little time to evaluating their ideas.

One test that measures this quality is called the Matching Familiar Figures Test. The child is shown an outline drawing of an object (say, an airplane) and six other drawings of planes. One is identical to the original; the other five are similar but have minor variations. The child is told to look at the six variations and to pick the one that is exactly like the original. Reflective children study all the pictures carefully, perhaps for ten or twenty seconds, before selecting the correct one. Impulsive children make their choices before they have scanned all the pictures carefully, usually respond in less than ten seconds, and, as a result, make more errors.

On some intelligence tests, the form in which the question is asked produces a great deal of response uncertainty, while the question form on other tests generates minimal uncertainty. If a test of vocabulary, for example, requires the child to select from a set of six pictures the one picture that matches the word spoken by the examiner (as in the Peabody Picture Vocabulary Test), the impulsive child obtains a lower score. But if the test of vocabulary requires the child only to respond verbally to a question like "What is a potato?", there is little difference in vocabulary score between reflective and impulsive children.

Socialization experiences during the preschool years are an important determinant of whether a child will be reflective or impulsive. Japanese children show a reflective attitude earlier than American or Israeli children, and Japanese parents communicate to their children a concern with proper behaviour earlier and more consistently than American or Israeli parents. However, temperamental factors might make a small contribution to this style. Japanese infants show a greater vulnerability to inhibition and fearfulness than do Caucasian children and Caucasian infants who show a tendency toward inhibition in unfamiliar situations are more likely to be reflective as older children than are less inhibited infants. When the extremely inhibited twenty-month-olds were tested at four or five years of age, they were much more reluctant than the uninhibited children to offer guesses to different problems, presumably because they felt unsure about their answers and did not want to be wrong.

Because most societies socialize their children to avoid error, most children become more reflective as they grow older. Lowerclass children, however, tend to be slightly more impulsive on intellectual tasks than middle-class children, due, in part, to less concern with error on these tasks. As might be expected, children with academic problems in school tend to be a little more impulsive than a comparable group without academic difficulty. Being pessimistic about their ability to solve different problems, the former adopt a "devil-may-care" attitude. Since they do not believe they will be able to solve a problem correctly or do not care-they do not find it useful to take the time to weigh carefully each possibility. Academically more successful children have higher standards for avoiding error on cognitive problems and believe it is worthwhile to evaluate the potential validity of each solution.

The Executive Processes

The number of problem situations in which an actual competence will be actualized increases dramatically during the interval from two to twelve years. Consider the actual competence, reflective evaluation of alternative solutions. Although two-year-olds will inhibit a potentially incorrect response when recalling the location of a toy hidden under one of five cups, and three-year-olds will evaluate the accuracy of their answers on a test in which a picture of an animal is disguised in a set of distracting lines, four-year-olds will not behave reflectively on the Matching Familiar Figures Test. Why is this so?

One reason is that four-year-olds do not yet understand that ten seconds of reflective study of the different pictures will make an initially correct answer more probable. The application of an actual competence to a broad array of problems is accompanied and perhaps explained by the growth of a set of executive processes. I call these processes *executive* in order to imply that each is superordinate to the processes of perceiving patterns of features, inferring categories, generating solution hypotheses, and remembering information. John Flavell might call some of these processes *metacognitive functions*. I now discuss some of these functions.

1. **Articulation of a problem and its solution.** The first step in any problem is to generate an idea of the solution. Although sixmonth-old infants will reach for a nearby toy, and newly hatched turtles will crawl to the sea, most scholars are reluctant to award to infant or turtle any awareness of the terminal state toward which each is moving. But a two-year-old playing with a doll will ask the mother where a doll's dress is or initiate a systematic search for the dress, even though she is not mature enough to generate an idea of what actions another child might expect of her if they were playing together. The seven-year-old, by contrast, automatically seeks to determine what a friend might mean by an unusual gesture. With growth, the child becomes increasingly familiar with a broader array of problems and, as a result, is able to specify the solution sought in a large variety of situations.
2. **Awareness of the cognitive processes necessary to solve a problem.** A second executive process is awareness of the factual knowledge and abilities necessary to solve a problem, and the ability to adjust cognitive effort to match the difficulty of the problem. Although middle-class six-year-olds appreciate

that recognizing a past event is easier than recalling it, young children do not appreciate all of the processes that might facilitate recall memory. Children in kindergarten and third- and sixth-graders were asked specifically to pick words that they believed would be easy to remember. The older, but not the younger, children suggested words that are easy to recall, like rhymes, antonyms, or words belonging to the same conceptual category.

Young children also fail to appreciate that an investment of attention will aid memory. Four-year-olds who were told that they had to remember a series of photographs for a week did not prolong their inspection times; eight-year-olds did because they understood that looking at the pictures longer was necessary to hold the information in memory for a period as long as a week.

3. **Activation of cognitive rules and strategies.** The third executive process follows naturally from the first two. If the child is aware of the cognitive units and processes necessary to solve a problem, he should activate them. And older children do spontaneously generate strategies and rules that aid solution. For example, adults cannot hold more than seven unrelated items of information (for example, numbers) in working memory if they do not have the opportunity to rehearse that information or to organize it. Consider this string of numbers: 1 2 4 8 1 6 3 2 6 4 1 2 8 2 5 6

   If one notices that the string is organized so that each number after the first is twice that of the preceding number, one can remember an infinite string, for all one has to do is recall the first number and the rule of doubling. Six-year-olds who know certain rules often fail to use them when they are appropriate for a problem. For example, many six-year-olds know the rule of alternation right, left, right, left, or up, down, up, down but do not activate that knowledge in a memory problem where such knowledge would help them. In one experiment, children had to remember whether each of a series of identical dolls was right side up or upside-down when the dolls were laid out in a horizontal row. When the orientation of the dolls was random, six-year-olds remembered a series of four or five, and eight-year-olds could remember six or seven dolls. But if the series of dolls had an organized pattern (say, alternating up and down), older children detected that pattern and remembered a longer string. Most of the six-year-olds possessed the rule "alternate" but were unlikely to impose that rule in this particular situation.

4. **Increased flexibility.** The ability to discard inefficient solutions that are not working and to search systemically for better alternatives also grows with age. This quality is often seen when the young child is working on a puzzle. A three-year-old who is trying unsuccessfully to fit two pieces that do not belong together will persist and eventually withdraw from the task. The eight- year-old is able to recognize the flawed hypothesis sooner and will begin to search for a better solution.
5. **Control of distraction and anxiety.** A fifth quality of the executive is to keep attention focused on a problem, to resist being distracted by extraneous stimulation (outside noises, the behaviour of other people), and to control the anxiety that mounts when a problem is difficult. Older children seem better able to prevent fear from overwhelming the system and interfering with productive thought.
6. **Monitoring the solution process.** As the child matures, he more consistently relates his ongoing performance to his idea of the correct solution and makes appropriate changes if he decides that his performance is too slow or unlikely to reach a successful solution. This function is similar to the cognitive process we called evaluation.
7. **Faith in thought.** A seventh characteristic of the executive is the belief that when one is having difficulty solving a problem, thought may help one to generate the correct solution. If an initial solution does not work, young children stop trying in part, because they do not appreciate that mental work may be useful. I recall an unusual five-year-old boy who was shown two identical pieces of clay that he acknowledged to be equal in quantity. I then rolled one piece of clay into a thick sausage and asked him if one piece had more clay or if the two pieces were equal. The child looked at the two pieces of clay, put his head down on the table, and remained quiet for almost two

minutes. When I repeated the question a bit impatiently, the boy looked up and said, "I'm thinking."

8. **Desire for the best solution.** The young child seems to lack a generalized standard for the best solution to a variety of problems. Although the two-year-old will, on occasion, want to imitate the mother exactly and become upset if he cannot, he is not usually concerned with finding the most elegant, error-free solution to most problems. Indeed, that is one reason the young child is impulsive on tests like Matching Familiar Figures. The five-year-old offers a hypothesis quickly because he does not regard an error as a serious violation of a standard of performance. By contrast, tenyear-olds have a general desire to perform with the greatest possible elegance on many tasks.

Although many of these executive processes eventually develop in all children, conditions of rearing have a profound influence on their rate of growth. Generally, children growing up in modern societies with good schools and continual exposure to events that challenge existing beliefs show faster development of these executive processes. Performance on memory tests is one index of the appearance of some of these processes. In one study, recall memory for a series of ten to twelve pictures, words, and orientations of dolls was better in American than in rural Indian children. The American children reached maximal performance around nine to ten years of age, with the greatest improvement between seven and nine years of age. The children living in an isolated village with inadequate schools, minimal variety in everyday life, and parents who felt impotent to change their lives, did not begin to approach maximal performance until late adolescence. The children growing up in a more modern Indian village a few kilometres away reached maximum performance on the test by thirteen years of age.

Piaget's Theory and the Executive Processes

Although the executive processes are important accompaniments of the changes in cognitive performance during the half-dozen years prior to puberty, they seem, on the surface, to be unrelated to the operations that, according to Piaget, bear the burden of explaining the improvement in thought over the same interval. Consider the operation of the conservation of quantity: knowing that the quantity of clay in a ball remains the same even though the examiner changes the shape of the clay. As I noted in the earlier discussion of Piaget's ideas, children who interpret the examiner's question literally would give answers regarded as nonconserving because tiny pieces of clay were left behind on the examiner's hand. But that is not what Piaget had in mind. The question the child is actually being asked is: "Ignoring very tiny pieces of clay, is it or is it not true that, generally, changing the shape of the piece of clay does not, theoretically, affect its mass?"

It is possible that the eight-year-old answers correctly because she has acquired an appreciation of the intention behind the examiner's question. Recognizing the problem is one of the executive processes. The child is always interpreting an examiner's question in a specific social context and trying to make sense of what the examiner asks in light of what has happened in the immediate past. In the conservation procedures, the examiner shows the child two balls of clay, two containers of liquid, or two linear arrays of beads, asks a question about their equality, and receives an answer. Then the examiner changes a feature of the array in a deliberate manner and asks the same question. The child is trying to understand the entire context, not just the words, and may regard the fact that the examiner changed the clay, the liquid, or the beads as a condition requiring a different answer. Although the isolated string of words that forms a question may seem to have a constant meaning, the meaning of any sentence that is part of a continuing conversation does not.

Similar problems surround Piaget's claim that the five-year-old cannot regard two complementary categories simultaneously. When shown three black cows and only one white cow lying on their sides and asked, "Are there more black cows or more cows?", most six-year-olds, but no ten-year-olds, say there are more black cows. According to Piaget the child cannot mentally compute the equation "All cows equal three black cows plus one white one." But when the question is changed to, "Are there more black cows or more sleeping cows?", many more of the six-year-olds answer correctly and reply,

"More sleeping cows". That simple change in the question makes a dramatic difference because the six-year-old is likely to think that the original question was, "Are there more black or white cows?" The child does not expect the examiner to ask him to compare a part (the black cows) with the whole. By adding the adjective sleeping to the question, the examiner calls the child's attention to the property belonging to all the cows, and so the child answers correctly.

This suggestion gains force through a different demonstration in which children were shown ten blue and five red building blocks and were asked, "Who would have more toys to play with, someone who owned the blue blocks or someone who owned the blocks?" Many six-year-olds replied that it would be the child who owned the blue blocks. But when the question was changed to, "Who would have more toys to play with, someone who owned the blue blocks or someone who owned the pile?", many more children answered correctly and said, "The pile." The use of the word *pile* called the children's attention to the whole collection of blocks. The set to consider more than one dimension in a statement or problem is a major characteristic of development (recall the "face-hands" test where young children had to be reminded that they might be touched in two places).

Piaget made the error of not taking into account the young child's subjective frame of understanding. He treated the five-yearold's understanding of a question about quantity as if it were the same as that of an older child, and assumed that the different answers offered by younger and older children were due to differences in how the same understandings were manipulated – that is, operated upon. The young child's frame is so special he will often agree with propositions he knows are not possible. For example, children between three and five years of age were read a story, an extract of which follows:

She would like to work in the big Post Office, but she works in a branch. As they were driving along, they saw a hare run across a field. Then they got back into the car and drove to the seaside. When they got there, they went for a walk along the quay. "Look at this castle," said Jane's Daddy. "The oldest wing is over 500 years old.".

They got held up behind a lot of other cars all going very slowly. "I hope we get out of this jam soon," said Jane's Daddy.

When the children were asked to draw the branch, the hare, the quay, the wing, and so on, many drew a branch of a tree, a head of hair, a key, and a bird's wing. When questioned, "What does a hare look like?", a child touched his hair. "Do you think it would be running across a field?" "Yes." When asked, "What sort of thing is a quay?" or "What's a quay for?", a child would answer, "For opening doors." But to "Do you think they could walk along a key?", a child would nod Yes. About one third of the responses had this curious quality. "We have repeatedly seen that young children's interpretations of language may be powerfully influenced by contexts so that they fail to show adequate respect for the words themselves".

Although three-year-olds are able to infer some mental states of adults like sadness, anger, or joy it is not until the years before adolescence that children are able to understand the specific intent of many adult questions and to offer appropriate answers. From the subjective frame of the respondent, a child's replies to intelligence test questions or a schizophrenic's answers to a psychiatrist are rarely wrong or irrational, although they may be treated as such by an interrogator who does not know how a question is being interpreted. One essential characteristic of cognitive growth is an increasing ability to appreciate the mind of the other, so that one knows at once the unspoken assumptions that surround a question.

Conclusion

In order to understand the ways children and adults react to problems, psychologists have invented units like *schema* and *concept*, and processes like *retrieval*, *inference*, and *evaluation*. These theoretical inventions seem reasonable because psychologists conceive of the human mind as composed of entities that represent experience and functions that manipulate these entities. An analogy from early twentieth-century physics illustrates how powerful a *priori* conceptions can be. The idea of an atomic nucleus was posited by Ernest Rutherford to explain why a sheet of zinc sulfide, after being struck by energy originating in a sample of radium and passing through a thin piece of gold foil, emitted brief flashes of light that were occasionally deflected by more than 90 degrees, when the angle of deflection of most of the light flashes was usually much smaller. Rutherford assumed that particles coming from the radium must have first struck something in the gold foil which had a mass as heavy as their own and, like a car hitting a truck, bounced far from the target they encountered. Rutherford suggested that this mass was the nucleus of the gold atom. If one considers only the observed facts a piece of radium, gold foil, and brief light flashes on a sheet of zinc sulfide the inference that atomic nuclei in the foil are the reason for the deflected light flashes is likely only if the concept of an atomic nucleus is a deeply held premise.

In a typical psychological experiment on cognitive development, the investigator presents information to a child, and the child displays some public reaction. A one-year-old, for example, is shown eighteen different pictures containing a pair of dogs of different shapes, sizes, and colours, and looks equally long at each of the dogs. On the nineteenth trial, the infant is shown a new dog, but one paired with a bird, and looks much longer at the bird than at the dog. Unless the scientist assumes that the infant possesses a concept "dog," to which he relates each of the eighteen pairs of different dogs, and is eager to look at a member of a new concept, the infant's looking behaviour will seem mysterious. The notion of a *concept* generated from experience is as reasonable to psychologists as the idea of an atom with a dense nucleus was to Rutherford.

Ideas like schema, concept, and proposition are deeply held premises psychologists use to explain how humans react to information. Let us hope that these ideas are as valid for psychology as the notion of an atomic nucleus has turned out to be in the physical sciences. The ideas and evidence presented in this chapter have implications for those concerned with the intellectual development of children. Teachers, parents, and psychologists should conceptualize the child's cognitive competences as intimately yoked to narrow rather than to broad classes of problems. The five-year-old who knows that a mosquito remains small in size, even though it appears large under a magnifying glass, does not know that the amount of water in a large, flat dish remains unchanged after all of it has been poured into a tall, thin cylinder. On the one hand, the psychologist can attribute to the five-year-old the general competence Piaget calls *conservation of quantity*, and rationalize the child's failure with the containers of water as being due to his inability to extend the principle to this specific problem. On the other hand, the psychologist can deny the general competence and treat the conservation of size or quantity as a set of highly specific competences tied to highly specific situations. The ancient Greeks thought the world was made of only fire, water, air, and earth and treated the extraordinary variety of objects in the world as derivative of these four abstract substances. Oil was simply a derivative of water; pebbles, of earth. Although physicists eventually may derive all matter from a few basic particles, chemistry still finds it valuable to assume the existence of over one hundred different basic chemical elements whose properties and functions can change with alterations in temperature, pressure, electromagnetic field, and the presence of other elements.

Developmental psychologists investigate key questions, such as whether children are qualitatively different from adults or simply lack the experience that adults draw upon. Other issues that they deal with is the question of whether development occurs through the gradual accumulation of knowledge or through shifts from one stage of thinking to another; or if children are born with innate knowledge or figure things out through experience; and whether development is driven by the social context or by something inside each child.

The modern form of developmental psychology has its roots in the rich psychological tradition represented by Aristotle and Descartes. William Shakespeare had his melancholy character Jacques (in As You Like It) articulate the seven ages of man: these included three stages of childhood and four of adulthood. In the mid-eighteenth century Jean Jacques Rousseau described three stages of childhood: infans (infancy), puer (childhood) and adolescence in

Emile: Or, On Education. Rousseau's ideas were taken up strongly by educators at the time.

In the late nineteenth century, psychologists familiar with the evolutionary theory of Darwin began seeking an evolutionary description of psychological development; prominent here was G. Stanley Hall, who attempted to correlate ages of childhood with previous ages of mankind.

8

CHILDREN'S LEARNING, THINKING AND REMEMBERING

Introduction

We first examine traditional topics of learning: classical and operant conditioning, followed by a look at Bandura's influential social cognitive theory, the contemporary version of his earlier social learning theory. Piaget's account of cognitive development is then reviewed. We next look at information- processing perspectives of development, stressing the topics of strategies, memory, metacognition, and theory of mind. We conclude the chapter with a very different perspective on cognitive development, Vygotsky's sociocultural approach, which focuses not just on the child's intellectual development, but views the child and his or her social environment as the level of analysis for cognitive development.

Learning

Classical and Operant Conditioning

Thinking and remembering imply learning the acquisition of new knowledge through experience. In the early part of this century, the primary theoretical approach to learning was *behaviourism*, which held that behaviour and development are shaped by environmental influences. Two principal types of learning were described: classical conditioning and operant conditioning.

In *classical conditioning*, discovered experimentally by Russian scientist Ivan Pavlov, a previously neutral stimulus is paired with another stimulus that elicits some response. For example, a particular tone might be paired with a puff of air to the eye. The tone is initially neutral in that it elicits no response from a person. The puff of air to the eye, however, does elicit a response an eye blink. After repeated pairings of the tone with the puff of air, eventually the tone will produce an eye blink even without the puff of air. In this example, the puff of air is referred to as the *unconditioned stimulus* and the tone as the *conditioned stimulus*. Emotional responses seem to be learned through classical conditioning. When a child associates a previously neutral stimulus with a stimulus that already elicits some response, eventually the new stimulus will elicit the emotion.

The most famous study of classical conditioning of emotion was performed nearly 80 years ago. In that study, Watson and Raynor conditioned a young boy named Albert to be afraid of a white rat by sounding a loud gong each time the boy was shown the rat. Albert's innate fear of the loud sound quickly became associated with the rat. After the experimental trials, the child showed fear to the rat alone, a conditioned or learned response to a previously neutral stimulus.

The other basic form of learning is operant conditioning, or learning through reward and punishment. In operant conditioning, some behaviour of the child is reinforced, or rewarded, causing a change in the probability of that behaviour in the future. For example, children who receive a reward (candy, money, praise) for good behaviour can be expected to continue to show good behaviour in the future. Patterns of reinforcement that is, the distribution or frequency of rewards received for particular behaviours can greatly affect learning; aversive stimuli (mild shocks for rats, spankings or a reprimand for children) can also affect behaviour.

Learning in Infancy

Although infants were once thought to be dumb, passive creatures, oblivious to the world around them, research over the last 50 years has clearly shown that babies are actively learning about their world from birth and before. Research has shown that infants less than a week old can learn to discriminate between the odor of their mothers and other women and that some learning of basic auditory patterns occurs prenatally.

Operant conditioning of newborns is relatively easy: They will modify their behaviour in order to receive some type of reward. The trick is to find a behaviour that infants can control themselves and something that they find rewarding. Behaviours that newborns can control include sucking, head turning, and kicking, all of which have been used in operant-conditioning experiments. Reinforcements have included milk, human voices, and music. For example, in one experiment, newborns would suck on a pacifier in order to hear music as opposed to nonrhythmic noise, demonstrating both an ability to learn and an innate preference for patterned sound.

Classical conditioning also seems to be within the capability of newborns, although it is limited to a few biologically prepared reflexes, such as sucking and blinking. However, the length of time between the neutral stimulus and the unconditioned stimulus must be shorter in young infants than in older children for conditioning to occur. Presumably, young infants cannot process information as efficiently and require more time to make the connection between the conditioned and unconditioned stimuli before learning takes place.

Behaviour Modification

Principles of classical and (especially) operant conditioning are used frequently by parents and teachers to control children's behaviour and establish discipline. In fact, *behaviour modification* the use of operant conditioning principles to change behaviour is the basis of many patenting programmes and popular books aimed at instructing parents in how to manage their children. Yet although the principles of conditioning are as valid today as they were 50 years ago, contemporary researchers believe that operant and classical conditioning alone are not adequate to account for most of the learning that children do. One complaint about behaviour-modification techniques is that children who are rewarded for desired behaviours often resort to earlier behaviours once the rewards are removed. That is, although behaviour-modification techniques clearly work in controlling a child's current actions, they are less successful in shaping future behaviour when rewards are no longer provided. In fact, children who are induced to comply by rewards (or punishments) may lose their intrinsic motivation for the behaviour in question and be less likely to engage in it on their own. For example, a study by Fabes and his colleagues investigated the relationship between experience with instrumental rewards (if you do X, you get Y) and prosocial motivation in elementary school children. To assess mothers' attitudes and practices regarding the use of tangible rewards for activities that children did not find attractive, the researchers asked mothers to respond to items on a 5-point scale, depending on how well it described their beliefs or behaviour. Some examples of the items are:

- The use of rewards to motivate children can be considered a type of bribery.
- The use of rewards to motivate children can help produce desired behaviour.
- The use of rewards to motivate children makes them stop working when the rewards are no longer available.
- To what extent do you provide your child with a reward for behaving properly? To what extent do you give your child a reward for doing something he or she does not like to do?

The children of these mothers were seen separately and given the opportunity to help make a game for kids in the hospital by arranging pieces of paper according to colour. Some of the children were offered a reward for helping (a small toy); other children were not. Later in the session, all children were given a second chance to "help the sick children," but rewards were not offered to anyone (free-choice period). Fabes and his colleagues reported that the offer of rewards increased helping behaviour in the first situation. However, during the free-choice period, previously rewarded children were less likely to help, and this effect was greatest for those children whose mothers put a high value on instrumental rewards. Thus, although the use of rewards may enhance prosocial behaviour immediately, "they may also undermine subsequent prosocial motivation in situations where rewards are no longer forthcoming".

These results do not mean that children should never be offered a reward for good behaviour. They mean that the desired behaviour is more likely to occur if rewards for prosocial behaviour are used with other techniques, such as modelling prosocial behaviour. In fact, modelling has been found to be a very effective technique for inducing prosocial behaviour in children, especially when the model is perceived as warm, influential, and powerful.

Social Cognitive Theory

The primary limitation of operant and classical conditioning in explaining how children learn is that children (and adults) learn much about their world simply by watching. We do not need to be explicitly reinforced to learn something new. We can simply watch a model, retain the observed behaviour, and be able to reproduce it at some later time. Not only can we learn overt behaviours from observing models, we can also learn attitudes and standards of judgement.

Recognizing the importance of learning by observation, a group of psychologists in the twentieth century developed a new theoretical approach known as "social learning theory". According to this theory, imitation is the primary learning mechanism for most social behaviours. Social learning theory was later championed by Bandura and his colleagues, who initially proposed that children learn through observation by experiencing vicarious reinforcement; that is, they feel good (or bad) watching someone else get reinforced and modify their behaviour accordingly. Over more than three decades, Bandura's theory has become less behavioural and more cognitive until, in its latest version, he has renamed it social cognitive theory. It is now the dominant approach to studying children's social development.

Unlike earlier social learning theory, social cognitive theory proposes that children play an active role in interacting with their environment. Bandura believes that children have as much effect on their environment as their environment has on them; he refers to this interaction as *reciprocal determinism*. Bandura proposed that children's thoughts, feelings, and behaviours interact with the external environment. Children's emotions and thoughts will affect their actions (and vice versa), which, in turn, will affect how others perceive and act toward them. It is a human characteristic to make sense of our behaviour (we rarely do anything for "no reason"), and we often modify our thinking and beliefs to make them consistent with our actions. Bandura theory recognizes the complex web of factors that affect children's behaviours, from their own internal thoughts and feeling, their actions, and the thoughts, feelings, and actions of others in their environment.

Bandura proposed five abilities that influence children's learning about their social world, each of which develops: *symbolization, forethought, self-regulation, self-reflection, and vicarious learning*. Symbolization is the ability to think about our social behaviour in words and images. Forethought is the ability to anticipate the consequences of our actions and the actions of others. Self-regulation involves adopting standards of appropriate behaviour for ourselves aspirations, or hoped-for levels of accomplishment, as well as social and moral standards. A capacity for self-reflection allows people to analyze their thoughts and actions. The fifth ability, vicarious learning, is the cornerstone of social cognitive theory. In contrast to earlier versions of social learning theory, children do not have to receive reinforcement for their modelling efforts nor even attempt to reproduce modeled behaviour for learning to occur. They can watch a model and represent mentally what the model did; this mental symbol can then serve to guide their subsequent behaviour, even if they never actually imitate what they observed. Bandura referred to this process as *observational learning*.

Bandura proposed four subprocesses involved in observational learning: *attentional processes, retention processes, production processes,* and *motivational processes*. For observational learning to occur, to-be-learned behaviour must first be attended to, then represented in memory for later retrieval, and finally the behaviour must be performed at the appropriate time. Each of these factors develops, and problems in any one area (retention, for example) will impede successful observational learning.

Children can learn from observation without ever actually producing the behaviour. For instance, although we "know" at some level what is appropriate male and female behaviour in a range of contexts, most of us display only same-gender behaviour. It is important for children to learn not only the behaviours and attitudes of same-gender adults in their society, but also the behaviours and attitudes of the opposite gender because it informs them what behaviours should complement their own. Yet despite "knowing" opposite-gender behaviour, children tend to code it negatively and not imitate it, whereas they code same-gender behaviour positively and incorporated into their behaviour.

Although imitation is not *necessary* for observational learning to occur, it is nonetheless an important component. Imitation is the clearest indication that children have learned through watching and the primary means by which children acquire new behaviours.

The Development of Imitation. Imitation begins early in infancy and changes in character with the advent of language and other symbolic tools late in the second year of life. Bandura's account of observational learning begins with children's ability to symbolically code events and actions they have seen, store them in memory, and imitate them at some later time. This is what Piaget referred to as deferred imitation. Such imitative abilities, although apparently present to a limited extent early in the second year, begin in earnest between 18 and 24 months of age.

Following Bandura's model there are many components to observational learning. It is well known that young children have limited attention spans. However, some things are more likely to be attended to than others. Events in which there is a lot of action, including aggression, are apt to catch children's attention, although keeping it is sometimes difficult. Educational television, such as Sesame Street, tries to keep young children's attention by limiting each segment to only a few minutes. Preschoolers may be able to attend to 2 minutes of "circles versus squares," but 4 and 5 minutes on such a topic would result in losing half, or more, of the audience. Young children's memory also shows substantial changes over early childhood, and how much and what children remember will influence greatly their ability to imitate.

Even if children pay close attention to some modeled behaviour, remember it accurately, and have the motivation to display it, it does not mean that they will be able to imitate it. A major limitation on children's imitation is their motor ability. Yet despite often obvious physical shortcomings, many preschool children believe they are more capable of imitating behaviour than they actually are. Young children, in general, overestimate their physical and intellectual abilities, and thus often believe that they can imitate behaviours that are actually beyond their abilities.

Young children's knowledge of their imitative abilities was investigated in a study by D. F. Bjorklund, Gaultney and Green. In that study, mothers questioned their preschoolers about how well they thought they would be able to imitate certain behaviours, and then recorded their attempts. Children's underestimation was rare, occurring on only 4.7% of the observations. In fact, the most common response was overestimation, which occurred 55.5%, with children stating that they would be able to imitate some action, which they did not.

Young children have great confidence in their own abilities. For them to get better at observational learning, however, they must learn to monitor their behaviour, compare their behaviour to their memory of the modelled action, and correct mismatches. As children get better at these production processes, the discrepancy between what think they can do and what they actually can do declines.

Television as a Model for Learning: Children learn not only from watching other people, but also from watching film, videos, and television. There can be no question that television is an important socializing agent in today's society. Most of children between 3 and 14 years of age watch more than 3 hours of television per day, with the amount of TV viewing time decreasing some over adolescence into young adulthood.

As a means of mass communication, television and its related technologies are the most important inventions of the 20th century. Television can serve as a great education tool, bringing knowledge in an easily understood visual form that doesn't require reading skills. But does it? What do children learn from watching TV?

TV and Education. Many programmes on public and commercial TV are aimed at educating children. Perhaps the best known and most successful of these is Sesame Street, which has the goal of fostering cognitive skills in preschool children.

Sesame Street has been a staple of children's television for nearly 30 years and is seen in more than 40 countries worldwide. Its intended audience was children from disadvantaged homes, with the goal of minimizing the gap in cognitive performance between advantaged and less advantaged preschool children. Its popularity has been enormous among children of all socioeconomic groups, and it is now viewed regularly by nearly 8 million pre-schoolers children in America.

Early studies that evaluated the effects of Sesame Street were impressive. During the first season of the show, Ball and Bogatz assessed preschool children's basic cognitive skills (including knowledge of letters, numbers, and geometric forms) prior to watching the programme. Some children were then encouraged to watch Sesame Street, whereas others were not. Ball and Bogatz then divided children into four groups, based on the amount of time they had watched the programme, and retested them. It was clear that watching the programme had had the desired effect: The amount of cognitive gain children showed was directly related to how much they had watched the show.

More recent research has investigated the effect of watching Sesame Street on children's vocabulary development. Children ages 3 to 5 and 5 to 7 were observed for 2 years, and changes in their vocabulary were related to their TV viewing habits. It was found that Sesame Street had a positive effect on the vocabulary development of 3- to 5-year-old children, with lesser benefits for children older than 5. Other types of children's programmes, such as cartoons, had no influence on the vocabulary of children of any age. These findings indicate that the programme format of Sesame Street is well suited for preschool children's vocabulary development.

The Sesame Street Generation. Television has been an everyday part of family life for the past 40 years. Many social critics blame television for the downslide in children's school performance. Even Sesame Street has been criticized for shortening children's attention spans and making classroom learning seem boring by comparison to its rapid-fire visual format. It is widely believed that children's comprehension of television is fragmented and passive, promoting a passive attitude to thinking in general. A number of authors have suggested that the more television children watch, the poorer their school performance is. However, D. R. Anderson and Collins, in reviewing the research evidence on the relationship between TV viewing and academic performance, found little evidence to support this assertion. They concluded that the impact of television is very small, particularly when children's IQs are considered, and that even for children most affected by television (those in low-ability groups), the effects are small and sometimes nonexistent. They conclude that "the most likely effects on schooling come directly from the central content of television programmeming most watched by children" and believe that television can have a major impact on what children know.

Piaget's Theory

Five-year-old Heidi was watching her father prepare lunch. After spreading peanut butter and jam on one slice of bread and topping it with another, Dad cut the sandwich in two and then again into quarters. Seeing her sandwich cut into four pieces brought an immediate frown to Heidi's face. "Oh, Daddy," she sighed, "I only wanted you to cut it in two pieces. I'm not hungry enough to eat four!"

To us it may seem obvious that the amount of sandwich is the same regardless of whether it is cut into 2 pieces or 4 pieces or 40 pieces. But that's not the way it appears to young children, who sometimes draw erroneous (and humorous) conclusions about how the world works. Taking such pronouncements by young children seriously, Swiss psychologist Jean Piaget formulated a grand theory to explain how thinking changes in quality over the course of development a theory that has had unparalleled influence in child psychology.

Assumptions and Principles of Piaget's Theory

Piaget's formal education was in biology, and he viewed intelligence as the way we as a species adapt to our environments. Basic assumptions of his theory include the concepts of intrinsic activity, organization, and adaptation.

Intrinsic Activity

A fundamental assumption of Piaget's theory is that of *intrinsic activity*. Babies are not passive creatures waiting to be stimulated by external forces before they respond, but are themselves the prime movers and shakers of their world. They actively seek stimulation, initiating action on objects and people who come in contact with them. Thus, the motivation to learn and to develop is within the child. In short, Piaget believed that children play the central role in their own development a view that minimizes the role of parents and teachers.

Children make sense of their surroundings by actively interpreting their experiences. Knowledge is not simply acquired; it is *constructed*, based on an interaction between the child and his or her environment. As a result, children of different ages hold very different beliefs about the world. A 3-month-old believes that a rattle that falls out of sight under the crib no longer exists; 4-year-olds believe that the sun follows them as they walk; 6-year-olds believe that in a group of seven dogs and four cats, there are more dogs than animals. To Piaget these examples demonstrated the constructive nature of cognition: Reality is not absolute, but a construction based on one's past experiences and current mental structures.

Functional Invariants

Piaget believed that there were two general processes, or functional invariants, that characterize intelligence and operate throughout the lifespan. He referred to these two processes as *organization* and *adaptation*.

Organization refers to the fact that every intellectual operation is related to all other acts of intelligence that intellectual abilities are coordinated with one another. Organization thus implies a tendency to integrate mental abilities into higher order systems, or *structures*. A structure, or *scheme*, is some enduring knowledge base through which children interpret their world. It is these structures that are intrinsically active and that construct reality. For Piaget, cognitive development is the development of structures.

Piaget's second functional invariant, adaptation, refers to the fact that the child (or, more properly, the child's structures) must adjust to environmental demands. This simple concept has two complementary components: *assimilation* and *accommodation*.

Assimilation refers to the incorporation of new information into already-existing structures. This should not be viewed as the passive registration of new information, however. Assimilation is an active process, with the child sometimes distorting information to fit existing cognitive schemes. For example, after being read "Jack and the Beanstalk" the night before, 22-month-old Kristin greeted her parents in the morning with "Fee, Fi, Fo, Fum. I smell bacon and eggs." The line in the story "I smell the blood of an Englishman" made no sense to Kristin, so she distorted what she remembered in order to assimilate it into her current world knowledge.

The complement of assimilation is accommodation changing a structure in order to incorporate new information. When children are confronted with something they cannot quite understand, they can modify their structures to make use of this new information. For example, a 2-year-old given a magnet for the first time would have difficulty understanding it if she treated it as she did any other small metal object; she would have to alter her underlying structures in order to take advantage of its special properties. In other words, she can incorporate the special properties of magnets into her behavioural repertoire only if she changes the way she thinks. This, according to Piaget, involves accommodation.

For another example of assimilation and accommodation, consider the 2-year-old who calls all men "Daddy." This child is using the verbal label she acquired for her father to refer to all adult males (assimilation). Now she must learn to restrict her use of the term "Daddy" to her father and find new terms for other men (accommodation), lest she cause embarrassment to her mother.

Piaget stated that all acts of cognition involve both assimilation and accommodation, although not always in equal portions. The purest form of assimilation is play. When playing, children assimilate whatever objects or people they are playing with into their own self-defined schemes. The chair is an engine, the table is the rest of the train, and the hassock is the caboose. At the other extreme is imitation, which Piaget believed was the purest form of accommodation. When successfully imitating another person, the child must modify his or her behaviour to match that of the other person.

Piaget used the concepts of assimilation and accommodation to explain how thought develops. According to his theory, children strive to maintain a balance, or equilibrium, in their cognitive structures. When faced with information that does not fit their current thinking, they experience a state of disequilibrium, which is intrinsically unpleasant. To reestablish balance, they alter their cognitive structures, using accommodation to incorporate new information. Accommodation occurs, however, only when the discrepancy between new information and the child's present thinking is small; if it is too great, the child will either ignore the information or distort it. Piaget referred to this process of changing structures to maintain a cognitive balance as *equilibration*.

Piaget's view of development has important consequences for education. A teacher with a Piagetian perspective strives to present children with tasks that produce slight degrees of disequilibrium. Problems that are too easy can simply be assimilated, and thus no development has occurred. Problems or information too discrepant from what a child already knows cannot be accommodated, and thus they are either distorted or ignored. Learning and development are most apt to occur when problems are of some optimal level of discrepancy from what a child already knows.

Piaget also believed that the role of teachers should not be to *instruct* children (that is, to transmit knowledge), but rather to provide opportunities to *discover* knowledge. According to Piaget:

Children should be able to do their own experimenting and their own research. Teachers, of course, can guide them by providing appropriate materials, but the essential thing is that in order for a child to understand something, he must construct it for himself; he must reinvent it.

Unlike conventional Western approaches to education, in which teachers are authority figures who transmit information to children, Piaget believed that the authority status of teachers actually hampered learning

It is despite adult authority, and not because of it, that the child learns. And also it is to the extent that the intelligent teacher has known to efface him or herself, to become an equal and not a superior, to discuss and to examine, rather than to agree and constrain morally, that the traditional school has been able to render service.

As these quotes indicate, Piaget did not believe that children learn or develop much from interacting with adults. For Piaget, development is a process of discovery, and one cannot discover if one is instructed by an authority figure. However, Piaget proposed that children can learn and develop by interacting with peers. Peers are people of equal status, and it is through the inevitable conflict that comes with peer interaction that children's minds develop. The ideas of other children often conflict with a child's own. This results in disequlibration, which children seek to resolve. Because peers are equal in status, they must work together to resolve these conflicts and cognitive development is the consequence.

Stages of Development

The cornerstone of Piaget's theory is the idea of stages, with functioning at one stage being *qualitatively* different from functioning at other stages. Thus, children at any given stage have a unique way of viewing the world that is consistent with the rules they have derived so far and consistent with the reasoning of other children their age.

Piaget insisted that stages cannot be skipped. He believed that every structure in the psychology of intelligence is based on earlier structures, making it necessary for children to master the accomplishments of one stage before advancing to the next. Children may go through stages at different rates, and development may be arrested at a certain stage for some individuals, but the order in which children go through the stages is unalterable.

Piaget divided cognitive development into four major stages, or periods: *sensorimotor*, *preoperations*, *concrete operations*, and *formal operations*.

The Sensorimotor Period. The first stage, which extends from birth to about 2 years, is known as the *sensorimotor period*. Mental functioning changes more drastically during these 2 years than during any other period in development. First, there is a change from an intelligence based on action to one based on symbols that is, from cognition based on overt actions to one based on internal representations. Second, there is a related change in personal perspective from an undifferentiated world with no notion of a separate self to one in which self and other are clearly distinguished.

At the earliest stage, that of *basic reflexes* (birth to 1 month), infants know the world only in terms of inherited reflexes. Piaget used the term reflex broadly to include not only behaviours such as sucking and grasping, but also behaviours such as eye movements, orientation to sound, and vocalizations. Basically, infants during this first stage apply their reflexes to objects. If an object, such as a nipple, fits a reflex, such as sucking, the infant applies the reflex to the object and assimilates the object to an existing scheme in other words, the baby nurses.

In stage 2, *primary circular reactions* (1 to 4 months), infants extend their reflexes to acquire new patterns of behaviour that were not part of the basic biological package they were born with. For example, there is no basic reflex for thumb sucking. However, there are inherited patterns for moving one's arms and hands and for sucking. When, as a result of chance, babies find their fists or thumbs in their mouths, sucking ensues. Because sucking is intrinsically pleasing, the infant attempts to re-create the pleasurable experience. Much trial and error follows, but the result is an infant who can suck its thumb at will. Although this may not seem an impressive act of intelligence, it is an example of infants' learning to control some aspect of their behaviour.

Infants' control of their world expands during the third stage, *secondary circular reactions* (4 to 8 months), as they learn to control not only their own bodies, but events in the external world. For example, Bjorklund and Bjorklund described the behaviour of their daughter during this stage of sensorimotor development:

When our daughter Heidi was about 4 months old, she was lying in a playpen with a "crib gym" strung over it a complex mobile with parts that spin when they are struck. While flailing her arms and legs, she hit the mobile, causing it to spin. She happened to be looking at the mobile, and its movement caught her attention. She immediately stopped moving and stared intently at the object over her head. When it ceased moving, she began to shake her arms and legs, to squirm, and finally, to cry. Again she hit the mobile, and again she froze and quieted, staring straight ahead at the wonderful event she had caused.

This is an important step in intellectual development. In this stage, babies begin to realize that they have some control over their world. Although the initial event occurs accidentally, once under their control, the action is theirs to use whenever and wherever they please. Not only could Heidi spin the mobile in her playpen, she could apply this new behaviour to other objects in other locations. She could switch hands or adjust the strength of her stroke to produce slightly different outcomes. She had begun to master her world by acting intentionally on objects around her.

Table 8.1. Piaget's Four Stages of Cognitive Development

Period	Approximate Age	Major Characteristics
Sensorimotor	Birth-2 years	Intelligence is limited to the infants' own actions on the environment. Cognition progresses from the exercise of reflexes to the beginning of symbolic representation.
Preoperations	2-7 years	Intelligence is symbolic; use of language and imagery enables children to represent and compare objects mentally. Thought is intuitive rather than logical.
Concrete operations	7-11 years	Intelligence is symbolic and logical, and less egocentric, but still limited to concrete phenomena and past experience.
Formal operations	11-16 years	Children are able to generate and test hypotheses, introspect about processes, and think abstractly.

Next in development infants learn to coordinate several of these accidental behaviour patterns to achieve a goal. Piaget labelled this fourth stage *coordination of secondary circular reactions* (8 to 12 months). Suppose, for example, that a toy is set in front of a baby and an obstacle placed between the baby and the toy. At 6 or 7 months, babies are unable to get the desired toy, even though they are perfectly capable of moving the obstacle. Somewhere around 8 months, however, babies develop the ability to use one behaviour (pushing an obstacle) in the service of another (retrieving a toy). This achievement of goal-directed behaviour is a major advance in the development of intelligence.

Cognition takes a turn again beginning at about 12 months. Now, for the first time, infants invent slightly new behaviours to achieve their goals. They no longer have to wait until chance provides them with an interesting event; they can make interesting things happen themselves. Piaget called this fifth stage *tertiary circular reactions* (12 to 18 months). Sometimes these "interesting things" involve getting into things they should not, such as kitty litter, the bathroom cabinet, and the living room CD player. Children are discovering as much about their world as they can and are learning more about the control they have over their environment. They learn that their action is independent of their parents and that they do not have to comply if they don't want to. They also learn the consequences of this defiance, as they must, and they modify their behaviour accordingly most of the time.

Table 8.2. Substages of the Sensorimotor Period

Stage	Approximate Age	Major Characteristics
Basic reflexes	Birth-1 month	Cognition limited to inherited reflex patterns
Primary circular reactions	1-4 months	First acquired adaptations extension of basic reflexes
Secondary circular reactions	4-8 months	Beginning of control of objects and events external to infant
Coordination of secondary	8-12 months	Coordination of two previously circular reactions acquired schemes to achieve a goal (goal-directed behaviour)
Tertiary circular reactions	12-18 months	Discovery of new means through active experimentation, trial and error
Mental combinations	18-24 months	First signs of symbolic functioning (language and imagery)

Although children at this stage are wonderful problem solvers, their intelligence is still limited to actions on objects. Babies know things by acting on them; they cannot make mental comparisons or represent objects and events symbolically. It is not long, however, before infancy is left behind and a totally new way of understanding the world develops. Somewhere between the latter part of the second year and the beginning of the third, children become symbol users.

They are able to make mental comparisons between objects, to retrieve memories from the past, and to anticipate the future. They no longer depend on their own direct actions to understand things; they can know the world through language and other symbols. This final stage of the sensorimotor period, *invention of new means through mental combinations* (18 to 24 months), is a transition between the action-oriented world of the infant and the symbol-oriented world of the child.

Perhaps the most studied aspect of Piaget's sensorimotor period is the concept of *object permanence*. According to Piaget, infants under 4 months have no concept of object permanence no idea that objects have an existence in time and space independent of their own perceptions of or actions on those objects. Thus, for example, 2- or 3-month-olds will follow their mother with their eyes, but when mother leaves their visual field, they will continue to gaze at the point where she disappeared and not anticipate her reappearance somewhere else.

The development of object permanence is gradual over infancy. For example, at around 4 months of age, infants will attempt to retrieve objects that disappear, but only if the object is still partially visible. Beginning at about 8 months, infants are able to retrieve a completely hidden object. To do this, infants must be able whether there ever is a period in life when children totally lack symbolic representation.

Despite the evidence that infants have greater cognitive abilities than we once believed, Piaget's description of their thinking and behaviour still provides an accurate description, we believe, of how most infants think and behave most of the time, although his account does greatly underestimate the actual cognitive abilities of infants and toddlers and may not focus on some important dimensions of cognitive development.

Preoperational Thought. The transition from the action-based cognition of the sensorimotor period to the symbol-based thinking of the *preoperational period* is seen most obviously in the child's use of language. Beginning around 18 months, children start stringing words together into sentences. Other examples of symbol use in young children are deferred imitation, drawing, imagery, and symbolic play (for example, pretending a shoe is a telephone or feeding imaginary cereal to a doll). Each of these forms of cognition is available to most 2-year-olds, although how they use these symbols will improve dramatically over the next dozen years or so.

During the preoperational period, children's thinking, although symbolic, is not logical. For example, if a red stick is taller than a blue stick and a blue stick is taller than a green stick, then logically the red stick must be taller than the green one. This, however, is not an inescapable conclusion to 4- or 5-year-olds, who base their conclusions on what *seems* to be, regardless of what, by logic, must be. For example, if water is poured from a tall, skinny glass into a short, fat glass, the preoperational child is likely to say that the amount of water has changed. There seems to be less water in the short, fat glass because the height of the water is lower. For preoperational children, appearance is stronger than logic; they find no contradiction in stating that the amount of liquid changes when poured from one container to another. This is the intuitive nature of thought characteristic of the preoperational period.

Piaget described a number of characteristics of preoperatonal children's thought. For example, he stated that preoperational children's perception was centered on the most obvious dimension of a situation and that they attend to and make judgments based solely on that dimension. In the water-level problem, for example, their attention is centred only on the difference in height of the waterlines; according to Piaget, they are unable to consider the two dimensions of height and width simultaneously. Evidence of young children's perceptual *centration* can also be found in their everyday thinking. For example, Piaget noted that preoperational children often use people's height as a means to estimate their age. Tall people are older than shorter people. This developmental difference in how two children judge age is illustrated in the following transcript.

Nicholas, age 5½

Interviewer: "If a grown-up came into your classroom and asked you to guess how old he was, how do you think you would do it? What sort of things would you look at?"

Nicholas: "I don't know. I'd measure. I'd measure by how high he is."

Interviewer: "What if he was big?"

Nicholas: "He'd be old, like 15 or 100."

Interviewer: "OK. What if a new kid came to your school? How could you tell how old he was? What sort of things would you look at?"

Nicholas: "His fingers."

Interviewer: "His fingers? How could you tell by his fingers?"

Nicholas: "I'd see how many fingers he held up."

Interviewer: "Oh. What if he didn't hold up any fingers? How could you tell how old he was just by looking at him?"

Nicholas: "I don't know. How big he is. If he was big, he'd be old, like Russell. If he was like me, he'd be 5. If he was little, he'd be 4. Or maybe 3. If he was a baby, he'd be real tiny."

Kristina, age 8½

Interviewer: "If a grown-up came into your classroom and asked you to guess how old he was, how do you think you would do it? What sort of things would you look at?"

Kristina: "I would usually look at his hair. If he has a lot of hair or is bald. And if his legs are hairy, and whether he had hair coming out his nose. And his skin and stuff. If he would be old, his hair would be gray and his skin would be wrinkled."

Interviewer: "OK. What if a new kid came to your school? How could you tell how old he was? What sort of things would you look at?"

Kristina: "Usually, if they're tall like me or if they're like Marci's size, they'd be like 8. If they were smaller, they'd be like 7 or 6."

Interviewer: "So if they're taller they're older?"

Kristina: "Yes."

Interviewer: "Can you do the same thing with adults? Use how tall they are to tell how old they are?"

Kristina: "No. With the height you can't really tell with a grown-up. And also kids don't have gray hair and wrinkled skin."

This doesn't mean that children can't judge age on the basis of other features, such as faces. When the conditions are right they can. But when differences in height are present and substantial, young children have a difficult time ignoring the them.

Another characteristic of preoperational children's thought is their *egocentricity*. Piaget used this term to refer to the tendency to interpret objects and events only from one's own perspective the inability to put oneself in someone else's shoes, as it were. Preoperational children are less egocentric than the sensorimotor child, but more self-centered in cognitive perspective than concrete operational children. According to Piaget, this egocentric perspective permeates the lives of young children, influencing their perceptions, language, and social interactions. For example, much research has examined young children's ability to take the visual perspective of another. In classic research by Piaget and Inhelder, young children sat on one side of a display of three mountains and asked to tell what a doll placed at various positions around the mountains saw. Piaget and Inhelder reported that most children under 8 years of age gave an egocentric response and simply said that the doll saw what they saw. Other researchers have criticized Piaget and Inhelder's three-mountain task as overly difficult, and more recent research has shown that children will make nonegocentric responses when provided with less complicated visual displays. Some everyday examples of egocentricity in young children are given here:

Egocentrism is easy to spot in young children. A kindergarten child will tell her parents a story about what happened to Billy at school and leave out much of the relevant information. Everyone knows about Billy. Surely that must include Mom and Dad.

A telephone conversation with a 4-year-old can be interesting, but in the absence of face-to-face visual cues, much important information is often lost. For example, the voice on the other end of the phone asks, "What are you wearing today, Kelly?" and in response Kelly says "This," while looking down and pointing at her dress.

Allen, the son of a high school math instructor, asks another 7-year-old, "What does your daddy teach?" assuming that everyone's daddy must teach something. He knows there are other jobs in the world; in fact, he's going to be a fireman when he grows up. Nonetheless, daddies teach.

Even young children are not consistently egocentric, however. At 5, my daughter Heidi still frequently demonstrated the classic egocentric attitude described by Piaget. For example, one evening in her bath she placed her head under the running water and excitedly called me in to hear the new sound. "Listen to this, Daddy," she said as she lowered her head under the faucet again while I watched. In a different context, however, this same child showed a keen ability to take the perspective of another. One evening, sometime before the bath episode, she and I were beginning a prebedtime card game and I was exhorting her to hurry because, I said, the game is more fun when you play it fast. Her response to that was quick. "No sir, Daddy," she said. "You only want to go fast so we can finish and you can put me to bed!" I had been caught. This child, who thought I could hear the rushing water when her head was under the faucet, in this instance, saw my perspective quite clearly.

In general, each of us sees the world from a slightly different perspective, but with age and experience our perspectives expand, becoming less personal and more cultural. Our world and the world of the young child are not exactly the same, even though we may reside in the same house and live through the same events. We should not be surprised that in telling the story of an afternoon together in the park, the child comes up with a different account of things than her father does. This is not necessarily due to the young child's poor memory; she may be remembering things very well. She just didn't see or experience the same things that her father did standing beside her. They saw and felt different things at the same place and time. This isn't a scene from *The Twilight Zone*, just the normal differences in thinking and perspective between children and adults.

Concrete Operational Thought. By about the age of 7, children are no longer so easily taken in by appearances. They are able to *decentre* their perception – that is, they demonstrate *decentration*, the ability to separate themselves from the obvious aspects of a perceptual array and make decisions based on the entire perceptual field. They are also less egocentric than young children.

Perhaps the most critical difference between the preoperational and the concrete operational child is that the older child is able to think following rules of logic. The most important logical rule underlying mental operations is reversibility. In arithmetic, for example, subtraction is the inverse, or reverse, of addition. If 6 plus 3 equals 9, then 9 minus 3 must equal 6. Understanding this rule is critical for children to learn arithmetic, and children who do not appreciate the logical necessity of reversibility in arithmetic will be doing little more than rote memorization. Reversibility, more generally, is the logical idea that for any operation there exists another operation that compensates for the effects of the first. For example, if water is poured from a short, fat glass into a tall, thin one, the increased height of the water is compensated for by a decrease in the width of the column.

Piaget developed many tasks that differentiate the thinking of the preoperational from the concrete operational child, but perhaps the most studied, and for Piaget the most important, were tasks that assessed conservation. Conservation refers to the understanding that an entity remains the same despite changes in its form. A classic example of a conservation task is the water-level problem. Do children realize that the amount of water remains the same after pouring it into a different container, even though there seems to be more (or less) than there was originally? The concept of conservation applies to any substance that can be measured and has been studied with respect to dimensions of length, number, mass, weight, area, and volume.

With respect to conservation, as with other aspects of his theory, Piaget believed that he was assessing children's competencies – their fundamental abilities. If this were the case, it should not be possible to train children to conserve unless they are in a transition stage, almost ready to learn to conserve on their own. However, a number of researchers, using a variety of techniques, have demonstrated that nonconservers as young as 4 can be trained to conserve. Training effects are greater for older than for younger children and few studies have successfully trained conservation in 3-year-old children. However, about three quarters of all published studies in which preschool children were taught to conserve have been successful, with a smaller percentage showing generalization to other materials and over delays of a week or longer.

Formal Operations. Formal operations advance the logical rules acquired during the concrete operational period to the point that children can think about objects, ideas, events, and relations independent of their prior experience. As one Piagetian scholar put it, "Concrete operations consist of thought thinking about the environment, but formal operations consist of thought thinking about itself". Formal operational thinkers are able to introspect about their own cognitions and produce new knowledge merely by reflecting on what they already know. They are also able to solve complex problems and to reason inductively, going from specific observations to broad generalizations, much as a scientist does when conducting experiments.

The hallmark of the formal operational period is the ability to think hypothetically or, as Piaget put it, *hypothetico-deductive reasoning*. Possibilities are more important than what is real. Such thinking is critical for most forms of mathematics beyond arithmetic. If $3x + 3 = 15$, what does x equal? The problem does not deal with concrete entities such as marbles and pencils, only with numbers and letters.

Another characteristic of formal operational thought is *inductive reasoning* going from specific observations to broad generalizations. This is the type of thinking that characterizes scientists, who generate hypotheses and then test them systematically in experiments. In other words, the ability to set up an experiment, test the effects that different variables have on an a dependent measure, and interpret the results properly, are abilities that children who have attained formal operational abilities posses, but children who are still in the concrete operational period have not yet mastered.

There has been controversy concerning whether concrete operational children are capable of solving problems requiring scientific reasoning. In fact, researchers have been able to train young children to solve many formal operational problems, although they demonstrate these abilities only under limited conditions.

In other situations, however, research has shown that Piaget overestimated the tendency of adolescents and adults to use scientific-type reasoning. For example, Kuhn and her associates, using 265 adolescent and adult participants in a longitudinal study, administered a battery of formal operational tasks adapted from Inhelder and *Piaget*, including tests of scientific reasoning. Based on these tests, only about 30% of the adults were classified as having completely achieved formal operations. Most adults were classified as transitional between concrete and formal operations, and 15% demonstrated no formal operational abilities at all.

Piaget and Individual Differences in Children's Thinking

Piaget was concerned with cognitive development age-related changes in children's thinking that typify the species. He was less interested in individual differences, differences in thinking among children of the same age. This has not stopped other psychologists and educators, however, from applying Piaget's theory to the problem of assessing individual differences in children's thinking. For example, several researchers have reported that how well children perform on a battery of Piagetian tasks (for example, conservation) predicts their academic performance.

Perhaps the most impressive research relating children's performance on Piagetian tasks to academic performance and measures of IQ was performed by Humphreys and his colleagues. Humphreys and his associates administered IQ tests and batteries of Piagetian tasks to children of varying intellectual aptitudes (mentally retarded and normal children) and ages (6 to 18 years). The tasks included those that assessed early concrete operational abilities (*e.g.*, conservation) to those evaluating formal operations (*e.g.*, scientific reasoning).

Humphreys reported correlations between scores on the Piagetian tasks, IQ, and measures of academic performance in excess of .70. In fact, children's scores on the Piagetian tasks predicted academic performance nearly as well as IQ scores. Based on the pattern of correlations, Humphreys proposed that IQ tests and the Piagetian batteries are both valid measures of intelligence. Although there was overlap in the type of intelligence the two measures tapped, Humphreys noted that there were some differences between the tasks in terms of the intellectual skills they assessed. Humphreys was not able to specify the nature of these differences, but he stated that each measure is a valid index of intelligence.

Information-processing Perspectives of Children's Cognition

Piaget's theory has been enormously influential, both in terms of providing scientists with a better understanding of child development and by helping educators to focus on ways in which children of different ages learn. But there is another approach to children's thinking that has also provided important insights into cognitive development, and that is the information-processing approach. Basically, this perspective views the human mind as being like a computer. We have certain hardware, such as limited-capacity memory stores, and are limited in how quickly we can process information. There are also aspects of our cognition that are analogous to software, for example, the strategies we use to solve problems. Both hardware (for example, how much information children can keep in mind at one time, speed of processing) and software (for example, knowledge that children possess and the strategies they have to act on that knowledge) change with age.

We examine several aspects of children's information processing. We will start by taking a look at the information-processing system, followed by an examination of strategies, focusing mainly on young children's early arithmetic strategies. We devote a bit more space to the important factor of memory, which influences all aspects of children's thinking. We conclude with a look at metacognition, and a particular type of metacognition termed theory of mind.

The Information-Processing System

Most contemporary theories of cognition assume that we have a limited capacity for thinking a finite amount of mental resources. We can only think about one thing at a time, and many of our mental operations are effortful, in that they consume a portion of these resources, leaving less behind for other aspects of thinking. Most theories also make a distinction between the shortterm and long-term stores. The *long-term store* is our repository of permanent memories. Presumably, it can hold an infinite amount of information for an infinite amount of time, although forgetting does occur. The *short-term store*, on the other hand, can only hold a limited amount of information (in adults, 7 plus or minus 2 items) for a matter of seconds. The short-term store has also been referred to as primary memory, working memory, and the contents of consciousness. It is in the short-term store that information is consciously evaluated. The short-term store is where we live, cognitively speaking.

Memory Span. One issue that has concerned developmental psychologists is age differences in the capacity of the short-term store. Can older children hold more information in consciousness at any one time than younger children? Early research found what appeared to be substantial and regular age differences, based on memory-span tasks. Memory span refers to the number of items one can recall perfectly after only a brief exposure (for example, hearing one item per second). Memory span for digits (digit span) is commonly used on tests of intelligence and shows very regular developmental changes.

Despite these impressive and robust findings, more recent research has seriously questioned the idea that the capacity of the short-term store increases substantially with age. For example, in one often-cited study, a group of graduate students at the University of Pittsburgh were given two simple memory tests. On one, they were read a series of numbers quickly (about one per second) and asked to recall them immediately in exact order. On a second test, they were shown briefly chess pieces on a chess board (again, about one chess piece per second), then given the pieces and asked to place them at their previous positions on the board. Their performance on these tasks was compared to that of a group of 10-year-olds. But, in all fairness, these were not typical 10-year-olds; they were all chess experts winners of local tournaments or members of chess clubs. When memory for the chess positions was tested, the children outperformed the adults. This finding was probably not surprising, given the expert status of the children. But the critical question was, How would they do when remembering the numbers? Does being a chess expert cause one's memory capabilities to improve overall, or was the children's remarkable performance limited to what they knew best? The results support the latter interpretation. The adults, despite being outdone by the children when memory for chess positions was tested, were superior to the children when the test stimuli were numbers.

What results such as these indicate is that children's short-term memory is not fixed but flexible. Under certain conditions, they can remember things as well as adults; in other situations, however, they act like kids. What this suggests is that the capacity of children's and adults' short-term stores is comparable; adults just make better use of it than do children (usually).

Efficiency of Processing. This brings us to the idea of efficiency of processing. If that actual capacity of short-term memory is not much different between children and adults, what causes the substantial differences that are seen on most cognitive tasks? The simple answer is that older children and adults process information more efficiently than younger children. With age, children process information faster and faster processing translates directly into more efficient processing.

Why should having detailed knowledge about a subject result in improved memory performance? Bjorklund and his colleagues proposed that the better established information is in one's mind, the more easily it can be activated, bringing that information to consciousness. They are also able to integrate new information more easily the more they already know about a topic. In fact, when children are highly knowledgeable about a topic, they are able to learn and remember information about that topic very well. Because older children usually know more than younger children about things in general, they require less in the way of mental effort to activate common word meanings, leaving them with more mental space or mental energy to spend on the recall of additional words or on other cognitive operations.

We earlier gave an example of how chess-expert children have greater memory spans for chess position than chess-novice adults. Let us provide another example on a more complicated task of how children's knowledge for a topic can influence how much they remember and compensate for the effects of low academic ability. Schneider, Körkel, and Weinert compared the story comprehension of soccer expert and soccer novice third-, fifth-, and seventh-grade children on stories related to soccer. They also classified children as successful learners versus unsuccessful learners based on their classroom grades in German and mathematics and performance on IQ tests. This led to four groups of children at each grade: soccer experts/successful learners, soccer experts/unsuccessful learners, soccer novices/successful learners, and soccer novices/unsuccessful learners. Children were then read a story about soccer. Care was taken to ensure that most parts of the story would be easily understood even by the soccer novices. Children were then asked questions about the story or were asked to recall the story. The average number of idea units children remembered from the soccer story. First of all, expert children performed better than did novice children. What may be surprising, however, is that a child's learning ability did not influence performance; the soccer expert/unsuccessful learners remembered more than did the soccer novice/successful learners. In other words, what children knew about soccer determined how well they performed, independent of their general learning ability.

Strategies

Much of cognition is automatic, in that it is done without a person's awareness. We are not conscious of the mental gymnastics that must be done to read the words on this page or identify the noise outside the window as the barking of our neighbour's St. Bernard. But much that we consider "thinking" does have a significant conscious and intentional component to it. We actively try to remember a phone number, figure out which can of deodorant is the best buy, or solve the problem of how to store our jumbled spices on the kitchen shelves.

Strategies are effortful processes, in that they consume a portion of one's limited mental resources. But the effort is usually well worth the mental cost because using a strategy typically results in better thinking. Strategies are generally defined as goal-directed mental operations used to facilitate task performance that are deliberately implemented and potentially available to consciousness. According to some theorists, age differences in strategy use more than any other single factor are responsible for age differences in thinking.

Even infants seem to show some signs of strategic, goal-directed behaviour as they search for missing toys or try to make their way around obstacles. But the strategies of the infant and young child are ineffective compared to the strategies of older children and adults. In fact, a popular view in cognitive development was that young children did not use strategies, at least not of their own accord. Most of these nonstrategic children could be easily trained to use simple strategies, and this resulted in improvements in their performance. This observation led Flavell to describe young children as having a *production deficiency* they have ability to use a strategy but fail to produce one spontaneously. In contrast, children who showed a *mediation deficiency* could not use a strategy even if it was demonstrated to them.

Today it is recognized that even young children use strategies, although the strategies of the preschool child may differ considerably from those used by older children. P. H. Miller has identified a third "deficiency," which she called a *utilization deficiency*, meaning that children are able to use a strategy but the strategy doesn't help them much. For example, in a memory study by D. F. Bjorklund, Coyle, and Gaultney, many third-grade children showed increases in a memory strategy over five trials, but no corresponding increases in how much they remembered. If the purpose of the strategy is to help children perform better, why do they use an effortful strategy when it doesn't help them? Utilization deficiencies are not rare, but have been found in most of the studies examined in which strategy use and performance can be evaluated independently.

There have been several explanations utilization deficiencies, the most common one being related to the effortful nature of strategies. Strategies use up a child's limited mental resources, and young children use their resources less efficiently than older children. That is, strategies have a cost in terms of mental effort, and young children exert so much mental effort carrying out the strategy that they do not have enough left to perform other aspects of the task effectively, such as remembering. However, children eventually show improvement in performance after repeated use of strategies. It has been proposed that many children are unaware that the strategy they are using is not doing them any good, and as a result don't get discouraged when their performance is actually not enhanced. One suggestion has been that children's lack of awareness of the relation between their strategy use and task performance is adaptive, and that a more cognitively aware child might stop using strategies that don't provide immediate benefits.

How Do Strategies Develop? One perspective that has gained much attention lately proposes that children have a variety of strategies available to them at any one time and use combinations of these strategies. That is, children do not simply develop from using a simple and ineffective strategy to using a more complicated and efficient one. Rather, both the simple and complicated strategies coexist with one another and compete for use. Such multiple- and variable-strategy use has been championed by Robert Siegler and his colleagues and has been observed on a large variety of tasks including arithmetic, spelling, memory and tic-tac-toe, among others.

Perhaps it is easiest to appreciate how children's multiple-strategy use by providing an example from children's early arithmetic. When children first learn to add, they often use a strategy that involves counting out loud both addends, starting from 1. So, for example, for the problem 4 + 2 = ?, a child might say "1, 2, 3, 4 [pause], 6, 7." This is called the sum strategy. A more sophisticated counting strategy involves starting with the larger addend (in this case, 4), and counting up from there (for example, saying, "4 [pause], 6, 7"). The most sophisticated strategy for solving simple arithmetic problems is "just knowing" the answer, retrieving it directly and quickly from long-term memory. This strategy is called *fact retrieval.* A number of researchers have shown that as children get older they are more likely to use the more sophisticated strategy. However, these arithmetic strategies do not change like stages, with one replacing another. Rather, Siegler and his colleagues have shown that even after children are able to use fact retrieval for most problems, they still use some of the less sophisticated strategies more characteristics of younger children. In fact, even college-educated adults will fall back on simpler counting strategies occasionally.

Memory

Memory plays a central role in thinking. We believe that it is safe to say that no complex cognitive task, and few simple ones, can be executed without involving memory. However, the act of remembering is also influenced by simpler cognitive operations, such as directing one's attention and storing information efficiently. Thus, memory represents a central stage around which both simple and complex processes revolve.

Recognition Versus Recall. *Recognition* is the simplest form of remembering. When we recognize something, we realize that what we are experiencing now is the same as something we have experienced before. Recognition requires relatively little mental effort. A stimulus, such as a song heard on the radio, either matches something one has heard before or it doesn't.

A more demanding form of remembering is *recall.* Unlike recognition, where a stimulus is presented and the person must simply state whether it has been experienced previously or not, recall involves the active retrieval of information. Who was the third president of India? How many chromosomes does a normal human have? Who are all the cousins on your father's side of the family? What are you supposed to buy at the grocery store for the big party this weekend? The retrieval question, or cue, can help a person focus on the right information. If you were cued, for example, by being reminded of the names of your father's brothers and sisters or that the big weekend party was to be a barbecue, you might have an easier time remembering the desired information.

Recognition memory is usually easier than recall memory, with *cued recall* falling somewhere between recognition and *free recall* (recall without specific prompts). A similar picture emerges when we look at development. Children's recognition memory is relatively good, and age differences are often quite small. When recall is required, however, age differences are larger. In general, the ability to recall information increases with age, and as they get older children require fewer prompts to produce successful memory performance. D. F. Bjorklund provided an example of the distinction between free and cued recall in a preschool child:

A 5-year-old boy who had spent the afternoon with his grandparents seeing his first play, The *Little Shop of Horrors*, was asked by his mother, "Well, how was your afternoon?" The child replied "OK." The mother persisted, "Well, did you have a good time?" The child said "Yeah." However, when prompted by his grandmother "Tell your mother about Audrey II, the plant" he provided copious details, telling how the plant ate some of the main characters, talked, sang, and how it took three people underneath it to make it move. The child had a wealth of information, but it could only be accessed when specific cues were provided.

The Development of Event Memory. There are many memory tasks that children are asked to perform on a regular basis. In schools, they may be asked to remember the names of all the Indian Prime Minsiters or the characteristics of the food pyramid. More commonly, however, children are asked to recall *events*, such as the 5-year-old in the example recalling the play he had seen. In most cases, children remember events from a personal perspective. That is, the events are something that happened to them, or that they witnessed. When we remember things that are related to the self is called *autobiographical memory*. Research over the past 30 years has made it clear that children learn to remember events by incorporating new events in terms of what they already know. For example, children learn what happens when they go to a fast food restaurant. The develop a *script* for the event. A script is a form of representation that organizes real-world events in terms of their causal and temporal characteristics. For example, a fast-food restaurant may include driving to the restaurant, going into the restaurant, standing in line, ordering, paying, taking your food on a tray to a table, sitting down, eating, and throwing away the trash when finished. Children learn what usually happens when, and use these scripts to interpret and then recall novel events.

In recalling information about events, children need to learn to focus on the important parts of the event to remember the who, what, where, and when of the event and the order in which things happened. How do they learn to do this? In large part, they seem to be guided by their parents. Several researchers have shown that parents (especially mothers) provide their children with cues and ask the relevant questions to help their children recall events. Consistent with Vygotsky's position on cognitive development, Hudson has proposed that children learn how to remember by interacting with their parents, and that remembering can be viewed as an activity that is first jointly carried out by parent and child and then later performed by the child alone".

Let us provide an example of joint remembering between a young mother and her 2 year old daughter, Shikha, after returning home after a trip to the zoo:

Mother: Shikha, what did we see at the zoo?
Shikha: Elphunts.
Mother: That's right! We saw elephants. What else?
Shikha: (shrugs and looks at her mother)
Mother: Panda bear? Did we see a panda bear?
Shikha: (smiles and nods her head)
Mother: Can you say "panda bear?"
Shikha: Panda bear.
Mother: Good! Elephants and panda bears. What else?
Shikha: Elphunts.
Mother: That's right, elephants. And also a gorilla.
Shikha: Go-rilla!

These observations make it clear that, parents play an important, and perhaps unconscious, role in helping children form narratives, or stories, in order to remember.

Children's Eyewitness Testimony. Ever since the Salem Witch Trials of 1692, when children testified to seeing people transform themselves into animals or fly into the night, children have generally not been welcomed into the courtroom as witnesses. One major reason for this is the belief that children are highly suggestible and thus not reliable witnesses. Research over the past decade has shown that young children can often be reliable witnesses. When asked free-recall questions for events they witnessed or experienced they rarely provide incorrect information. However, the absolute amount of information they do provide is low, making the use of leading questions necessary. When young children are asked more specific questions, such as "Tell me what the man looked like," they recall more correct information, but they also recall more incorrect information, reducing the overall accuracy to their recall.

Most research indicates that preschool children are indeed more suggestible than older children and adults. For example, in research by Ornstein and his colleagues, 3-and 6-year-old children were asked misleading questions about a visit to a doctor's office 3 weeks earlier. Although both groups of children were generally correct, the 3-year-olds were less likely to reject the misleading suggestions of the interviewer than the 6-year-olds, suggesting somewhat greater suggestibility for the younger children. In other research, children watched a video of a theft and were asked sets of leading questions. If children did not agree with a question, they were immediately asked a more strongly worded follow-up question ("You do remember, don't you, that the girl said it was okay for the boy to take the bike?"). Five-year-olds were more likely to agree with the misleading questions than either 7-or 9-year-olds, with this difference being particularly large for the follow-up questions.

Although young children frequently comply with the misleading requests made by interviewers, this does not mean that they are actually "remembering" information incorrectly. At least a portion of young children's compliance with the misleading questions seems to be due to a desire to conform to the wishes of an adult. For example, after agreeing to the misleading questions of an interviewer, 5- and

7-year-old children later correctly identified the central factors in a bike theft, indicating that, although they changed their answers, they did not change their minds.

Although much research indicates that children's long-term memories for events are only moderately influenced by misleading questions, another line of research shows that it can be relatively easy to get young children to create false memories. In research by Ceci, Loftus and their colleagues, preschool children were asked to remember a series of events. Some of the events had actually happened to them, whereas others were invented by the interviewer (for example, "Got finger caught in a mousetrap and had to go to the hospital to get the trap off. Think real hard, and tell me if this ever happened to you. Do you remember going to the hospital with a mousetrap on your finger?"). Children were interviewed over a series of 10 or 11 weeks. In one study, 58% of the children produced at least one, often very detailed, false account, with one quarter of the children producing false stories to a majority of the false events. Moreover, many of the children in these studies refused to believe the interviewer and their parents when later debriefed and told that these events had not actually happened. In short, it was relatively easy, merely by repeatedly suggesting that an event had happened to them, to get preschool children to generate false descriptions of these events, and many came to believe them to the extent that they disbelieved their parents when told that the stories were made up.

Recall from Infancy and Early Childhood: The longer the delay between experiencing an event and recalling it, the less likely we are to remember it correctly, if at all; this is best illustrated by our general inability to remember events from infancy and early childhood. In fact, when we do have memories of such long ago events, they are often not accurate:

I have one vivid memory from my infancy. We were living at my grandparents' house, and I had the croup (I think it's called bronchitis today). My crib was covered by a sheet, but I remember looking past the bars into the living room. I can hear the whir of the vaporizer, feel the constriction in my chest, and smell the Vicks Vaporub. To this day the smell of Vicks makes my chest tighten. I can claim no other memories until close to my third birthday, and they are not as real for me as this memory is.

Some years back, I related this memory to my mother. "Romy," she said, "you were such a healthy baby. You never had the croup. That was your brother, Rony. You were almost three years old then."

The fact that my earliest memory is of an event that never happened doesn't make it any less real for me. The feelings it invokes are intense, and knowing that they didn't happen, at least not to me, does not lessen their impact. It's still *my* infant memory. It's just that the infant was my younger brother, and I was only an observer.

Few of us have memories from our infancy, and for those of us who do, most can be explained as mine was. It's not a memory of infancy but a memory about infancy. In my case, it wasn't even a memory about my infancy, but rather about my brother's.

This inability to remember events from infancy and early childhood has been labeled *infantile amnesia*. There have been a number of hypotheses concerning why our recall of events from the early years of our life is so poor, including Freud's idea that the events of infancy are so painful that we actively repress them. The most reasonable hypothesis, we believe, is that information is represented differently by very young children than it is by older children and adults. This perspective is consistent with the views of stage theorists such as Piaget, who contended that the nature of representation changes over childhood. The minds that reside in our heads now interpret information differently than did the minds that experienced the world when we were infants and toddlers. Other researchers have suggested similar explanations for infantile amnesia. For example, K. Nelson proposed that it is the ability to use language to form narratives that is responsible for autobiographical memory. Until we're good at forming and telling stories about our lives, something that happens at about 4 years of age, we won't be able to remember much of what we experience. In a similar vein, Howe and Courage proposed that autobiographical memory requires that children have a well-developed sense of self, and this, they propose, develops gradually over the preschool years.

Metacognition

Metacognition refers to a person's knowledge about his or her cognitive abilities. For every form of cognition, it is possible to think of a corresponding form of metacognition. Thus, for example, metamemory refers to one's knowledge about the working of one's memory, meta-attention refers to a knowledge of the factors that affect one's attention, and so on. Metacognition requires a conscious awareness. It is one thing to have complicated mental operations for solving problems, but it is another to know that you have these operations, to know when to use them, and to know how effective they are in arriving at answers.

Flavell and Wellman described three major classes of metacognitive knowledge variables: person, task, and strategy. Person variables include a person's knowledge of his or her own abilities and the abilities of other people with respect to thinking – for example, a knowledge that you can solve certain problems faster with visual than verbal information. Task variables involve knowledge of the requirements of tasks. Is there enough information provided to solve the task, or is more information needed? Strategy variables include a knowledge of what cognitive techniques one has available to solve a particular task and which strategies would be most appropriate for the task at hand. Does this task require my full concentration, or can it be accomplished with only a little study? What knowledge do I have that can be brought to bear on arriving at a solution?

One robust finding over the past 30 years has been age differences in children's metacognitive knowledge. Some research findings include: the ability to distinguish important from unimportant aspects of a written story improves with age; an understanding of the factors that influence attention increases developmentally; and young children do not effectively monitor information they have in memory, causing them to poorly predict their memory performance. In general, age-related differences have been found on person, task, and strategy variables, with children becoming more aware with age of their own knowledge and how it can be applied.

Contemporary researchers stress the bidirectional relationship between cognitive and metacognition development. Metacognition is obviously an important component in children's cognitive development and certainly influences cognition; but the relationship also works in reverse, with competent cognition influencing metacognition. The two are intimately entwined, and the relationship varies depending on a child's age and the task involved.

One aspect of metacognition we have addressed earlier in this chapter concerns children's ability to predict how well they are able to perform certain tasks. Recall that preschool children greatly overestimated their imitative abilities, thinking they would be better able to imitate a model than they actually were. Children's poor prediction skills have been found for a broad range of physical and cognitive tasks, from how accurately they can throw a ball or who are the smartest children in their class, to how many items they will remember on a memory task.

A good demonstration of developmental changes in metacognitive skills is seen in a study by Yussen and Levy, in which children were asked to predict their own memory spans. Yussen and Levy presented children and college students with a set of 10 pictures and asked them to predict how many items they could recall in exact order; then they measured their actual recall. They found that 4-year-olds greatly overestimated their memory spans estimating, on average, that they would recall slightly over 8 of the 10 items, whereas their actual recall was slightly greater than 3 of the 10 items (overestimation = 152%). Half the 4-year-olds predicted that they would recall all 10 items. Predictions were closer to reality for third-grade and college students (overestimation = 40% and 6%, respectively), and only 10% of third graders and 2% of college students predicted perfect recall. After the memory test, the preschoolers were aware of their failure to recall according to their predictions, but many were unperturbed, saying things such as, "If you gave me a different list like that, I could do it".

Young children's tendencies to overestimate their abilities is apparently not due entirely to a cognitive inability to make judgements of competency. For example, Stipek and her colleagues reported that young children can make relatively accurate assessments of other children's abilities and are overly optimistic only about their own performance. Stipek proposed that children's overly optimistic self-perception is due to *wishful thinking*, a concept originally introduced by Piaget: children wish to hit a home run the next time at bat, and therefore they *expect* to hit a home run. By 8 or 9 years of age, children's evaluations of their own abilities are more in line with those of their teachers and other children.

Several people have proposed that young children's poor metacognition with respect to their abilities may actually be adaptive. Bandura has stressed the importance of developing a positive sense of *self-efficacy* for success in life. Self-efficacy refers to the extent to which people view themselves as effective individuals, as having some control over their lives. Young children's overly optimistic (and unrealistic) opinions of their own abilities may foster their developing sense of self-efficacy. If they knew how poorly they did on most tasks, young children may get discouraged and quit. Being out of touch with their own abilities believing that they know more than they actually do and can do more than they actually can may provide them with positive perceptions of their own skills and encourage them to attempt things that they would not try if they had a more realistic idea of their abilities. In fact, rather than seeing these poor metacognitive skills of young children as deficits to overcome, we should perhaps "try harder to design educational environments which maintain their optimism and eagerness".

Although we believe that overestimating one's cognitive and physical abilities is generally adaptive for young children, there is a potential cost to such poor metacognition. For example, Plumert has shown that 6-year-olds who greatly overestimated their physical abilities in a laboratory task had a greater number of serious accidents than other children. Thus, young children's overly optimistic perspective of their abilities is a double-edged sword, and parents and teachers should be cautious neither to thwart young children's adventurous explorations nor to let them let them try anything they set their minds to.

Children's Theory of Mind

Over the past decade, perhaps the hottest research topic in the area of cognitive development has been children's *theory of mind*. In particular, researchers have been interested in when and how children appreciate that other peoples' behaviour is motivated by their beliefs and desires, which are often quite different from their own. Most research has focused on children 4 years of age and younger.

A frequently used task in theory-of-mind research is the *false-belief task*. In this task, children watch as a toy or some other treat is hidden (in a box on a table, for instance). Another person, John, is there when the toy is hidden but leaves the room. Then, the toy is moved to another hidden location. When John returns, will he know where the toy is hidden? On this and similar tasks, most 4-year-olds are correct and state that John will look where the toy was originally hidden. In contrast, most 3-year-olds state quite confidently that John will look for the toy at the new hiding place, apparently not realizing that John had no way of knowing this.

One reason why 3-year-olds fail the false-belief task may be due to a failure to remember what they had originally believed before any switch was made. For example, in a modification of the false-belief task, called the "Smarties" task, children are shown a box of Smarties (a type of candy in a distinctive box) and asked what they think is in the box. Children, of course, say "Smarties." But when the box is opened, the children see that it is filled with pencils. They are then asked what they believed was in the box before being shown the contents and to predict what another child (who doesn't know about the trick) will think is in the box. The correct answer to both of these questions, of course, is "Smarties," but most 3-year-olds say "pencils" to both questions. In other words, these young children seem to "forget" their earlier belief.

Interestingly, children 3 years of age and younger seem to be able to "read" another's mind when they are deliberately trying to deceive that person. For example, children played a game similar to the false-belief task but part of the game involved the intentional deception of another person. Under these conditions, even 2 ½-year-old children were able to use deception, implying that they had some idea of what the other person knew. Chandler concluded that these findings "leave little room for doubt that even children as young as 2 ½ are already capable of engaging in a variety of well-crafted deceptive practices, best interpreted as strategies aimed at instilling false beliefs in others". The picture is a complicated one, but it seems that 3-year-olds do have a limited "theory of mind";

however, one that is not nearly as sophisticated as it will be within a year.

Vygotsky's Sociocultural Approach

The theories and research we have examined to this point in the chapter have all focused squarely on the child as the unit of analysis. Information-processing approaches, Piaget's theory, and even Bandura's social-cognitive theory all view the child as processing or discovering information and changing mentally as a result. Each theory, of course, recognizes the environment as playing an important role in shaping development, but it is the child in active interaction with the environment that is responsible for development. A different perspective is represented by the sociocultural approach, emanating form the theory of the Soviet psychologist Lev Vygotsky. Vygotsky, whose theories have come to light in the Western world only recently, proposed that cognition develops through the collaborations of members of one generation with another, and that one cannot examine the individual without also taking into consideration the community and activities that the individual is involved in. The child and his or her development are entwined with interactions with others in a culture, and development proceeds as children are guided through life in collaboration with others. Bandura's theory emphasized social learning, but his approach sees the child as internalizing social roles and behaviours from observation, and not as the result of active participation in social life. Piaget stressed that children develop through interactions with peers; but this was a minor part of his broader theory that emphasized the development of the child's individual structures and not the development of cultural understanding through participation of social life.

From a sociocultural perspective, it is children's participation in the social life of the community in which cognitive development occurs that must be considered. Vygotsky acknowledged maturationally paced differences in children's cognitive abilities, but proposed that children in different cultures have available to them different tools of intellectual adaptation, particularly suited for life in that culture. For example, it is common for children in

Western cultures to be asked questions by a parent for which the parent already knows the answer (*e.g.*, "What did we do at the park today?", "What's the name of Becky's new baby?"). This prepares children for life in school, where teachers ask children for information the teachers already know. Such a practice is not found in other parts of the world where formal education of the Western type is not practiced In fact, for the Wolof people, asking questions for which they already know the answer suggests a riddle or an aggressive challenge. Another example of how middle-class parents prepare their children for life in their culture was provided earlier in the section on memory development. Middle-class mothers "teach" their children how to remember events by asking them questions, structured so that children learn the components that are important in constructing and remembering stories.

Barbara Rogoff, a leading sociocultural theorist, sees development as a process of *transformation of participation*. From this perspective:

> Evaluation of development focuses on how individuals participate in and contribute to ongoing activity rather than on "outcome" and individuals' possessions of concepts and skills. Evaluation of development examines the ways people transform their participation, analyzing how they coordinate with others in shared endeavors, with attention to the purposes and dynamic nature of the activity itself and its meaning in the community. The investigation of people's actual involvement and changing goals in activities becomes the basis of understanding development rather than simply the surface to try to get past.

Such a perspective makes clear the impossibility of separating the child's cognitive development from the greater social context.

Zone of Proximal Development

Vygotsky proposed that cognitive development occurs in contexts in which a child's problem solving is guided by a more knowledgeable or skillful person, usually an adult or older child. Children are encouraged to participate in a sociocultural activity by someone with greater expertise, who assists them to perform an activity in a way they could not do on their own. Learning and development thus take place as the expert guides the novice in the execution of some task. Vygotsky referred to such a process as the *zone of proximal development*, defined by Vygotsky as the difference between a child's "actual developmental level as determined by independent problem solving" and his or her level of "potential development as determined through problem solving under adult guidance or in collaboration with more capable peers". Learning in the zone of proximal development is an active and dynamic process. Not only do children learn, and thus change, as a result of interactions with adults, but adults modify their behaviour as children change.

Rogoff has described the transaction between children and adults as reflecting an "apprenticeship in thinking," with novice children improving their "skills and understanding through participation with more skilled partners in culturally organized activities". This apprenticeship is not the sole responsibility of the adults, however. Vygotsky, like Piaget, saw children as playing an active role in their own development, and children frequently seek out adult attention in sociocultural contexts, increasing the level of engagement between themselves and adults, which in turn fosters development.

Scaffolding. Related to the concept of the zone of proximal development is the concept of *scaffolding*. Scaffolding refers to a process in which experts respond contingently to novices' indications of understanding on a problem, gradually increasing the novices' grasp of the problem. Scaffolding is not just something that teachers do with students, but something that parents spontaneously do with their children. Scaffolding occurs when adults tailor their instructions to children, guide children to a level near the limits of their performance, and adjust instructions and feedback as a function of children's responses. For example, mothers of preschoolers gave their children more responsibility for solving a counting task as their children's performance improved, but provided more specific instructions following inaccurate trials.

An example should help clarify the concept of scaffolding. A mother and her 5-year-old daughter Silvy are playing a game of Chutes and Ladders, but instead of a spinner to compute moves, players must determine their moves from a throw of two dice. After explaining the game to the child, Silvy throws the dice. She just stares at the dice, saying nothing, and then looks at her mother. Her mother says, "How many is that?" Silvy shrugs her shoulders. "Count them," her mother says. Silvy shrugs again. Her mother then points to the dots on the first dice saying, "One, two, three," then to the dots on the second dice, saying "four, five. You have five. Now you count them." Silvy does and moves her piece five spaces on the board. The mother then throws the dice and asks Silvy, "How many do I have?" Silvy shrugs, and her mother says, "Count them," which Silvy does. The next five sets of moves continue this way. Then, on Silvy's sixth move, she immediately counts the dice after her mother's question of "How many do you have?" She does the same on her mother's turn. Her mother then hesitates on the next several trials before asking Silvy any questions. Eventually, Silvy throws the dice and counts the dots herself, without her mother making any request, and this continues throughout most of the game. The mother corrected Silvy when she counted wrong, but became less directive as Silvy took more of the responsibility for the game herself.

Adults and children jointly determine the extent to which children are capable of functioning independently. More specifically, children who are less capable of independent problem solving will elicit more directive and less demanding strategies from parents. More competent children elicit less directive and less demanding strategies from parents. In short, with development, children assume more responsibility for the dyad's work. The more competent child is less in need of adult support, or scaffolding in order to solve a problem.

An important qualification here is that competence in this model is contextspecific to the extent that learning and development occur by interacting around tasks that have very specific rules. Competence is not a psychological absolute in the Piagetian sense as a "central cognitive processor"; it is competence in specific tasks.

Guided Participation: Rogoff developed the concept of *guided participation* to extend Vygotsky's concept of zone of proximal development. She defined guided participation as "the process and system of involvement of individuals with others, as they communicate and engage in shared activities". Although guided participation would include instances of scaffolding, where instruction is the explicit goal, it is not limited to such situations.

Rather, it applies to all contexts in which "human learning occurs through people's diverse processes of participation in the activities of their varying communities". These would include the day-today activities in children's lives, such as helping to prepare meals, discussions around the dinner table, and eavesdropping on parents. It is during such mundane activities that children's cognition develops, as much or more so than in formal "educational" settings.

Peers as Collaborators: Vygotsky's primary focus was on children learning from adults. In recent years, the idea that cognitive development may occur as a result of collaboration among peers has caught the imagination of researchers and educators. Recall Piaget's proposal that cognitive development occurs only when peers interact, and not when children interact with adults. This perspective is not shared by the practitioners of sociocultural theory. In fact, when comparing the effectiveness of peers versus a parent in collaborative learning, parents usually provided better support, and thus better fostered learning, than slightly older children.

However, in many situations, peers do learn to solve problems together in collaborative learning better than when trying to solve problems alone and the children who gain the most are typically those who were initially less skilled than their partners. In a meta-analysis of 378 studies that contrasted achievement of people working alone versus cooperatively, fewer than 10% of the studies produced better results when working individually, whereas working cooperatively yielded significantly better performance for greater than half of all studies.

Why does cooperative learning work? One reason seems to be motivation. Children working together on problems seem to be more motivated to work on the problems. The process of cooperative learning requires children to explain their ideas to one another, to attempt to persuade, and to resolve controversies. Each of these requires children to evaluate more closely what it is they actually believe and to convey that knowledge to someone else. The adage that one learns information best by teaching it is likely true in cooperative learning among peers. D. W. Johnson and Johnson also reported that cooperative learning promotes the use of high-quality cognitive strategies and metacognitive approaches. This results in children creating new ideas that none in the group could have created alone.

Peer collaborative learning is not a panacea for school systems, however. Fewer teachers cannot be hired based on the hope that they can be replaced by peer tutors. Collaborative learning does not always result in better performance, especially if the more competent peer lacks confidence in his or her knowledge or fails to modify instruction appropriately for the less skilled partner. In fact, research suggests that shared decision making is difficult for many American children, although their abilities to make decisions cooperatively improves with practice. One reason for their difficulty is apparently related to the structure of American schools and the experience of teachers. Schools are not organized to promote cooperative learning, and children, accustomed to competitively structured individualistic classroom, have a difficult time knowing how to behave when cooperative techniques are use. When the structure of schools change to support peer collaboration, with teachers as participants in and not directors of the learning experience, cooperatively learning produces improved performance.

■ ■ ■

BIBLIOGRAPHY

Abravanel, E. The development of intersensory patterning with regard to selected spatial dimensions. *Monographs of the Society for Research in Child Development, 1968, 33, No. 18.*

Armstrong, T.D., & Costello, E.J. (2002). Community Studies on Adolescent Substance Use, Abuse, or Dependence and Psychiatric Comorbidity: A Literature Review. *Journal of Consulting and Clinical Psychology, 70,* 1224-1239.

Bates, J. E., Pettit, G. S., Dodge, K. A., & Ridge, B. (1998). Interaction of temperamental resistance to control and restrictive parenting in the development of externalizing behaviour. *Developmental Psychology,* 34(5), 982–995.

Beitchman, J.H., Douglas, L., Wilson, B., Johnson, C., Young, A., Atkinson, L., Escobar, M., & Taback, N. (1999). Adolescent Substance Use Disorders: Findings From a 14-Year Follow-Up of Speech and Language Impaired and Control Children. *Journal of Clinical Child Psychology, 28,* 312-321.

Bell, J. A., & Livesey, P. J. (1985). Cue significance and response regulation in 3– to 6–year-old children's learning of multiple choice discrimination tasks. *Developmental Psychobiology,* 18(3), 229–245.

Berlin, L. J., Brady-Smith, C., & Brooks-Gunn, J. S., & Rapoport, J. (2002). Links between childbearing age and observed maternal behaviours with 14–monthholds in the Early Head Start Research and Evaluation Project. *Infant Mental Health Journal,* 23(1–2), 104–129.

Campbell, S. B., Pierce, E. W., March, C. L., Ewing, L. J., & Szumowski, E. K. (1994). Hard to-manage preschool boys: Symptomatic behaviour across contexts and time. *Child Development, 65,* 836–851.

Canfield, R. L., Wilken, J., & Schmerl, L. (1991). Speed of reaction, expectancies, and mental processing in young children. Poster presented at the XVIIth Biennial Meeting of the *Society for Research in Child Development,* Seattle, WA.

Casey, B. J., Cohen, J. D., Noll, D. C., Forman, S., & Rapoport, J. L. (1993). Activation of the anterior cingulate during the Stroop concept paradigm using functional MRI. *Society for Neuroscience Abstracts, 19,* 1285.

Cicchetti, D., & Rogosch, F.S. (1999). Psychopathology as Risk for Adolescent Substance Use Disorders: A Developmental Psychopathology Perspective. *Journal of Clinical Child Psychology, 28,* 355-365.

Clark, D.B., & Winters, K.C. (2002). Measuring Risks and Outcomes in Substance Use Disorders Prevention Research. *Journal of Consulting and Clinical Psychology, 70,* 1207-1223.

Clark, D.B., Parker, A.M., & Lynch, K.G. (1999). Psychopathology and Substance-Related Problems During Early Adolescence: A Survival Analysis. *Journal of Clinical Child Psychology, 28,* 333-341.

Compton, S.N., Egger, H.L., Burns, B.J., & Robertson E. (2002). Review of the Evidence Base for Treatment of Childhood Psychopathology: Internalizing Disorders. *Journal of Consulting and Clinical Psychology, 70,* 1240-1266.

Costello, J.E., Erkanli, A., Federman, E., & Angold, A. (1999). Development of Psychiatric Comorbidity With Substance Abuse in Adolescents: Effects of Timing and Sex. *Journal of Clinical Child Psychology, 28,* 298-311.

Diamond, A., & Taylor, C. (1996). Development of an aspect of executive control: Development of the abilities to remember what I said and to "Do as I say, not as I do." *Developmental Psychobiology, 29,* 315–334.

Drewe, E. A. (1975). An experimental investigation of Luria's theory on the effects of frontal lobe lesions in man. *Neuropsychologia, 13,* 421–429.

Farmer, E., Compton, S. N., Burns, B.J., & Robertson E. (2002). Review of the Evidence Base for Treatment of Childhood Psychopathology: Externalizing Disorders. *Journal of Consulting and Clinical Psychology, 70,* 1267-1302.

Glantz, M. D. (1992). A Developmental Psychopathology Model of Drug Abuse Vulnerability. In M. D. Glantz & R. Pickens (Eds.). *Vulnerability to Drug Abuse.* (pp. 389-418). Washington, D.C.: American Psychological Association.

Glantz, M.D. (2002). Introduction to the Special Issue on the Impact of Child Psychopathology Interventions on Subsequent Substance Abuse: Pieces of the Puzzle. *Journal of Consulting and Clinical Psychology, 70,* 1203-1206.

Glantz, M.D., & Leshner, A.I. (2000). Drug Abuse and Developmental Psychopathology. *Development and Psychopathology, 12,* 795-814.

Glantz, M.D., Weinberg, N.Z., Miner, L.L., & Colliver, J.D. (1999). The Etiology of Drug Abuse: Mapping the Paths. In M. D. Glantz & C. R. Hartell, (Eds.). *Drug Abuse: Origins and Interventions.* (pp. 3-46). Washington, D.C.: American Psychological Association.

Greenbaum, P.E., Foster-Johnson, L., & Petrila, A. (1996). Co-Occurring Addictive and Mental Disorders Among Adolescents: Prevalence Research and Future Directions. *American Journal of Orthopsychiatry, 66,* 52-60.

Greene, R.W., Biederman, J., Faraone, S.V., & Wilens, T. (1999). Further Validation of Social Impairment as a Predictor of Substance Use Disorders: Findings From a Sample of Siblings of Boys With ADHD. *Journal of Clinical Child Psychology, 28,* 349-354.

Kendall, P.C., & Kessler, R.C. (2002). The Impact of Childhood Psychopathology Interventions on Subsequent Substance Abuse: Policy Implications, Comments and Recommendations. *Journal of Consulting and Clinical Psychology, 70,* 1303-1306.

Loeber, R., Stouthamer-Loeber, M., & Raskin White, H. (1999). Developmental Aspects of Delinquency and Internalizing Problems and Their Association With Persistent Juvenile

Substance Use Between Ages 7 and 18. *Journal of Clinical Child Psychology, 28*, 322-332.

Michael, K.D., & Crowley, S.L. (2002). How Effective Are Treatments for Child and Adolescent Depression? A Meta-Analytic Review. *Clinical Psychology Review*, 22, 247-269.

Rende, R., & Weissman, M. M. (1999). Sibling Aggregation for Psychopathology in Offspring of Opiate Addicts: Effects of Parental Comorbidity. *Journal of Clinical Child Psychology, 28*, 342-348.

Webster-Stratton, C., & Taylor, T. (2001). Nipping Early Risk Factors in the Bud: Preventing Substance Abuse, Delinquency, and Violence in Adolescence Through Interventions Targeted at Young Children (0-8 Years). *Prevention Science*, 2, 165-192.

Weinberg, N.Z., & Glantz, M.D. (1999). Child Psychopathology Risk Factors for Drug Abuse: Overview. *Journal of Clinical Child Psychology, 28*, 290-297.

Weinberg, N.Z., Rahdert, E.Q., Colliver, J.D., & Glantz, M.D. (1998). Adolescent Substance Abuse: A Review of the Past 10 Years. *Journal of the American Academy of Child and Adolescent Psychiatry, 37*, 252-261.

INDEX

A

Acculturation and Second-
    Language Learning, 140
    Hypothesis, 140
Adult Attachment Interview, 177
    Speech to Infants, 127
African American Community, 139
Age in Learning a Second Language, 142
American Academy of Child and Adolescent Psychiatry, 150
Anxiety, 82
Arbitrariness, 116
Arguments for Connectedness, 45
    Against Connectedness, 49
Aspects of Language, 117
Assessment of Parent-Child Relationship, 149, 162
Attachment Behavioural System, 151
    Ethological Theory, 151
Attentional Processes, 242

B

Behaviour Modification, 239
Behavioural Research as "Science", 96
    Theories, 122
Benefits of Bilingualism, 143
Black English, 137
Bound Morphemes, 119

C

Campbell and Stanley, 105
Categories and Language, 210
Causality, 98
Cause-Effect Relationships, 94
Child Psychology: Assessing Infants and Young Children, 11
Child's Fear of the Father, 83
Children Acquire Language, 126
    Eyewitness Testimony, 270
    Learning, Thinking and Remembering, 237
    Theory of Mind, 275
Chomsky's Theory, 124

Chuang-Tzû Commentary, 79
Classes of Persons, 55
Classical and Operant Conditioning, 237
Clinical Presentation and Case Description, 24
Problem-Solving Procedure, 175
Cognitive Processes, 203
Communication System a Language, 116
Communicative Competence, 122
Conceptual and Theoretical Foundations, 151
Connectedness and Discontinuity in Development, 78
Connections between Stages, 40
Contributions of Child, 159
of Parent, 156
Cooing and Laughter, 129
Critical Period for Learning Language, 144
Cross-Cultural Psychology, 113
Cultural Assessment for the Child's Diagnosis and Care, 30
Assessment Framework for Infants and Toddlers, 22
Definition and Influence, 12
Formulations with Children, 20
Identity of Child and Caregivers, 26
Culture as Shared Meaning, 12
Influences Expressions of Distress, 17
is Experienced Subjectively, 13
is Transactional, 13
Occurs in An Ecology, 12
Operates Silently and with Voices, 14
Bound Syndrome, 20
Culturologic Interview, 21
Current Integration of Culture and Clinical Assessment, 18

D

Declarative Knowledge, 14
Development as a Sequence of Stages, 34
Developmental Psycholinguistics, 124
Diagnosis of Relational Disorders, 178
Diagnostic and Statistical Manual of Mental Disorders, 17, 150, 178
Classification of Mental Health and Developmental Disorders of Infancy and Early Childhood, 179
Process, 18
Differences in Behaviour, 56
Different Theoretical Perspectives of Language Development, 122
Discipline's Level of Progress, 53
Displacement, 116
Disturbed Parenting, 158
DSM-IV, 11
Approach, 19
Duality, 117

Dyadic Disorganization and Tension, 170

E

Early Nonlanguage Communication, 126
Ecological Validity, 111
Embryological Development, 70
Emotional Availability Scales, 174
Examples of Research Designs, 106
Executive Processes, 226
Experimental Environments, 44
  Methods in Child Psychology, 93
External Validity, 109

F

Fago, 48
Falsifiability, 46
Family Systems Theory, 156
Features of Language, 116
Feeling of Anonymity, 88
Field Experiments, 102
Frame, 76
Free Morphemes, 119
Freeman Dyson, 84
Functional Invariants, 247

G

Generation of Thought in Children, 184
Guided Participation, 14
Guiding Principles in Human Development, 71

H

Hawthorne Effect, 111
HOME Inventory for Families of Infants and Toddlers, 174
Hormones (Androgens), 103
Hostility, 82

I

Infant Positive Affect, 170
  Caregiving Network, 28
  Directed, 127
  Social Vocalization, 128
Inference and Categories, 208
Information-Processing
  Perspectives of Children's Cognition, 261
  System, 262
Inhibition to the Unfamiliar, 62
Insightfulness Assessment, 177
Integrating Culturally Sensitive Approaches, 182
Integrative Motivation, 140
Intellectual Ability, 65
Interference, 89
Intermediate Zones of Experience, 16
Internal Validity, 104
  Working Models, 151
Internally Valid, 94
Interview with Parents, 163
Intrinsic Activity, 246

J

J. J. Conger, 43
Jargon, 130

L

Laboratory Experiments, 100
Strengths and Weaknesses, 100
Language Acquisition Device (LAD), 124
Acquisition Support System (LASS), 128
and Thought, 145
Development in Child, 115
in Context, 136
Law of Effect, 39
of Practice, 39
Learning, 237
in Infancy, 238
Lower Socioeconomic Status (LESS), 100

M

Mean Length of Utterances (MLU), 133
Measure Preservation, 55
Medical Conditions, 161
Memory, 220, 267
Span, 262
Mental-Demand Characteristics, 111
Metacognition, 273
Metalinguistic Awareness, 144
Morpheme, 119
Morphology, 119
Motivational Processes, 242
Multiple Systems Theories, 155

N

Nativist Theories, 123
Natural Experiments, 103
Need for Achievement, 82
Nursing Child Assessment Satellite Training (NCAST), 176

O

Objective Frame, 86
Observations of Parent-Child Interactions, 164
Optimal Parental Care, 156-57
Origin of Species, 44
Overextensions, 121
Overregularization, 133

P

P. H. Mussen, 43
Paradigm War, 93
Paradox of Piaget, 188
Paradoxical Sleep, 85
Parent Subscale I, 170
Subscale II, 170
Subscale III, 170
Parental Intrusiveness, 170
Negative Affect and Behavioor, 170
Positive Affective Involvement and Verbalization, 170
Parent-Child Early Relational Assessment, 167
Infant Relationship Global Assessment Scale (PIR-GAS), 180
Parenting Stress Index, 176
Partial Pregnancy, 80
Person with a Motive for Power, 55

Phonology, 117
Piaget and Individual
  Differences in Children's Thinking, 260
  Theory and the Executive Processes, 230
  Theory, 246
Pragmatics, 121
Prediction and Feeling of Child, 33
Premises of Experimental Methods, 94
Preoperational Period, 254
Preservation of Individual Qualities, 52
Principles of Piaget's Theory, 246
Private Speech, 146
Production Processes, 242
Productive Language, 131
Productivity, 116
Propositions, 54
Psychodynamic/Object Relations Theory, 152

Q

Qualities and Quantities, 80

R

Real World, 101
Reality and Experience, 16
Reciprocal Determinism, 241
Reflection-Impulsivity, 225
Reflexive Vocalizations, 129
Regress Toward the Mean, 105
Relationship between the Parents or Caregivers and the Clinician, 29
Relative Dominance of Left over Right Hemisphere, 88
Remediation of Weaknesses, 113
Research Design, 104
Respiration Aerates the Blood, 52-53
Retention Processes, 242
Review of other Parent-Child Interaction Assessment Methods, 172
Robust Phenomenon, 89

S

Sangwish, 141
Scaffolding, 279
School-Age Children, 62
Second-Language Learning, 139
Secure Attachment, 58
Selection of Terms, 193
  Maturation Interaction, 106
Semanticity, 116
Semantics, 120
Sensorimotor Period, 250
Sesame Street Generation, 245
Social Cognitive Theory, 241
  Configurations, 111
  Interactive Theories, 125
  Learning Theory, 153, 241
  Relations with Native Speakers, 140
Speech Registers, 137
Spot, 120
St. Augustine, 122
Stages of Adulthood, 36
  of Development, 250
Strange Situation, 175
Strategies, 262

Subjective and Objective Frames, 86
Syntax, 119

T

Television as a Model for Learning, 244
The Decline and fall of the Roman Empire, 44
Newborn is Labile, 84
Three Essays on Sexuality, 44
Themata, 72
True Babbling, 129

U

Uncontaminated Conditions, 100
Underextensions, 121

V

Verbal Repairs, 135
Vocal Play, 129
Vygotsky's Sociocultural Approach, 277

W

Wechsler Intelligence Scale, 86
Working Memory, 82
Model of the Child Interview, 176

Z

Zone of Proximal Development, 14, 278

Other Books on

TEXT BOOKS

1. Philosophical & Sociological Foundations of Education(New)	225/-
2. Research Methods in Education (New)	225/-
3. Psychology of Learning & Human Development (New)	225/-
4. A New Approach to Teacher & Education in the Emerging Indian Society (New)	225/-
5. Safety and Disaster Management (New)	225/-
6. History of Medieval India	495/-
7. Measurement and Evaluation in Psychology and Education (New)	225/-
8. Special Education (New)	225/-
9. Principles of Office Management (New)	195/-
10. History of Ancient India (New)	395/-
11. Methodology of Educational Research (New)	250/-
12. Environmental Education (New)	195/-
13. Experimental Psychology (New)	195/-
14. Teaching of Home Science (New)	195/-
15. Select World Constitutions (New)	450/-
16. Educational Thought and Practice (New)	195/-
17. Guidance and Counselling A Manual (New)	195/-
18. School Organization and Administration (New)	195/-
19. Developmental Psychology (New)	195/-
20. Social Work Theory and Practice (New)	225/-
21. Modern Education for New Generation	195/-
22. Advanced Educational Technology	175/-
23. Comparative Education	195/-
24. Introduction to Educational Research	175/-
25. Computer Education	175/-
26. Teaching of Chemistry	175/-
27. Teaching of Physics	175/-
28. Handbook of Journalism & Mass Media	225/-
29. Advanced Educational Psychology	195/-
30. Educational Administration & Origanisation Management	195/-
31. Social Psychology	225/-
32. Teaching of Commerce	175/-
33. Educational Development & Technology	195/-
34. Disaster Management	195/-
35. Information Technology	195/-
36. Human Resource Development	195/-
37. Mass Media Communication Theory & Practice	225/-
38. Adult Education	195/-